Mastering

phpBB Administration

The Essential Guide to Installing, Configuring, Troubleshooting and Administering a phpBB Bulletin Board

Includes phpBB 3.3!

Mark D. Hamill

phpbbservices.com

Table of Contents

Chapter 1 | What is phpBB?

If you picked up this book, you probably know what phpBB is. Even if you don't, chances are that you've already used it.

phpBB is open-source bulletin board software for the web. It runs discussion forums on websites and is found widely on sites around on the web. If you've ever used online technical support, then chances are phpBB was used to drive the site's support forums (Figure 1.1). This also means that you probably already know the basics of phpBB: how to make a post and how to navigate around various forums and topics.

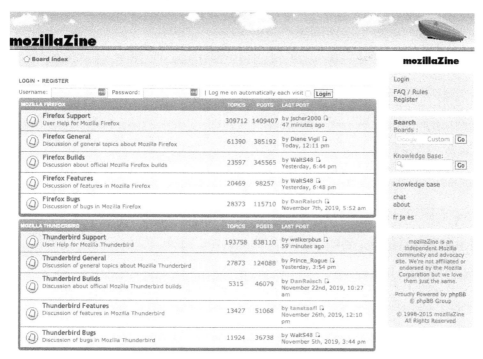

Figure 1.1: Mozilla's forums with over 4.8 million posts run on phpBB

Soon after it was introduced in 2000, phpBB dominated online bulletin board solutions. People liked it because it was free and used the *open-source* software model. This model usually allows anyone to install, use and inspect the software for free. And it works seamlessly with other popular open-source software that powers the web. That's because it is written in PHP, a programming language that became popular around the turn of the century and quickly spawned lots of PHP-based software.

Because phpBB was released under the GNU General Public License, Version 2, you can modify its code, but you can't sell your modification. It's community-developed software whose license requires that can't be sold.

phpBB is maintained by the phpBB Group, a nonprofit group of developers and others interested in promoting, maintaining and enhancing this bulletin board solution. Note that while phpBB's code is open source, it is still subject to copyright and is owned by the phpBB Group.

As you might have guessed, the "BB" in phpBB stands for bulletin board. In the software world, a bulletin board is a collection of forums, with each forum containing many topics with a similar theme or with a similar purpose. In the case of the Mozilla Foundation (Figure 1-1), its MozillaZine board allows users to ask questions and participate in discussions about its many products (such as the Firefox browser).

phpBB is not necessarily the best bulletin board solution out there, since that depends on your criteria. However, it definitely dominates the bulletin board solution marketplace.

phpBB is a bit unusual in one way: it presents British English. Of course, many of its developers are not British, but the bulk appear to be European. It's more typical to see software presenting American English, but only a British English language pack is provided in its default installation. An American English language pack is available for those who find British English spellings a bit jarring. Dozens of other language packs are available.

Why I wrote this book

Since 2006, I have been helping the phpBB community use and manage phpBB. As a phpBB consultant, I have helped over four hundred clients make their boards work better.

This book was written to help phpBB bulletin board administrators properly set up and better manage their bulletin boards. It provides useful documentation, best practices and little-known secrets to help administrators use the full spectrum of phpBB's capabilities. Armed with this knowledge, administrators should be able to configure, use and maintain their bulletin boards effectively.

Other phpBB documentation is out there. The phpBB Group has various user manuals that can be read online or downloaded that are reasonably thorough in describing its features. But they aren't necessarily written for ease of understanding. Pieces of the knowledge they offer are generally easy to grasp. Based on my many clients, board administrators are very challenged putting it all together.

As a paid phpBB consultant, I see many bulletin board administrators more than a little frustrated with phpBB. Usually, it works fine until you need to tweak something or your web hosting changes in some subtle way. Updates and upgrades to phpBB are often a hassle too. Many administrators stumble through the chore of administering their bulletin boards. In many cases, troubleshooting issues can have administrators feeling exasperated and flustered, forcing them to give up or hire consultants like me.

I wrote this book mainly for those administrators who can't afford a consultant like me. I want it to keep them from giving up.

If this sounds like you, take some comfort in knowing you are hardly alone. The truth is phpBB is great, but hardly perfect bulletin board software. Being chockfull of features makes it very useful, but it can feel overwhelming.

I expect that you will skip or skim chapters and sections of this book. If you feel you have a good grasp of the chapter's material already, it will help with the finer points. If you are looking to solve a specific issue right away, it may give you the information you need quickly.

phpBB can feel like a rabbit hole at times. The more you learn, the more you learn you have barely scratched its surface. At best, this book aspires to provide about twenty percent of what you could learn about phpBB. Fortunately, based on the work I do for clients, what I present is essential for board administrators to know.

So, come on down the phpBB rabbit hole with me. Don't worry. You'll always be able to find your way out, and we won't go down it too deeply.

Navigation conventions used in this book

In this book, I use certain acronyms and conventions—shortcuts for documenting how to navigate using phpBB. You will often see these conventions on phpbb.com as well.

ACP is an acronym for **Administration Control Panel**. As its name implies, the ACP is a set of screens that allow you to administer phpBB. To access the Administration Control Panel, you can select its link at the bottom of the bulletin board (Figure 1.2). Only administrators see this link.

Figure 1.2: Administration control panel link

Click on it and after authenticating yourself again you can access the ACP. If you have administrator privileges, the link should also appear on phpBB's navigation bar as **ACP** (Figure 1.4).

UCP stands for **User Control Panel**. Users use it to control their overall experience on the board, such as managing their profile (Figure 1.3). When you are logged in, you can find the UCP on the far right of phpBB's navigation bar. There is a dropdown menu attached to your username. When you click on the dropdown, you will see the link to the UCP.

Figure 1.3: User control panel link

MCP stands for **Moderator Control Panel**. Moderators have responsibility for ensuring that topics and users' posts adhere to the rules set by the administrator. These are often rules about using obscenities, posting spam, or making posts that are off topic.

Figure 1.4: Moderator control panel link

The MCP provides access to moderator functions (Figure 1.4). You will see the **MCP** link on the navigation bar, but you won't see it unless you have forum moderation privileges.

These three control panels are big discrete portions of phpBB, separate from the general bulletin board software. As an administrator, you will be spending most of your time in these areas.

I also use **>** to separate actions that are done in sequence.

ACP > General > Board configuration > Board settings > Site Name

This example can be interpreted as follows:

1. Click on the **Administration Control Panel** link.

2. Select the **General** tab.

3. Look in the **Board configuration** group on the sidebar.

4. Select the **Board settings** link within that group.

5. Select the **Site Name** field.

All actions that follow this convention are **bolded**.

In general, selectable links, fields, and button names on screens that allow some action are **bolded** as well.

Commands that must be typed in from a computer's command prompt are shown in a fixed width font. Italicized items in commands are unique information that you type in. Here's an example:

```
mysql --user=username --password
```

You should type in the value of the username desired after the equal sign.

Terminology

To be clear, I try very hard to distinguish between the terms *board* (or *bulletin board*) and *forum*.

When I use the term *board*, I am talking about all your forums and all the software that makes it work.

When I use the term *forum*, I mean a general topic area within the board. You can see a list of most forums on the board's index, such as in Figure 1.1.

It's common for people to say "forum" (as in "Check out my forum") when they mean "board," but this is incorrect.

How current is this book?

This book describes phpBB's features as of version 3.3.7, released in March 2022.

One good thing about phpBB is that its features change slowly. It's very unusual for new features to be added in a minor version, such as in phpBB 3.3, after its initial release.

New features generally show up in the next minor or major versions. No version 3.4 is planned. The next version should be a major version: 4.0. As usual, the phpBB Group won't say when this version will be released. So, most likely, the content of this book will remain almost entirely relevant for at least five years from the date of publication.

I do plan to update the book annually at least, and I am hoping that I can provide updated electronic versions to purchasers at little or no cost. You can see when this book was last updated on the copyright page.

Chapter 2 | Why phpBB?

If you are exploring phpBB for your bulletin board, then it's worth taking some time to discuss why you might want to use it and why you might not want to use it.

Figure 2: phpbb.com website

What is bulletin board software?

First, a thought experiment: is Facebook bulletin board software? You can make posts easily enough. And it's got an internal search engine.

If just making posts were the criteria for a bulletin board, Facebook would qualify, along with Instagram, WordPress sites and many sites and software solutions.

But Facebook is not bulletin board software. That's because true bulletin board software allows content to be tightly organized. Facebook is anything but tightly organized.

You need bulletin board software if you want to create an online space to allow a particular community of users to interact. You want the content to be organized with the help of the bulletin board's software and to persist indefinitely. You expect that people will use more than the built-in search engine and a post button. They might want to delve into areas full of similar content, but in one seamlessly well-managed web space.

For example, a bulletin board for Barbie® fans might have categories that discuss various doll types. The forums inside these categories might get into various iterations of Barbie dolls over time. There might be a Ken category too, with similar forums inside its category for Ken doll enthusiasts.

I'm sure there are many Barbie doll groups on Facebook. There are probably Ken doll groups too. But if you are in one, you probably won't know about the others. The communities in both groups will be different too.

The essential quality of a bulletin board solution is to corral a bunch of people into a general web space based on shared—but not identical—interests and to let them share their thoughts and knowledge in one or more forums using topics. It promotes the interaction of people within the community, allowing them to get into certain niches within their general area and into many other niches as their interests take them.

I've worked on hundreds of phpBB boards, and I can attest to the variety of interest groups out there. It's left me both surprised and humbled. Here's a sampling of some of the boards I have helped maintain, enhance and troubleshoot:

- A bulletin board for eye doctors doing a very specialized type of ocular surgery. It's so specialized that membership is by invitation only, and its boards cannot be publicly read.

- A bulletin board for Australian Bonsai fans

- A bulletin board for fans of a local Australian football (soccer) club

- A bulletin board for mothers who choose to have children on their own

- A community bulletin board for an English hamlet

- A very popular gardening board

- A bulletin board for "budding" marijuana entrepreneurs (where it's legal, of course). Yes, it's all about growing marijuana buds!

Some of these boards are truly bizarre. I keep client information confidential, so I won't mention them by name, but I've worked on many boards with unusual or bizarre adult content and boards with highly controversial content.

If the people running those boards were using a Facebook group, they'd likely be violating Facebook's terms of service, and their group could be gone tomorrow. Ultimately, Facebook owns the content posted on its site.

In contrast, *You* own your bulletin board. It's *hosted*, which means it belongs to whoever pays the bill for the web hosting. Moreover, if you are getting subpar web hosting, you can take it and move it somewhere else. In the case of phpBB, this is because it rests on top of common and free open-source software that is available from thousands of web hosts.

With Facebook, you don't have to do much thinking. A bulletin board, though, needs to be actively administered and probably moderated as well. Ultimately, you—the bulletin board administrator— take ownership of it and set its direction and rules. You also manage any technical issues that arise.

What are phpBB's strengths?

- **Longevity**. It's been around since 2000.

- **Market share**. According to the phpBB Group, phpBB is the #1 bulletin board solution in use. If you type "bulletin board software" into a search engine, generally phpBB is top ranked.

- **Support**. The phpBB Group's support forums are outstanding. Responses to questions are quick and almost always helpful.

- **Security**. While no software can guarantee that it is free of security vulnerabilities, phpBB's combination of open-source software, peer reviews of its code and the phpBB Group's extensive automated nightly test builds minimize unexpected security issues.

- **Rock solid**. While most phpBB boards are relatively small, with just tens of thousands of posts, some are huge with millions of posts. It works reliably on boards that range from tiny to enormous. As of this writing, phpbb.com's forums alone have over 4.3 million posts. It needs to work, and almost all the time, it does – at least if you use the latest version, stick with approved extensions, and your web host's technical infrastructure doesn't change too quickly. When phpBB fails, it's almost always due to hosting changes beyond its control.

- **Features**. If you need a feature, it's likely available in phpBB, with one major exception (see the next section).

- **Familiarity**. Since you have likely used it before without knowing it, there is no steep learning curve.

- **Fanatical devotion to open standards**. The phpBB Group goes to great lengths to ensure phpBB works across all modern browsers and devices. It does this by carefully adhering to the latest web standards and through running daily automated test builds. This helps make it a good SEO (search engine optimization) bulletin board solution.

- **Responsive**. It behaves seamlessly on mobile devices, intelligently sizing down to the device's screen size with no loss of functionality.

- **Uses top-tier integrated third-party libraries.** Under the hood, phpBB uses a host of other top-notch, enterprise-class software libraries. For example, it uses a templating library from Symfony for embedding web pages with dynamic content.

- **Supports many database types**. Typically, phpBB is used with the MySQL or MariaDB database management systems (DBMS). But if you want to run it on the Oracle, Postgres, Microsoft SQL Server or even the SQLite DBMS, it will work and function virtually identically. phpBB's code abstracts away the minor differences in these DBMSes through a database abstraction layer, ensuring portability.

- **Permissions system**. There is probably no better permissions system available anywhere. It's incredibly feature-rich, if more than a bit obscure.

- **Extensions**. Since version 3.1, phpBB supports *extensions*. Extensions are new features created by others that you can add to phpBB. Extensions can be turned on or off once you install them, all without affecting its base code. Extensions are currently not as easy to install and configure as WordPress plugins, but they are getting there. And the number of approved extensions keeps increasing with time.

- **It's maintained and updated.** If a security issue is uncovered, it tends to get fixed promptly with patch instructions made available until there is a new release. Over time, new releases will update phpBB so that it works with the latest changes to technology. Users can add bugs and feature requests to its tracker.

What are phpBB's weaknesses?

- **No multi-threading**. While a poster can quote from a previous post inside of a topic, you cannot see a group of related indented replies to a post within a topic. Hopefully this will show up as a feature one of these days.

- **New features are added slowly, if at all**. While phpBB is a rock-solid bulletin board solution, it is not easily changed. This is, in part, because it is so feature-rich. Features that are added tend to be relatively minor and incremental. Rarely will you see big new features. The extensions system introduced in phpBB 3.1 was one of these rare and big changes to phpBB.

- **Standalone**. phpBB doesn't integrate with other software solutions. For example, you can't integrate it into WordPress or Joomla, at least not elegantly, and it's not available as a WordPress plugin.

- **Updates and upgrades can be painful**. While better than it was, updating and upgrading phpBB is often a challenge. Most of my consulting business involves helping clients with these activities. Web hosting limitations also can introduce problems during these time-critical activities.

- **Configuring and maintaining a bulletin board is mysterious and somewhat painful**. This is one of the major reasons I wrote this book. Mostly bulletin board administrators learn by doing. It's so much better to do things the phpBB way, although you can get a hundred different opinions on what the best way is. I'll risk the wrath of the phpBB community (they are a passionate and very helpful bunch) by telling you what I think the best ways are, and why. I will help step you through these phpBB mysteries based on more than a decade of practical experience.

- **Complicated to administer**. While *using* a phpBB bulletin board is not complicated and is usually intuitive, *administering* a phpBB bulletin board can be very complex. With so many features, it's hard to know all of them or where to find them. Certain very powerful features, like its granular permissions system and its ability to bundle permissions into roles, are totally awesome but rarely delved into. Sometimes an administrator won't even know a feature exists. Fixing technical issues that arise can be very challenging.

- **Supports many database types**. Wait! Isn't this a strength? Yes, but it's also a weakness, in a way. phpBB is almost always installed using the MySQL DBMS or its effective clone MariaDB (which is based on a community edition of MySQL). You will occasionally see phpBB installed on Postgres, but it's rarely installed on Oracle or SQLite. You are only likely to see it on SQLServer if phpBB is running on Windows servers, where MySQL and MariaDB can also be installed. One of the reasons WordPress is successful is they support MySQL and MariaDB only, allowing them to be more agile and introduce new features more quickly.

My advice: know what you are getting into. If any of these are major issues, you might want to use another bulletin board solution, or just not bother to install phpBB in the first place.

Chapter 3 | Using phpBB: the basics

In this chapter, I go over the basics of how a typical user will use a phpBB bulletin board. These are just the basics. There is more to learn, such as subscribing to forums and topics or using private messaging, that I don't get into in this book. I also don't get into moderating phpBB forums in this book.

The reason I am focusing on the basics is because most of the time, bulletin board users are doing the same things over and over again: finding topics of interest, reading them and replying to them. These basics are quickly mastered and are generally intuitive. I include them here in the interest of completeness, in case you are new to phpBB. Also, if you don't understand these basics, you will likely flounder as a bulletin board administrator.

The Bulletin board index

In Figure 3.1, you can see the index, or main page, for the forums on a hypothetical Hampshire County Schools bulletin board. The index page (called the bulletin board index) links to the forums on the site and is typically the first page that users see. You know you are on the index page when you see "index.php" in the page's URL.

Below, I have highlighted some common elements and areas of interest on the bulletin board index:

- **Navigation bar**. A set area on the screen that appears on all pages and contains links that takes you to useful pages outside of the forums. The illustration shows the look of the navigation bar when you are logged in. It changes somewhat if you are not logged in.

- **Breadcrumb menu**. This bar, below the navigation bar, is sometimes called the Breadcrumb menu. This is because as you get into forums, or forums inside forums, it will show you the path back to the index, with each part of the path back delineated by the < character, the "crumb."

- **Category**. A broad wrapper, under which one or more forums are found. The forums under the category represent more specific topics of interest having to do with the category. You can think of a category as a wrapper around a set of related forums.

- **Forum**. A collection of topics having a common theme. You click on the forum name to see related topics.

If you find yourself many clicks into a forum's thread, you can return to the index by clicking on the **Board index** link in the breadcrumb menu. If you want to go to the parent forum or category, you can pick its link on the breadcrumb menu too.

Don't confuse the board index with the **Home** link that sometimes appears on the breadcrumb menu. The **Home** link takes you to the main page of a larger site.

Figure 3.1: Board's index page

Since phpBB 3.1, phpBB has implemented responsive design. This means that on mobile devices with narrower screens, the screens intelligently size down. You don't lose any functionality at all, but it may take a few extra finger presses to do something that is simpler to do on a laptop or desktop computer. Figure 3.2 shows how the same index might look on an iPhone in portrait mode.

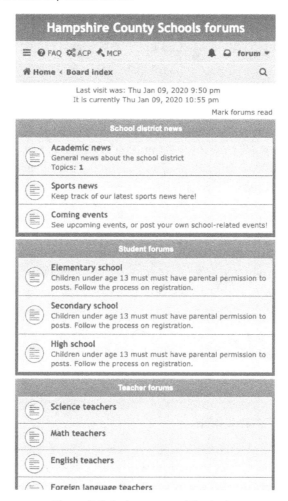

Figure 3.2: Index on a mobile device

Logging in and logging out

The first time you access a phpBB bulletin board, you are a considered a guest. Generally, you will see a list of the board's forums. In some cases, you will see a "This board has no forums" message. If you see this, it usually means the board does have forums, but guests don't have permission to see them.

Figure 3.3: Navigation bar when logged out

Figure 3.3 shows how the navigation bar's look changes when you are logged out. To join the board, you will usually find a **Register** link on the navigation bar next to where your username would normally be. If the link is missing, it's because registration is disabled. You can use the **Register** link to create an account on the bulletin board. You may get instant access after registering, you may have to confirm a link in an email to complete your registration, or you may have to wait for the board's administrator to approve your application.

If you already have an account, the **Login** link rightmost on the navigation bar allows you to login, usually with a username and password. Once authenticated, you can start reading or posting in forums where you have the privileges.

Once logged in, the **Login** link is replaced with a dropdown containing your username shown in Figures 3.1 and 3.2. Open the dropdown and select **Logout** to log out of the board.

The View forum page

Once logged in, you are on the index page. You normally pick a forum to read and perhaps post in. Figure 3.4 shows the View forum page, which comes up when you click on a forum link on the index. Here you see a list of topics in a forum, which are generally presented with the most recent topics shown first. This page is identified in the browser's URL as viewforum.php. Here you can select topics of interest within a forum by clicking on the topic links.

- **New topic button**. Press this button to create a new topic in this forum. You must have posting permissions in a forum to see this button. A new topic is a special form of a post. A *post* is simply some comments added to a topic by a poster. A new topic post is the first post of the topic.

- **Search board field**. You can search all the posts on the board by entering one or more search terms in the search field. The search field is optional in phpBB, but is usually present. If enabled, it almost always appears on all pages and for all classes of users. There is an **advanced search link** (the gear icon) that lets you more granularly define the search, such as limiting the terms to certain forums.

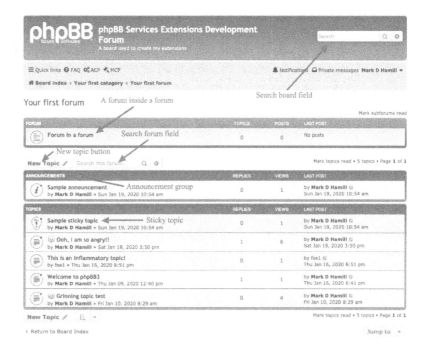

Figure 3.4: View forum page

- **Search forum field**. This is like the search board field, but instead searches for search terms in topics only in this forum. It also has an **advanced link** (gear icon) for a more granular forum search.

- **A forum inside a forum**. This demonstrates that it's possible for a forum to exist inside another forum, sometimes called a *subforum*. Such forums will appear as links within a group at the top of the View forum page. Forums can be nested inside of other forums or categories as deeply as desired. Having said this possible, most bulletin boards administrators keep it simple and don't nest forums other than putting them inside a collection of master categories on the board's index.

- **Announcement group**. With the right privileges, a user can create an *announcement*, which acts as its own special kind of topic, by clicking the announcement checkbox when creating the topic. Announcements are given the highest visibility by always appearing in a separate group at the top of the view forum page, above all other posts. If there are no announcements in the forum, this group will not appear.

- **Sticky topic**. With the right privileges, a user can also create a *sticky topic*. These topics "stick" to the top of the list of topics to give them prominence. Sticky topics are topics that should be read by everyone and often include important information, such as the rules for using the forum. Sticky topics are denoted with a special icon.

The View topic page

This is probably phpBB's most used page (Figure 3.5). It appears when you click on a topic link on the View forum page. You use it to read posts within a topic. It is identified in the URL with the name viewtopic.php.

- **Topic reply button**. Press the **Post Reply** button to reply to the current topic. Once posted, your reply will appear at the end of the topic. Replies are posts in response to a topic. They usually appear below the initial post, from first reply to last. Generally, up to ten posts will show on a page. If there are more posts than that, you will see topic navigation controls to take you to the first, last, next, previous or particular page of interest within the topic.

- **Post controls**. A variety of buttons can appear above a post. What appears depends on your privileges. They allow the post to be edited, deleted and reported. They also show information about the post and allow the post's text to be quoted in a reply.

- **Poster profile**. Some brief information about the poster appears here. After you create an account on the board, you can leave some information about yourself in a *profile* that could be of interest to other members of the bulletin board. phpBB also tracks the number of posts you have made automatically, which usually shows up in the poster's profile. A user can change their profile in the User Control Panel.

Figure 3.5 View topic page

Post a reply

When you click on the **Post Reply** button, you go to the Post reply page (Figure 3.6). This is identical to pressing the **New Topic** button, except that after pressing the new topic button, the subject field is blank. When you post a reply, a default subject line is created for you based on the topic title of the topic you are replying to, which can be changed. A subject line is simply a one-line summary of your post's content, like when you write an email. *Emojis* can easily be added to a subject by simply placing it in at the location of your cursor. Emojis are small images, symbols or icons used in electronic messaging to communicate information without using words.

In the posting window, you type whatever it is you want to write, aided by editing controls provided above and next to it that allow the text to be marked up.

Note that it's possible to embed images or attach other documents to the post if the forum's and the user's permissions permit it. (See the **Attachments tab** at the bottom of the screen.)

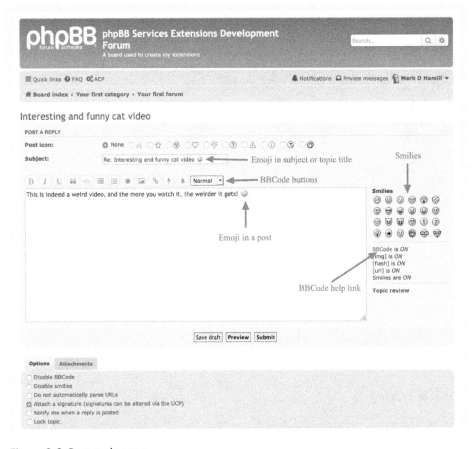

Figure 3.6: Post reply page

- **BBCode buttons**. These buttons add standard text markups to your post, such as bolding and italicizing text, among other types of markups. BBCode is a standard for marking up posting text, which is entered as plain text. It is discussed in more detail in Chapter 6.

The BBCode markup tags will appear wherever your cursor is in the posting window when you press the desired BBCode button. For example, press the **B** button and you will see [b][/b] in the markup. Text between these tags will be bolded when the post is submitted. You can also select some text in the posting window first, and then press the BBCode button and the text will be prefixed and suffixed by the BBCode tag.

- **Smilies**. Smilies are small icons that express an emotion and are placed in the post text wherever the poster wants. Press the button on one of these images and the BBCode to render that smiley will appear in the posting window at the location of the cursor in the field. For example, clicking on the Very Happy smiley will render :D as its BBCode short-code. When rendered, you will see the smiley substituted for the code.

- **BBCode help link**. This link often goes unnoticed, but if you want to learn more about the various BBCodes available and their syntax, click on the link.

- **Emoji in subject or topic title**. Since phpBB 3.2.9, it's been possible to add Emoji to a topic title or a subject field of the reply. Simply paste the Emoji in the field.

- **Emoji in a post**. Since phpBB 3.2, it's also possible to use an Emoji in a post by simply pasting it at the location of the cursor. At one time, only a limited Emoji set was supported. But since phpBB 3.2.9, virtually any Emoji can be added.

When you are ready to post your reply, press the **Submit** button. The **Preview** button allows you to make sure it looks right before you submit the post.

The User Control Panel

When logged in, on the right side of the navigation bar, there is a dropdown that you can open containing your username (Figure 1.3). The **User Control Panel** (UCP) link in the dropdown will take you to a page where you can monitor, view and update your board preferences, profile, and forum subscriptions using a set of tabs. This allows you to control phpBB more granularly and take other actions, like access private messaging. The dropdown also contains a **Profile** link. This allows you to view your profile, as others will see it.

Figure 3.7 shows the typical view rendered when you go into the User Control Panel. The Profile tab obviously lets you change your profile, which is visible on the view topic page, but also on the Members link under the Quick Links link on the navigation bar. Only administrators or moderators may see certain fields in your profile. The most useful part of the UCP is actually one of its least known (Figure 3.8).

UCP > Board preferences > Edit notification options

Figure 3.7: User control panel

Here you can control whether you want to receive emails when new topics or posts are made, just get a notification in the navigation bar, or both. You need to be subscribed to a forum or a topic to get these notifications, and in most cases, phpBB won't bother to send you emails. You also might want to change the default behavior of notifications, which are enabled by default. A link to see new notifications appears on the navigation bar, with the number of new notifications (if any) next to the bell icon.

For example, most people want email notifications if they get a private message. You can set that up on this screen. Moderators (users who are charged with moderating content on forums) and administrators will see other notification types they can control on this screen. Moderator notifications are among those shown in Figure 3-7.

With this basic understanding of how a user uses phpBB, the next chapter begins learning how to administer phpBB. We start by showing how to properly install phpBB.

Figure 3.8: Edit notifications

Chapter 4 | Installing phpBB

To install phpBB, first you need web hosting.

Web hosting are sets of co-located machines and infrastructure that provide web content to the world. Web hosting is too huge a topic to delve into here. However, if you need web hosting or just want to plumb my thoughts on web hosting (as I work on plenty of web hosts), read Appendix A.

Make sure your hosting meets phpBB's system requirements. This is rarely a problem and these are also detailed in Appendix A. But since the requirements might have changed, you should check phpBB's current system requirements before buying hosting.

Once you have acquired web hosting, you'll need to install phpBB. Let me distinguish between installing phpBB and configuring phpBB.

- *Installing* means getting it up and running. This chapter covers only installing phpBB.

- *Configuring* involves making phpBB look and behave the way you want it to. This is actually the harder chore. We discuss configuring phpBB in Chapters 5 and 6.

Avoid using an autoinstaller to install phpBB

Many web hosts have an autoinstallers in their web host control panels. You can use it to set up phpBB with only a few clicks. Figure 4.1 shows a phpBB autoinstaller that is often enabled in the cPanel web host control panel.

Figure 4.1: cPanel's phpBB autoinstaller

I do not recommend the autoinstaller approach. The phpBB Group does not recommend it either. Why?

- It might install older versions of phpBB.

- Often it is configured to automatically upgrade phpBB for you. You don't want to do this because it's not done correctly by these autoinstallers. It will often mess up your styles and perhaps cause other unexpected issues. You should always follow the phpBB Group's procedures for updating or upgrading phpBB. In Chapter 9, we'll discuss how to upgrade or update your board.

- You often can't choose where to place the bulletin board. Typically, it lives in a folder with the name they provide, like phpbb.

- It will create a database for the bulletin board to use you, but its name probably won't be intuitive.

Installation overview

There are a couple of ways to install phpBB properly. A lot depends on what tools are available to you by your web hosting.

If your web host can only be accessed using Secure Shell (SSH), a command line tool, it's going to be a bit of a hassle and is best avoided. It's generally much easier and faster to use a web host control panel and an FTP program instead. That said, with some types of hosting, you might not have a choice.

If you have a modern web host control panel like Plesk or cPanel, it's much easier.

Installing phpBB is usually straightforward. I'll demonstrate how to install phpBB using a web host control panel (easier method) and using SSH (harder approach). I won't delve into installing phpBB in cloud hosting. You might want to check my website, phpbbservices.com, as there may be posts that will help.

Web host control panels are front-end web pages provided by web hosts that make it much simpler to set up and control your web hosting. Web host control panels vary, so those shown in this book won't necessarily look like yours. I will use cPanel, a popular panel that is most frequently seen on shared web hosting. cPanel's arrangement and look can be tailored by your web host, so if you have cPanel, my illustrations won't necessarily match yours.

The steps to installing phpBB using a cPanel are:

1. Acquire a domain

2. Acquire web hosting

3. Decide where you want to place the bulletin board

4. Install an SSL certificate (optional)

5. Create a database for the bulletin board

6. Download phpBB

7. Decompress the phpBB archive

8. Upload the files

9. Set folder and file permissions correctly

10. Run the install program

11. Remove the install folder

12. Change the config.php file permissions

Step 1. Acquire a domain

You must acquire a domain for the bulletin board, if you don't have one already. A domain is the logical URL name for a web site, like yahoo.com. See Appendix A to learn how to acquire one.

Step 2. Acquire web hosting

Your web hosting must meet phpBB's system requirements, which is rarely a problem. See Appendix A to learn how to select and acquire hosting.

Step 3. Decide where you want to place the bulletin board

On virtual or dedicated servers, finding the right folder to place your web content in can be a real adventure. It may be in a /home, /opt or /var folder buried somewhere. Often it appears in a /home folder, inside another folder labeled with your web host control panel username.

Your domain's web content is usually placed in a public_html or htdocs folder, but it varies depending on your operating system's configuration. Ask your web host if you don't know which folder to use.

You have three choices of where to place your bulletin board within a domain:

- **Web root folder**. This is the folder that contains your domain's entire web content. With this approach, your domain is the bulletin board, like www.myspecialboard.com.

- **Subfolder**. This is a folder inside your web root folder, like www.myspecialdomain.com/forums. In this scenario, your bulletin board is part of a larger website.

  To actually create a folder for your board (if it doesn't exist), you can:

  - **Use the File Manager in your web host control panel.** The file manager is a web interface in your web host control panel used for manipulating your web space's file system. Make sure it is inside the domain's web accessible folder.

  - **Use an FTP client.** FTP stands for File Transfer Protocol and is used for sending and receiving files over the Internet. An FTP client is a program that makes using FTP easy. Read Appendix B.

  - **Use SSH.** SSH is a command line method of accessing and controlling content on the Internet securely. It is invoked with the ssh command (lowercase). Some versions of Windows don't have this command on the Windows command line, or it must be enabled. Once connected via SSH to your web server, use the cd command to change to the parent directory of the bulletin board and then use the Linux mkdir command to create the directory.

You may need to follow this with `chmod` command to set proper permissions to the folder, which is generally 755 for Linux-based systems. Sometimes you also need to use the `chown` command to set the owner and group for the folder to match those of other folders.

- **Subdomain**. A *subdomain* is a domain inside a domain. With this approach, your bulletin board is logically and physically walled off from the rest of your site in a subdomain. For example, forums.myspecialdomain.com. This approach implies that it's okay for the bulletin board to look and behave differently than the rest of your site. Since phpBB is a standalone application, this is what I recommend if you have other content on your domain. The subdomain precedes the domain name and is followed by a period.

  You can create a subdomain through your web host control panel. After creating it, look for where its files will be stored. Sometimes you get a folder outside of your public_html or htdocs folder with the full subdomain name. Sometimes it will be a folder inside these folders.

  To create a subdomain using SSH, you should check the knowledge base of your web host as procedures vary.

Step 4. Install an SSL certificate (optional)

Generally, you will want to serve your board's content securely using SSL (secure socket layer) technology. This means your board's URL can have https:// at its start, rather than http://. This is done by installing an SSL certificate. Once installed, the certificate can be used to serve content securely for your entire domain.

If you board is not going to be serving any confidential information, you don't have to do this. But it's a good idea anyhow:

- Search engines will rank your site higher in their search indexes

- There is virtually no performance penalty for using SSL

- You can often install a free certificate that renews automatically

- If you intend to do eCommerce on your site, a proper certificate will help legitimize and authenticate your site

Most web hosts provide automatic self-signed certificates. These are undesirable. When used, the browser will report a security exception and warn you that the connection may be compromised. To use it, a user will have to tell the browser to authorize an exception.

If you plan to do eCommerce on your site, you might want to buy a higher-quality certificate. Various classes of certificates are available. A highly trusted certificate will validate your credentials, much the way the DMV does to give you a license. For example, a certificate with organizational validation means that some human took the time to validate the organization associated with the certificate is legitimate and was requested by the organization.

Most web hosts offer free Let's Encrypt security certificates that work automatically with all browsers. Only the domain in validated, and it is done using a token exchange when the certificate is created. For most sites, this is sufficient. A Let's Encrypt certificate may be created for you automatically, so check with your web host.

Figure 4.2 Let's encrypt option in cPanel

Figure 4.2 shows an interface in cPanel often provided for creating free Let's Encrypt certificates. If using Plesk or WHM, you may have to install a Let's Encrypt package first.

Generally, web hosts will automatically handle the process of renewing Let's Encrypt certificates, but check to make sure. This is a convenient and free way to handle SSL for your domain.

For higher classes of certificates, you may need to work with your web host to install the necessary private and public keys provided with the certificate. There is often a web host control panel form where you can enter these keys.

Step 5. Create a database for the bulletin board

Your web host will have one or more database management systems (DBMS) that you can use for phpBB. A DBMS is software that stores and retrieves data in a centralized database. Your database will hold the board's dynamic content, such as its posts and private messages. It also keeps a lot of information on the bulletin board's configuration, such as its name and characteristics.

phpBB supports the following database management systems:

- MySQL

- MariaDB

- Postgres

- Oracle

- SQLite

- SQL Server

phpBB is almost always installed using a MySQL or MariaDB database. These two DBMSes are identical for most purposes, and your web host will generally provide either MySQL or MariaDB, but not both. Either is fine.

You might also see a PostgreSQL option. On Windows servers, there will probably be a SQL Server option. SQL Server is Microsoft's DBMS.

While any of these can be used, I recommend using MySQL or MariaDB. Since they are more often used with phpBB, it is less likely there will be database integration issues. Postgres is also a fine choice and is free.

Create the database with a database wizard

Your web host control panel usually has an interface that can be used to create a database. If you are using cPanel, there is usually a MySQL or MariaDB Database Wizard you can use (Figure 4.3). In the database wizard, you will be prompted to provide:

- **A database name**. Each database requires a unique name. Sometimes the database prefix is filled out for you and can't be changed. Make it something you will recognize, perhaps using "board" or "forums" as part of the name.

- **A database username**. This is the name of the database user that will be authorized to use the database. Sometimes the username's prefix is filled out for you and can't be changed. To keep it simple, you might want to make it the same as the database name.

Figure 4.3: cPanel databases group

- **A database username password**. This authenticates the database username with the database. A complex password should be used. Make sure the database username is given **all privileges** to the database you created.

- **A database host name**. Sometimes you are given a database host name to use. This is the name of the machine that contains your database. The database is usually on the same machine as your web server, in which case, you can use "localhost" or sometimes an IP address of 127.0.0.1 as the database host name.

Note: Write these down, as you will need them later.

Create the database without the wizard

If you don't use the wizard, there is generally a three-step process to perform if you select the **MySQL Databases** option (Figure 4.2) or a similar option like **MariaDB Databases** or **Postgres Databases** in the control panel. Once you choose one and click into it, there should be blocks on the screen where you can create the database, create the database user with a password, and finally give privileges to database users to a database, just as in the wizard example above.

Create the database using Secure Shell (SSH)

To create a database using SSH, you will first need to figure out how to access your web host using SSH. If you are new to SSH, expect some hassle figuring out what server name, port, username and password to use.

Your web host should provide these, but sometimes you will have to ask them or find the information in their knowledge base. These commands are typically entered using a terminal prompt. The typical syntax for the SSH command is:

```
ssh -l username hostname
```

Port 22 is used by default by SSH. But if given a different port to use, you must specify the -p parameter with the port number to use after it:

```
ssh -l username -p 2222 hostname
```

You will be asked if you want to accept the key provided by the server. If you say yes, the key is stored on your computer in a special file. Generally, you want to say yes because it will speed up subsequent SSH connections.

Occasionally, web hosts will require enhanced security, requiring you to create private and public keys to use with SSH. This is definitely complicated for a novice to do. The syntax of the SSH command will change as well.

On Windows computers, you usually download a program called Putty and use it to connect. Newer versions of Windows 10 and Windows 11 can support SSH natively, if the OpenSSH feature is enabled. When enabled, it is run from PowerShell. On Macs and Linux computers, the ssh command is used from the Terminal application.

When connected, you should get a successful login message and a Linux command prompt, possibly prefixed by your current path on the server. The prompt is usually trailed by a $ sign.

Once you are connected with SSH, you will need to interact with the database through its own command prompt. To do this, you may need credentials to the database. This is *not* the same thing as the username and password used to connect with SSH.

If your DBMS is MySQL or MariaDB, use the mysql command, although with MariaDB the mariadb command can also be used. You may have to hunt for mysql's location on your host's file system, because it may not be in the Linux path. You may also need to preface the command with sudo because it may require root privileges to run, in which case your SSH username must have privileges to act as the root user on the server. The root user has complete access to the machine. The syntax to login to MySQL or MariaDB is:

```
mysql --user=username --password
```

With MariaDB, you can also use:

```
mariadb --user=username --password
```

The `--password` option forces a prompt to ask for the database username's password.

If you don't know your credentials for accessing MySQL or MariaDB, ask your web host. If you are logged in as root, because root often already has credentials to the DBMS, sometimes you just have to type:

```
mysql or mariadb
```

When logged in, you should get a command prompt like:

```
mysql> or mariadb>
```

Commands are entered after the prompt. *Each command or statement must end with a semicolon.* Press **Enter** or **Return** to execute the command.

Next, I will show a MySQL/MariaDB syntax example with a database name and database user of "forums." These commands are standardized across most database management systems. I use upper case for the commands, a convention in SQL, but it is not required. To create the database named "forums":

```
CREATE DATABASE forums;
```

If you want to use the database username you used to invoke the mysql command for the bulletin board, you can skip the next step. I think it's cleaner to create a separate username for your bulletin board's database.

In this case, the database username is also "forums" with the password "abc123" (obviously, this is not a secure password). If your database is on a different machine than your web server, you should replace "localhost" with the machine name or the IP of the database server. So, in this example, to create a database user "forums" on a database server called localhost, use this:

```
CREATE USER 'forums'@'localhost' IDENTIFIED BY
'abc123';
```

phpBB requires that the database username has all privileges to the database. This is because when phpBB is installed, tables are created. Also, some extensions need to alter the database and will fail without these privileges.

To grant all these privileges for a database user named "forums" to a database named "forums" on a database server called localhost, use this:

```
GRANT ALL PRIVILEGES ON forums.* TO
'forums'@'localhost';
```

You can now type `quit` or `exit` to get out from the database command line interface. To exit SSH, type `exit`.

If you are using Microsoft hosting and Microsoft's SQL Server database, there is usually a separate interface for creating these credentials. Your web host can provide more information, but the procedures will probably vary considerably.

Step 6. Download phpBB

Make sure you download the latest version of phpBB, which can be obtained at:

https://www.phpbb.com/downloads/

Step 7. Decompress the phpBB archive

The archive containing phpBB must be decompressed. An archive is a collection of many files and folders stored in one file. To access the files and folders in the archive, it must be expanded (decompressed) with a program. Double-clicking on it usually starts the decompression process. From a local command prompt, the `unzip` command usually will decompress the archive as well. Either way, it will result in more than 4000 files extracted, all of which need to be moved to your web server.

The archive can also be uploaded then decompressed using your web host control panel's file manager on the web server itself, instead of on your local machine. The phpBB Group doesn't like this approach, but it has always worked for me, so I consider it safe. This approach is covered below and tends to be much faster. The procedures for doing this as discussed in the next step.

Step 8. Upload phpBB's source files

Uploading phpBB using FTP

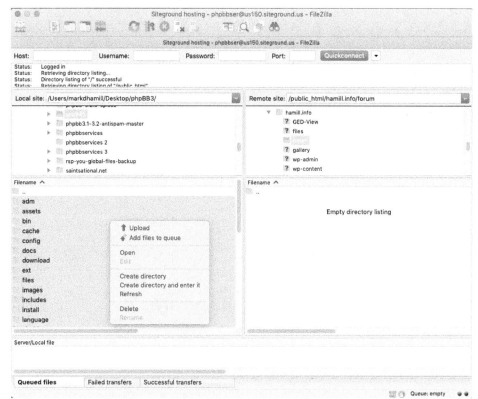

Figure 4.4: Uploading files with FileZilla

If you are unfamiliar with File Transfer Protocol (FTP), read Appendix B. Basically, an FTP program is used to move files between your computer and a computer on the Internet.

The phpBB archive should contain a folder with a single folder inside it called "phpBB3." You need to move only the files *inside* the phpBB3 folder to the web host. Figure 4.4 shows how this could be done using the FileZilla FTP program.

The left pane shows my local machine. It is focused inside a phpBB3 folder containing the uncompressed archive downloaded from phpbb.com. I selected all the files in the phpBB3 folder, which is easy to do by pressing CTRL-A (or Command A on a Mac) in that window.

The right pane shows my web server and the empty board folder, which will contain the phpBB bulletin board.

To move all these files into the board folder on my domain, all I need to do is click on the **Upload** link. In the FTP program FileZilla, I can get it by right-mouse clicking in the left window. It generally takes at least five minutes to move the files.

Using the File Manager to upload the files

There is a faster way to transfer the files if you have a web host control panel file manager. It's just a little trickier. Here are the steps:

1. Using the file manager, navigate to the folder where your bulletin board will be. Use the **Upload** button generally near the top of the file manager to select and upload the archive (.zip file).

2. Once uploaded, the archive should appear in the file manager. If not, press the **Reload** or **Refresh** button. It should have a name like phpBB-3.3.x.zip, where x is a number.

3. Make sure the archive is highlighted after you click on it. Then press the **Extract** button or link, which is usually near the top of the File Manager. Change the path for the extracted files, if necessary, and press **Extract File(s)**. When you do this, a window showing all the files and folders that were decompressed should appear. Close the window and press the **Reload** or **Refresh** button to see all the new files.

4. Now, there should be a subfolder named phpBB3 plus the original phpBB-3.3.x.zip file you uploaded. Select the .zip file then press the **Delete** button.

5. Double-click on the phpBB3 folder to go into it.

6. Select all the files. First click on the adm folder at the top, then scroll to the bottom, then while holding the SHIFT key, select the last file. All files should be highlighted.

7. Click on the **Move** button near the top of the page. Change the path to remove phpBB3 from the path, so the files are moved to the parent folder. Then press the **Move File** button.

8. Press the **Up One Level** button.

9. Get rid of the phpBB3 folder (*not* the phpbb folder) by clicking on it and then pressing **Delete**.

Step 9. Set folder and file permissions correctly

After uploading the files, they should be right where you need them.

While it's tempting to run the install program next, certain folders need to have public write permissions.

You can use your FTP client or the File Manager to check the permissions and change them if needed. Sometimes they inherit the right permissions. To change permissions using FileZilla, you right-mouse click on each applicable folder and select **File permissions**. In the typical File Manager, you select the file or folder and select **Change Permissions**. You may have to right-mouse click on the folder to see the option.

The following folders must have public write permissions (777). This means the owner, the group and the public should be able to read, write and execute the following folders:

- cache

- files

- images/avatars/upload

- store

You may also have to change the permissions of the empty config.php file temporarily to 666.

Getting these permissions correct on Windows hosting can be challenging and may require filing a support ticket. Windows goes out of its way to avoid giving any folder or file public write permissions.

Step 10. Run the install program

phpBB is usually installed with a web browser. I will demonstrate this approach. Just be aware that phpBB also has a command line interface, so it can be installed that way too.

It's more work to use the command line interface, but if you want to use the command line, here's a set of instructions you can use:

https://area51.phpbb.com/docs/dev/3.3.x/cli/getting_started.html

Note: If your bulletin board's domain is not already connected to your web hosting, you must either wait until it is or do a little-known trick. It's possible to tell your local computer to use the domain's IP address as if the domain is connected to your hosting. It won't work outside of your computer, however. Details are in Appendix E.

Otherwise, use the URL for your new bulletin board to start the installation process. The URL you will use will look similar to these:

- If your bulletin board is the website: http://www.myspecialforums.com

- If your bulletin board is a folder in a website: http://www.myspecialdomain.com/forums

- If your bulletin board is a subdomain: http://forums.myspecialdomain.com

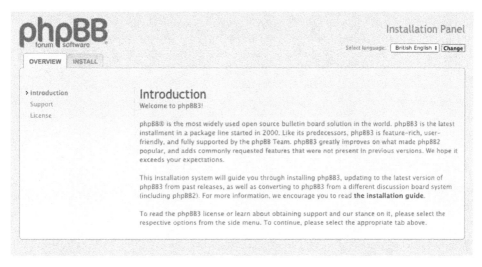

Figure 4.5: Introduction screen

You will be directed to the install program automatically. Simply enter the URL for your new board. If you want, you can add /install to the end of the URL and start it directly.

The URL will change as you are redirected to the install folder, where the installation program resides.

If you do not have a compatible version of PHP installed, you will get an immediate error. Your web host control panel usually has an interface that allows you to change the version of PHP used.

Then you will first see an introduction screen (Figure 4.5) where you can simply click on the **Install** tab, which will render the next screen (Figure 4.6). This next screen is only informational so click on the **Install** button to launch the rest of the installation wizard. If you made any errors, the installation process will catch them. For example, if you specify an invalid database name and try to submit the form, the page will refresh with the database name field highlighted and a message that it could not be found. Correct any errors and submit the form again, until the next page appears.

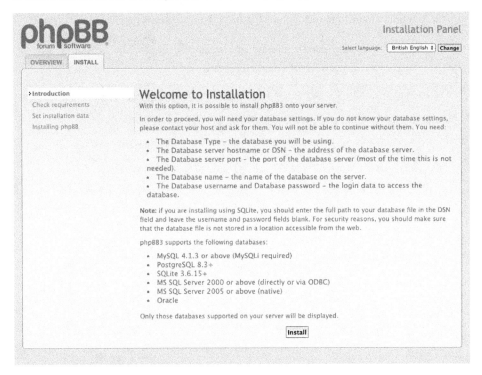

Figure 4.6: Installation introduction screen

Here are the rest of the Install Wizard screens:

See Figure 4.7. On this screen, you create the administrator's credentials to login to the bulletin board, along with the administrator's password. This administrator is special: it's a *founder*. Founders can do special things, like create forums.

- **Administrator username**. Avoid using "admin" for the administrator username.

- **Contact email address**. You also need to specify the administrator's email address. Ideally, this would be an existing email address associated with your domain. We'll get more into this in the next chapter, so you can save this detail for later if you want. For now, enter a valid email address that you use.

- **Administrator password**. The administrator's bulletin board password should be complex. Confirm the password in the next field.

*Note: Make sure you record the administrator's username and password before you press the **Submit** button.*

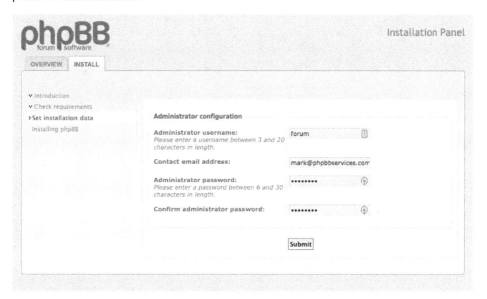

Figure 4.7: Installation administration configuration screen

See Figure 4.8. Next you will connect phpBB to a chosen database. The installation program writes to the empty config.php file in the bulletin board's root folder with the information you supply here, which is why the file has to be publicly writeable during installation.

- **Database type**. Generally, you select the default MySQL with MySQLi Extension. This should also work if your database management system is MariaDB. If you chose a different database management system, you will need to select it from the dropdown. All database management systems the server knows about will be shown in the dropdown.

- **Database server hostname or DSN**. Unless you were given a database machine name, enter "localhost." If neither works, try 127.0.0.1.

Figure 4.8: Installation database configuration screen

On Windows hosts, you can use a configured DSN (Data Source Name) to specify the database to use. This is basically an alias you create that allows Windows to reference the database more easily. This requires first setting up an Open Database Connectivity (ODBC) interface to the database. The DSN still needs to connect to a database management system that phpBB supports. So, if you have a DSN defined to connect to a Microsoft Access database, you could not use it.

- **Database server port**. Generally, leave this blank. Each database management system has a default port it uses. For example, MySQL uses port 3306 by default. If you were given a different port to use, enter it in the field.

- **Database username**. Enter the database username you created earlier with permissions to the bulletin board's database.

- **Database password**. Enter the password you created earlier for the database username.

- **Database name**. Enter the name you gave the bulletin board's database.

- **Prefix for tables in database**. Generally, you should leave the default phpbb_ unchanged. The same prefix is used to identify all phpBB tables in the database. For example, the default table containing users of the bulletin board is the phpbb_users table. If you use one database for lots of software solutions, you might want to change the prefix to something like board_.

  If you used phpBB before, the database may have a set of phpBB tables already in the database, probably for an earlier version of phpBB. If so, this might be a reason to use a different database prefix because the installer cannot create tables that already exist. Attempts will generate an error and could potentially alter data in these old tables.

Press the **Submit** button when done.

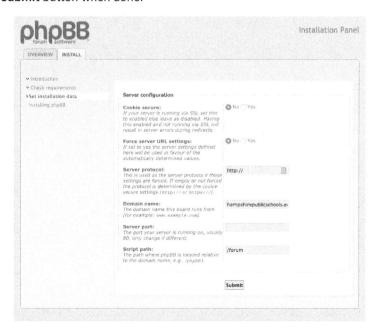

Figure 4.9: Installation server configuration screen

This will lead you to the Server configuration page (Figure 4.9). Here, you enter your server's configuration information.

Generally, you only need to review these settings if you set **Force server URL** settings to **Yes**. Most of the time phpBB will figure out the server protocol, domain name to use and the script path from the web server, which is usually authoritative.

Press **Submit** when done.

Figure 4.10: Installation email configuration screen

On the screen that follows, you can configure email settings (Figure 4.10). It's often sufficient to leave these settings unchanged when installing phpBB and come back to them later if you want to enable SMTP for sending emails. This will be covered in Chapter 5.

- **Enable board-wide emails**. You should enable this or no emails can be sent, including account activation emails. It's enabled by default.

- **Use SMTP server for email**. This will be covered more in the next chapter. If you have a set of tested SMTP server credentials, you can set this to **Yes** and fill in the other fields. Otherwise leave the other fields blank and leave the setting **No**. It's very easy to get SMTP settings wrong, so it's best to leave these as is for now. There are some powerful reasons to use a SMTP server that we'll get into later.

Press **Submit** when done.

In this last screen, you name your bulletin board and tell the world a little bit about it (Figure 4.11).

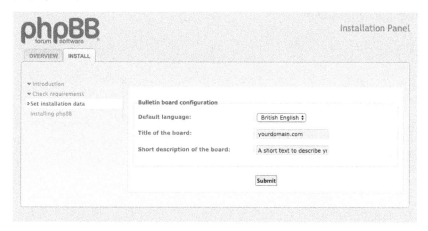

Figure 4.11: Installation bulletin board configuration screen

- **Default language**. Unless you proactively uploaded a different language pack for phpBB, you won't be able to change this. In the next chapter, we will cover adding different language packs.

- **Title of the board**. This is how your board will be advertised to the world. Whatever you enter here should appear in the bulletin board's header. It will also appear in the HTML <title> tag on the board's web pages. This is easily changed later. It should probably not be your domain name, as by itself that's pretty meaningless.

- **Short description of the board**. This is an optional one-line description that tells a bit more about the purpose of your bulletin board. It will also show up on the bulletin board's header. This is easily changed later too. You should remove the default text if you don't plan to type something in this field.

Press **Submit** when done.

It takes about a minute or less to create and populate all the tables that phpBB will use with some basic data. When you see Figure 4.12, you are done with installation.

Note: If you are connected properly for sending out emails, you should get a confirmation email in your inbox containing your username and a login link. Save it for future reference. If you don't get an email, first look in your Spam folder. It may be there. Then make a note that this is an issue for later analysis.

Next, click on the link to **the ACP**.

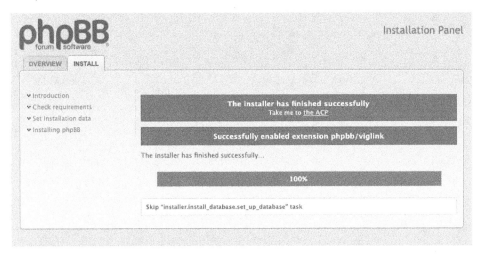

Figure 4.12: Installation completion screen

With your first access into the Administration Control Panel, you are asked if you want to share your statistics with the phpBB Group and whether you want to enable the VigLink extension. These questions should appear only once. Both are enabled by default. (Figure 4.13)

Figure 4.13: Help support phpBB screen

Enabling the VigLink extension (we'll discuss extensions later in the book) is a way to help fund the phpBB Group, which depends on donations, but its presence is unobtrusive. You can also use it to potentially monetize your bulletin board. If you want to do this, enable the extension and make a note to configure the VigLink extension later.

Press **Submit** after making your choices, which will lead you to a confirmation screen (Figure 4.14).

Figure 4.14: Confirmation screen

Step 11. Remove the install folder

One more step must be done manually to complete the install process. The /install folder, which contains the installation programs, is still present. Until removed, the bulletin board is inaccessible to users, and you will be nagged with a warning message about removing the install folder every time you go into the ACP (Figure 4.15).

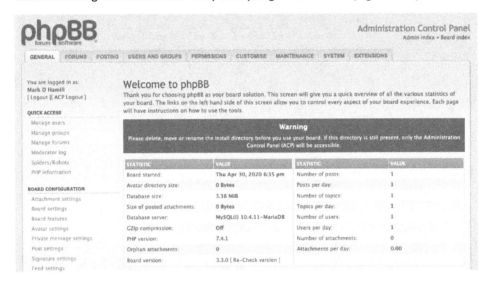

Figure 4.15: Warning to remove install folder

To remove the /install folder, use either FTP or the web host control panel's File Manager. If you use SSH and are in the bulletin board's main folder, it is easily removed with the following Linux command:

```
rm -rf install
```

You can now see your new, hot-off-the-press bulletin board! Simply click on the Board index link in the top right corner of the ACP to preview the default set up.

Step 12. Change the config.php file permissions

If your board's config.php is publicly writeable, you will get a warning message encouraging you to change the file's permissions to 640 or 644 when entering the ACP.

After installation, its permissions are normally set to 644, which means it can be read but not written to by phpBB. 644 permissions are safe, but 640 is better. It just takes a minute; so, take the time to use FTP or your web host file manager to remove group and public read permissions by making its permissions 640.

Chapter 5 | Basic phpBB configuration

Figure 5.1: phpBB board index after a default installation

If you chose all the defaults during installation, your new board will look like Figure 5.1.

At this point, it's not yet tailored to your needs. To set it up the way you want:

- Change your bulletin board title and bulletin board description.

- Change "Your first category."

- Change "Your first forum" and its description.

- You probably need to create more forums.

- You may want to give your board a different look by installing a different style, if the default prosilver style is unappealing.

- You will likely want to use a different logo.

- You may want the bulletin board to present a language other than British English.

In this chapter, we'll look at how to get your board up and running in a rather basic way. In Chapter 6, we'll look at how to add the polish and get phpBB tuned just right.

Refining your board settings

To start to make a useful board, refine your board's settings (Figure 5.2).

ACP > General > Board configuration > Board settings

The Board settings page has three sets of fields in it. We're going to concentrate on the first set, and ignore the Board style and Warnings groups.

You already set an initial site name and site description during installation, but these can be changed at any time. The first two fields, **site name** and **site description**, are the most important. This is because they succinctly tell both people and search engines what your board is about.

- **Site name.** This is the name for your bulletin board. The name is shown in the header of most pages of the board. Since it appears in the title of your browser tab, it is also in the HTML <title> tag on almost every page of your board, a key tag scanned by search agents.

  The site name should succinctly brand your board. It's how your page will show up in search engines. You are allowed 255 characters, but you should use less than that. No more than sixty characters are ideal.

- **Site description**. Here you may write a couple of short sentences about what your board is about. You're limited to 255 characters. Feel free to leave this blank if your site title is sufficiently informative. In most styles, the site description appears below the site title, in a smaller font.

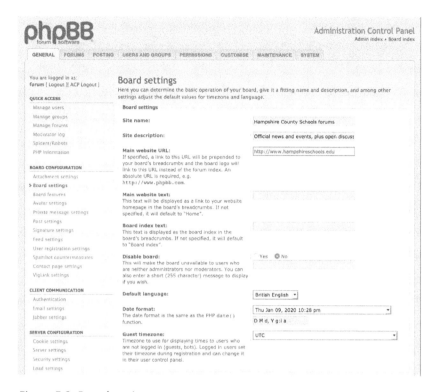

Figure 5.2: Board settings screen

- **Main website URL.** If your board is part of a larger website, this is the link that takes you back to the larger website, which is typically the main page for the board's domain. This is optional, but if specified, it dynamically adds a **Home** link to your breadcrumb menu (Figure 5.3). Click on the **Home** link and you are taken to that page, which is outside of the bulletin board. Leave it blank and the link will not appear on the breadcrumb menu.

Figure 5.3: Home page link

- **Main website text**. If you prefer to give a name to the home link other than "Home," you can specify it in this field. *Note: This text will be substituted for all language packs used on your board.*

- **Board index text**. If you don't want the words "Board index" to show on your breadcrumb menu, you can call it something else by changing this text. *Note: This text will be substituted for all language packs used on your board.*

- **Disable board**. Normally this is left at **No**. When disabled, no one can make posts on the board, and users will see a message saying the board is disabled. You should disable the board if there is a serious technical issue or before updating or upgrading the board's software. If you are concerned about getting registrations before having the board all set up, you might want to set this to **Yes**, just make a note to change it to **No** when your board is fully set up.

- **Default language**. Normally only one language pack is activated because few boards can assume everyone is multi-lingual. Initially, only British English is available. Adding additional language packs is covered later in this chapter.

- **Date format**. This displays how dates and times are rendered on the board by default and to guests. A user that doesn't like the format can change it in the User Control Panel.

  The syntax for expressing dates is a little strange. Since phpBB is written in the PHP programming language, it uses syntax for the PHP <u>date</u> command to format dates for display. If you want to change the date format, you need to look up this syntax with a search engine and change this field accordingly.

- **Guest timezone**. This is the time zone that is assumed if you are not logged in. If your board is a regional one, change this to your local time zone. It defaults to Coordinated Universal Time (UTC).

As with all these forms, you need to press a **Submit** button at the bottom for the changes to take effect.

Do you need to create any special groups?

Before you start creating forums, consider whether or not you need to create special groups. All forums are tied to the various groups given permissions to access them.

Life is much easier for an administrator if you only use phpBB's built-in groups. You can see these at:

ACP > Users and Groups > Groups > Manage groups (Figure 5.4)

Let's study phpBB's built-in groups:

- **Administrators**. Initially, you are the only administrator, and you are a special type of administrator called a *founder*. You can create other administrators who can be assigned all sorts of finely tuned administrator permissions.

- **Bots**. phpBB recognizes most popular bots (search agents) automatically. You can add more manually if you want. Using phpBB's permission system, you can limit what these bots can do. For example, you can keep these bots from indexing your board in their search engines. More on this later.

- **Global moderators**. A global moderator can moderate the content of any forum they can access. You became a global moderator when phpBB was installed, but you can create others. You generally don't need moderators right away when starting out, but it's good to know that phpBB cleanly separates administration from moderation. If you want an administrator to also be a global moderator, you will need to manually put them in this group.

- **Guests**. These are any humans looking at your bulletin board that aren't registered or any existing user that is logged out. There is no reason to add additional members to this group, as all use the one account called "Anonymous."

- **Newly registered users**. After you open the bulletin board to the public, people will register. By default, newly registered users appear in this group until they make three posts, which must pass moderation before being publicly available. On the fourth post, they are automatically removed from this group. You can change this: **ACP > General > Board configuration > User registration settings > New member post limit**

- **Registered users**. Registered users include anyone who has registered on the bulletin board. This includes users that haven't completed registration yet or haven't yet had their registration approved. What's curious is that newly registered users go into this group as soon as they register too, which means they appear as Newly registered users *and* as Registered users. By default, phpBB's permissions system will apply Newly registered users' permissions before those for registered users are applied. So, everyone who gets past the registration screen is automatically placed in this group. In addition, you, as an administrator, are also considered a registered user.

- **Registered COPPA users**. The United States has a law called COPPA (Children's Online Privacy Protection Act). If you have a bulletin board used in the United States that allows children to register, they should be in this group. This allows you to fine-tune their privileges, perhaps limiting them to a kids-only, highly moderated forum. This feature is rarely used. When it is enabled, whoever registers has to indicate if they are age 13 or above. If under age 13, the administrator must receive a signed parental permission, either by mail or fax, before making the user active, and keep records of minor users. The COPPA feature is off by default. If you want to use it, turn it on: **ACP > General > Board configuration > User registration settings > COPPA**

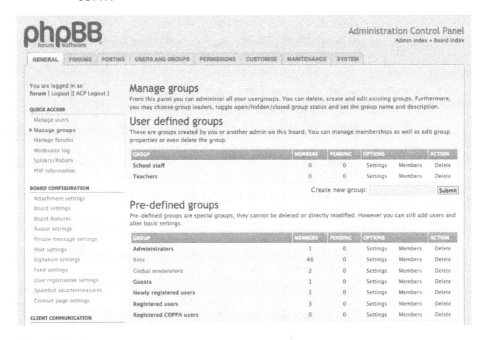

Figure 5.4: Manage groups screen

You need to figure out if you need other groups in addition to these. phpBB calls these *user defined groups.* You only need to create user-defined groups if they will have special forum permissions that registered users will not.

An example might be a school district's bulletin board. Students should not be able to access forums used by teachers, so you might want to create a teacher's group. Ideally, the teachers' forums would be visible to teachers only, or anyone who works for the school system. phpBB's permission system allows this.

Note: If you anticipate needing groups like these, you should decide the group names needed now. Write these down. You will create them later.

I frequently see forums that only administrators or moderators can access. These behind-the-scenes forums are not of interest to others, or are too sensitive to share more publicly. They can be created later, if you find you need them.

Server configuration

The server configuration group (**ACP > General settings > Server configuration**) has a number of screens that help your server work optimally with your board. Once set, they can generally be ignored.

Figure 5.5: Cookie settings screen

There are many options on these pages, and most are best left initially undisturbed. So, I'll concentrate on the ones to pay attention to during the configuration process.

Cookie settings

Cookies help a browser remember a user's relationship with a website. phpBB creates a number of cookies that the browser uses, mostly to remember who logged in.

ACP > General settings > Server configuration > Cookie settings (Figure 5.5)

The defaults shown are probably good to start out.

- **Cookie domain**. Do not change this unless your board is in a subdomain. If the cookie applies to the whole domain, it should always start with a period. But if your board is in a subdomain like myboard.mydomain.com, the cookie domain is myboard.mydomain.com, without the period at the front.

- **Cookie name**. This can be anything you want. The cookie name is hidden, so it can be a string of random letters. If you have other software on the domain, you don't want the cookie name to conflict with any existing cookie names.

- **Cookie path**. This controls where the cookie can be used in your domain or subdomain. Generally, there is no reason to change it from / (which means it can be used anywhere in your domain), but if your board is in a folder called "board" off your web root and you want your board's cookies only to work inside that folder, you might want to change this to /board. Leave a trailing slash in the cookie path, like /board/.

- **Cookie secure**. If you already have a working security (SSL) certificate installed, and insecure (http) access is not allowed, you should click **Enable**. This means the cookie can only be used if the web traffic on your board is encrypted.

- **Cookie notice**. If you don't want to present a notice that your board uses cookies, disable this. It's enabled by default. The cookie notice shows up as a banner across the bottom of the index until the user confirms the cookie notice. It's considered a good practice to let users know your site uses cookies. In some countries, you may be legally required to display a cookie notice.

Note: If you change the board cookie name, users must login again.

Server settings

You don't usually need to change server settings, although it's a good idea to review them to make sure they are set the way you want.

ACP > General settings > Server configuration > Server settings (Figure 5.6)

In most cases you don't need to change server protocol, domain name, server port and script path fields on the page, even if the values in these fields are incorrect. Only if you select **Yes** for the **Force server URL settings** option will the data in these fields be used. For example, if the server protocol field says http:// but you are using https, phpBB will detect this and create URLs that use https://.

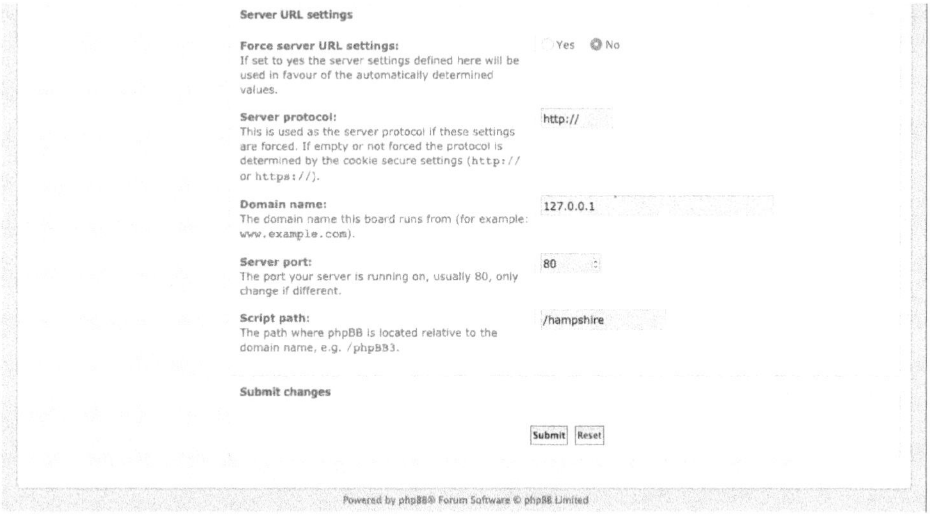

Figure 5.6: Server settings screen

If you want to force server URL settings and have installed an SSL certificate to use https (encrypted http), such as a free Let's Encrypt certificate, then you should:

- Change the **server protocol** from **http://** to **https://**

- Change the **server port** from **80** to **443**

Why is this? This is because normally phpBB gets this information from the web server, which is authoritative. Also, if you make a mistake (like enter an invalid script path), the URL becomes invalid and will return an error.

In the server settings block (not shown), you might want to change the **Enable Gzip compression** to **Yes**. Look for the field at the top of the page. Web pages and other content will be sent compressed to users if Gzip is configured with your version of PHP. It usually is. An easy way to see if your web server supports Gzip compression is to go to this web page and enter the URL for your board in the search field:

https://www.whatsmyip.org/http-compression-test/

The cost of compressing the content is usually less than sending the data uncompressed across the Internet. All browsers can decompress compressed web pages and files.

Security settings

ACP > General settings > Server configuration > Security settings

There are a lot of options on this page, most of them quite advanced and, ironically, most of which won't do much to improve security. We'll discuss these more in the next chapter. In the meantime, here are a two fields worth considering changing when configuring your board:

- **Password length**. You might consider changing this from a minimum of six characters for the password to eight. The more characters, the harder it is to crack the password.

- **Password complexity**. Change this from the default **No requirements**. **Must contain numbers and letters** is a pragmatic choice. Obviously, simple passwords are easier to crack.

Load settings

ACP > General settings > Server configuration > Load settings

These settings help keep your board available if traffic is high. Normally this is not a problem with a new board, but over time you may want to tweak some of these settings. A fuller discussion of these settings will be covered in the next chapter.

Search settings

ACP > General settings > Server configuration > Search settings

phpBB automatically indexes the content of your posts so content can be found using its search engine. The mechanism used depends on your database management system and your search indexing choice.

Use the **Search backend** dropdown field to select the type of search index. By default, the phpBB Native Fulltext index is used. This means that phpBB uses a set of its database tables as its search index: phpbb_search_results, phpbb_search_wordlist and phpbb_search_wordmatch.

If you change the search engine, you will be prompted to re-create the search index:

ACP > Maintenance > Database > Search index

On small boards, this takes only a few seconds. On very large boards, it can take hours, so it's a good idea to disable your board if you know it will take a while:

ACP > General > Board configuration > Board settings > Disable board > Yes

If you are using MySQL or MariaDB for your database management system, you can opt for the MySQL fulltext index. While it's faster to create a MySQL fulltext index, choosing it won't save a significant amount of space in your database.

With this option, the search tables are not used. Instead, three MySQL fulltext indexes are added to the phpbb_posts table and are used to perform searches.

As posts are made, it takes a little time to add the words in the post to the search index. This may result in a short lag when submitting a post.

The search index is uses up about 50% of a database's total space. So removing the search tables can be a quick way to address database quota issues, but at the expense of losing the ability to search your board.

ACP > Maintenance > Database > Search index

Press the **Delete** button for the search index that is populated. Afterward, you should disabled the search feature for the board: **ACP > General > Server configuration > Search settings > Enable search facilities > No**

However, with the search engine disabled and the search index removed, you will get an annoying message on the ACP's main page saying the search index for the chosen search engine doesn't exist.

It's important to note that if you are changing the search engine you should remove the old search index to save space:

ACP > Maintenance > Database > Search index

We'll discuss this more in the next chapter.

Decide the forums and categories you need

Before creating new forums, you first need to create a plan that answers these questions:

- What are the names of the forums I need?

- What category should each forum be placed into? (Technically, a forum on the index doesn't need to be inside a category, but usually is.)

- Which groups should be able to *read* the forum?

- Which groups should be able to *post* to the forum?

- Should the forum be a subforum (a forum inside another category or forum)? If so, what forum or category should it belong to?

- How should the forums and categories be arranged from the top to the bottom on the index? If forums are to be nested inside a category or another forum, what should their order be?

| | | Pre-defined groups | | | | | | User defined groups | |
Category	Forum name	Administrators	Bots	Guests	Global moderators	Newly registered users	Registered users	Teachers group	School staff group
School district news	Academic news	Read – yes Post – yes	Read – yes Post – no	Read – yes Post – no	Read – yes Post – yes	Read – yes Post – no	Read – yes Post – no	Read – yes Post – yes	Read – yes Post – yes
	Sports news	Read – yes Post – yes	Read – yes Post – no	Read – yes Post – no	Read – yes Post – yes	Read – yes Post – no	Read – yes Post – no	Read – yes Post – yes	Read – yes Post – yes
	Coming events	Read – yes Post – yes	Read – yes Post – no	Read – yes Post – no	Read – yes Post – yes	Read – yes Post – no	Read – yes Post – no	Read – yes Post – yes	Read – yes Post – yes
Student forums	Elementary school	Read – yes Post – yes	Read – yes Post – no	Read – yes Post – no	Read – yes Post – yes	Read – yes Post – yes	Read – yes Post – yes	Read – yes Post – yes	Read – yes Post – yes
	Secondary school	Read – yes Post – yes	Read – yes Post – yes	Read – yes Post – yes	Read – yes Post – yes	Read – yes Post – yes	Read – yes Post – yes	Read – yes Post – yes	Read – yes Post – yes
	High school	Read – yes Post – yes	Read – yes Post – yes	Read – yes Post – yes	Read – yes Post – yes	Read – yes Post – yes	Read – yes Post – yes	Read – yes Post – yes	Read – yes Post – yes
Teacher forums	Science teachers	Read – yes Post – yes	Read – no Post – no	Read – no Post – no	Read – yes Post – yes	Read – no Post – no	Read – no Post – no	Read – yes Post – yes	Read – yes Post – yes
	Math teachers	Read – yes Post – yes	Read – no Post – no	Read – no Post – no	Read – yes Post – yes	Read – no Post – no	Read – no Post – no	Read – yes Post – yes	Read – yes Post – yes
	English teachers	Read – yes Post – yes	Read – no Post – no	Read – no Post – no	Read – yes Post – yes	Read – no Post – no	Read – no Post – no	Read – yes Post – yes	Read – yes Post – yes
	Foreign language teachers	Read – yes Post – yes	Read – no Post – no	Read – no Post – no	Read – yes Post – yes	Read – no Post – no	Read – no Post – no	Read – yes Post – yes	Read – yes Post – yes
	Teaching assistants	Read – yes Post – yes	Read – no Post – no	Read – no Post – no	Read – yes Post – yes	Read – no Post – no	Read – no Post – no	Read – yes Post – yes	Read – yes Post – yes

Figure 5.7: Forum plan

Since phpBB allows forums to be nested inside of other forums and categories, they can be layered quite deep. Your tendency might be to have dozens of forums that go many levels deep.

Broadly speaking, this is not a good strategy, in part because nested forums are harder to notice. Keep it simple at first. You can always create new forums and categories later, or move a forum on the index inside other forums or categories.

Figure 5.7 shows a potential plan for a school district's forums, including how they will be arranged on the index and the planned privileges for each group.

Each forum exists within a category, so the category "School district news" will contain three forums: "Academic news," "Sports news" and "Coming events." The idea in this example is to limit the teachers' forums to teachers, administrators, global moderators and the school staff groups *only*. Students would be ordinary registered users, so they would not be able to see, read or post to the teachers' forums, the same should be true with parents or the general public.

Two user-defined groups are planned: a teachers' group and a school staff group. phpBB has dozens of forum permissions. To keep it simple, the plan concentrates on two big permissions: Can members of a group read a forum? And can members of a group post to the forum?

If you put together a plan like this, you can save yourself a lot of time and effort later.

Create the forums and categories you need

With a plan defined, you know the forums you need to create and how they should be organized. So, let's create them! We'll save getting the forum permissions correct for later. What we'll do instead is use the default permissions created for "Your first forum" for the forums we want to create. This will simplify things considerably.

Rename "Your first category"

Let's start with renaming the category titled "Your first category":

ACP > Forums > Manage forums

"Your first category" is a default name. To change its name, click on the green edit wheel (see Figure 5.8). This brings up the Edit forum screen.

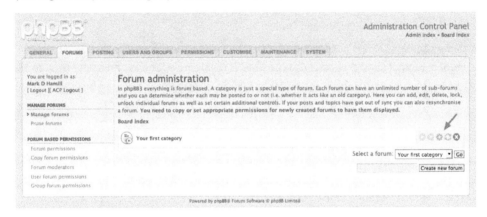

Figure 5.8: Manage category screen

Here you are actually editing a category, but the screen is identical to editing a forum (Figure 5.9).

We'll concentrate on the first section of the page: the forum settings block. The other sections contain settings that are rarely used but can be added at any time.

Let's look at some of these fields (Figure 5.9):

- **Forum type**. You can choose either **category**, **forum** or **link**. A *category* is a collection of similar forums. A *forum* contains a set of related topics. You cannot make posts in a category, as it is a wrapper. Posts are made in forums.

A *link* is a pseudo-forum which links to a URL you specify, which is generally outside of the board. It can be any URL that you want.

- **Parent forum**. Since this is your first category, it has no parent, so it will appear on the index. If you wanted to create a category or forum that belonged inside another category or forum, you would set the parent's name here.

- **Copy permissions from**. Since this category was created for us during installation, it has a set of default permissions already. We don't need to change it for this category. But as we create forums, we'll discover that we generally want to copy permissions from another forum, just not in this case.

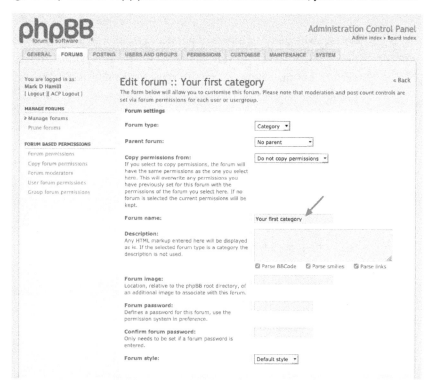

Figure 5.9: Edit forum screen

- **Forum name.** In this case, we are not renaming a forum, but a category. Based on your plan, change the name "Your first category" to the category name you've decided on. In my example plan, this becomes the "School district news" category. Do not imbed HTML tags because they will be interpreted literally.

- **Description**. Here, you can give more information about the category or forum. If you do, it will show up on the index. Or you can leave it blank. Do not imbed HTML tags because they will be interpreted literally.

- **Forum password**. It's very unusual to use a forum password. If used, to access the forum, all users must enter the same password. The password becomes a shared secret for everyone using the forum. Users must enter the password to access the forum.

  phpBB's permission system is typically used to control access to various users and groups, making this extra level of security unnecessary. Given this, it's unclear why this is a feature of phpBB. Just because a forum is accessed by a password, doesn't mean anyone can see the forum. Other phpBB permissions may make it unseen to groups like guests. So, the password becomes an additional security measure in addition to phpBB's robust permission system.

- **Forum style**. To start, only the default prosilver style is installed. Installing additional styles is covered later. If you install additional styles, it's possible to select a style to apply to a particular forum. This is rarely seen, as most administrators prefer their board to have a consistent look across all pages.

Press **Submit** after you have renamed "My first category." After a dialog page appears, confirming the settings are saved, you can click on a link and return to the Manage forums screen.

Rename "Your first forum"

Now let's change the name of "Your first forum."

First, click on the **category** link, which should now be using the name you chose for the category.

Since I renamed "Your first category" to "School district news," the screen shows us "Your first forum" is now inside the renamed "School district news" category (Figure 5.10).

To go to the Edit forum screen, click on the green wheel beside "Your first forum."

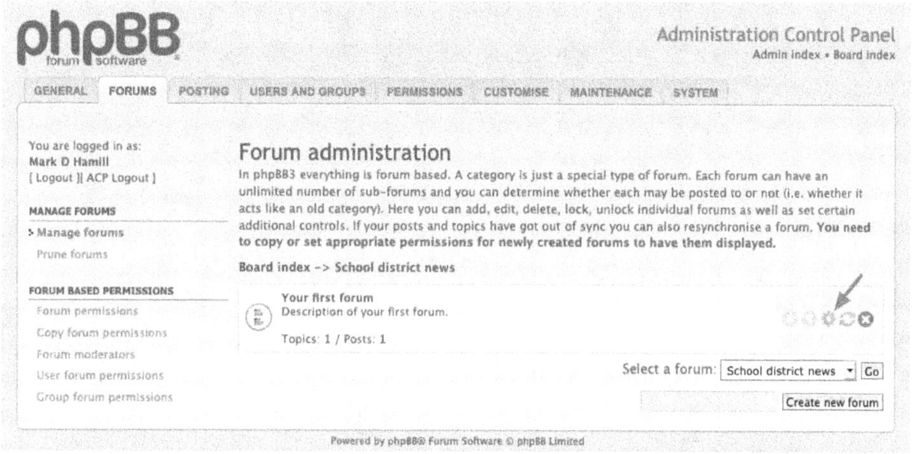

Figure 5.10: Edit forum screen, for a nested forum

Here we change the name of the forum based on your plan. In my plan, this becomes "Academic news." I also want to change the description field to something that better describes the forum. This can be left blank.

Again, I don't need to copy permissions at this time, as the forum already had some default permissions when it was created during installation. We can fine-tune them later.

Pressing **Submit** brings you to a confirmation screen, and then clicking on the link returns you to the Manage forum screen, though we are now within the forum's category.

Creating additional categories and forums

You need to create additional categories and forums based on your plan. Hopefully, you now understand the process for doing this.

Check your navigation. Make sure you are at the right location in your forum hierarchy. You are either at the top level or inside a category. Use links in the breadcrumb menu on the Manage forums screen or the **Select a forum** dropdown with the **Go** button to get to the proper part of the hierarchy quickly.

Then go to the Edit forum screen (Figure 5.9). The name of the forum or category is filled in based on what you entered in the last screen.

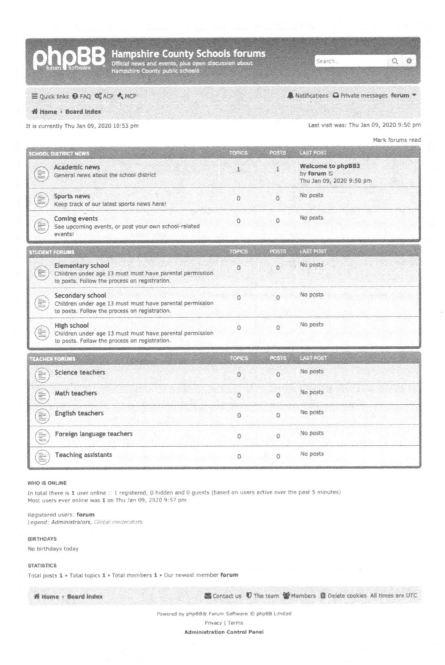

Figure 5.11: Index page, after creating categories and forums

On this screen:

- **Select the correct forum type**. Make sure to specify if you want a forum or a category. Pick the right dropdown option.

- **Enter the forum or category name**. Enter it in the **forum name** field. Use the name in your plan.

- **Copy permissions**. *You will want to copy permissions from another forum for now.* If you don't, no one can access the forum. The best thing to do is copy permissions from what was "Your first forum." We'll refine these later, but for now, enter an optional description, and then press **Submit**.

Continue the process for all your planned categories and forums until you are all done.

The Manage forums screen has controls that allow you to reposition forums and categories easily. Each click on the blue up or down arrow icon will move the row up or down in its position on the index or within a category.

The easiest way to check everything is to go to the Board index and see how the forums and categories lay out. They should match your plan. Using my plan, the index now looks like Figure 5.11.

Clean up: edit or delete the first post

During installation, phpBB created a test post in "Your first forum," which should now have been renamed.

Create the user-defined groups you need

As an administrator, you should edit or remove this post:

1. Go to your board's index.

2. Click on the link to the forum.

3. Once in the forum, click on the topic.

4. Once in the topic, select the **Delete post** icon (X icon) if you want to delete it, or the **Edit post** icon (pencil icon) if you want to edit it. If you want to edit it, you will want to change both the topic's title and its content.

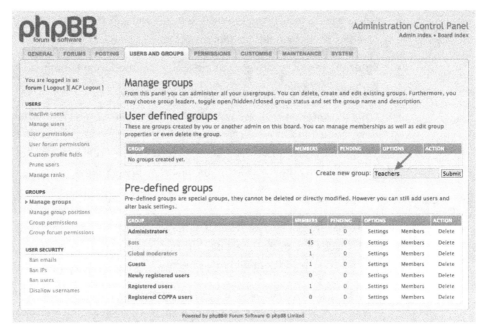

Figure 5.12: Manage groups screen

5.   Pressing the **Submit** button will affect the changes.

In your forum plan, you decided If you needed any user-defined groups in addition to the pre-defined groups. If so, now you need to create them.

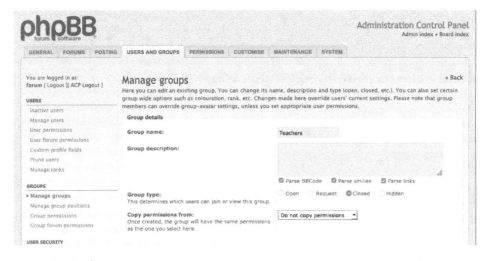

Figure 5.13: Edit group screen

ACP > Users and groups > Groups > Manage groups

Enter the group name in the **Create new group** field then press **Submit** (Figure 5.12). This returns a second screen with lots of fields that can be entered (Figure 5.13).

In this example, only part of this screen is shown. You might want to scan through all the fields on the screen, but here are some of the critical fields to consider:

- **Group name**. This should be what you entered on the last page.

- **Group description**. If there is any ambiguity about the purpose of the group, you can describe it in this field. In particular, if there are any special criteria for membership in the group, you should describe it here.

- **Group type**. There are four types of groups.

    - **Open.** This means that any registered user can get access to the group. They just have to request access, and the system will instantly grant it. How does a user request group access? **UCP > Usergroups**, if the group type allows it.

    - **Request**. This means a moderator or administrator reviews access requests and either approves or rejects them.

    - **Closed.** In this case, no one can petition to join the group, even though it is listed. In my example, administrators will know which users are teachers and can read the teacher forums, so students and the public can't petition to join these groups.

    - **Hidden.** The group exists, but is not listed, so most users won't know it exists.

- **Copy permissions from**. *I recommend copying the registered users' permissions to start.* This provides a base set of permissions to these groups that you can add to or subtract from.

Groups and users can have an avatar (small image) assigned to them, if board permissions allow. Skip this step for now. We will discuss adding avatars in Chapter 6.

Press **Submit** to save your changes. You will get a confirmation screen saying your changes were saved and a link that will take you back to the Manage groups screen.

Continue creating your user-defined groups using these procedures for each group until you are done.

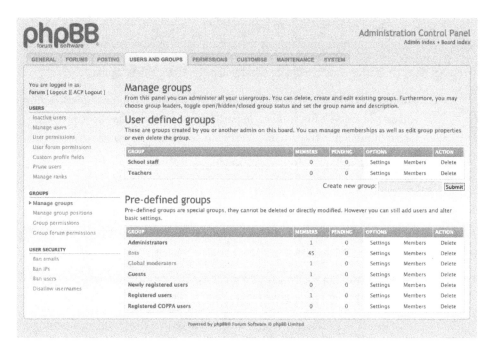

Figure 5.14: Manage groups screen, with user defined groups

Later you will add users to these groups. There's no point in doing that now, as you have not advertised your board yet. Except for you, there is no one to add to these groups.

At this point, your Manage group screens should look similar to Figure 5.14.

Change the forum permissions for your user-defined groups

You need to ensure that members in these user-defined groups and the built-in groups have correct forum permissions.

phpBB's Administration Control Panel has many ways of accessing the same screen. This can be done from links on the Forums, Users and Groups, or Permissions tabs in the Administration Control Panel. I'll use:

ACP > Users and Groups > Groups > Group forum permissions

For each group, you need to decide which forum permissions will apply for your user-defined groups.

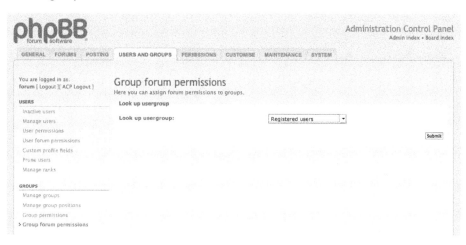

Figure 5.15: Group forum permissions, screen 1

In my plan, what's critical is to keep bots, guests, newly registered users and registered users from accessing these five forums for teachers and school staff only. They should not be able to read or see these forums.

Let's start with the forum permissions for the registered users group. Select the Registered users group from the **Look up usergroup** dropdown, and then press **Submit** (Figure 5.15).

On the next screen, I'll choose the forums that need their permissions changed for the registered users group. There are two forum lists to pick from. Since all these forums are in the same category, the simplest way is to go to the second **Select a forum** dropdown and pick Teacher forums [+Subforums] then press the lower **Submit** button (Figure 5.16).

On the third screen, I can set the forum permissions for this group. Roles are usually the easiest way to set these permissions. We'll talk more about roles and finely tuning permissions in Chapter 8.

The default role is probably **Read only**, but I changed it to **No access** for each forum instead. Only employees of the school district should be able to access these forums, so this role is appropriate. Then I pressed **Submit**. See Figure 5.17.

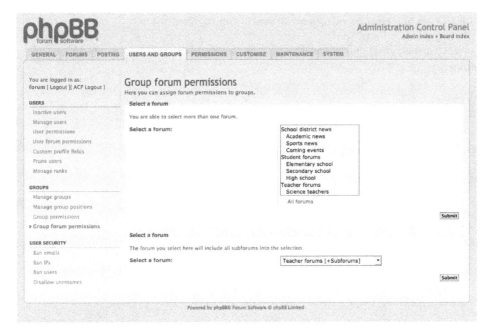

Figure 5.16: Group forum permissions, screen 2

Press **Apply all permissions** to save these changes.

Next, I do this for each of the other groups that shouldn't have access to these forums: Bots, Guests, Newly registered users and Registered COPPA users.

What about the permissions for the Administrators and Global moderators' groups? You would think that administrators in particular would have full permissions to everything by default, but they don't. phpBB doesn't have a role applied to them, so it defaults to **No role defined**.

Strange as it may seem, to keep to my plan, I must explicitly give permissions to these groups too. Since **No role defined** could amount to no access, you need something better. I chose the **Full access** role for each forum for each of these groups, since they are trusted users.

As for your user-defined groups (teachers and school staff, in my example), you need to explicitly set permissions for them too for these forums. There are two major roles to consider: **Full access** and **Standard access**. Generally, **Standard access** is better. With **Full access**, posters can create announcements and stickies. This is something generally reserved for power users like moderators and administrators.

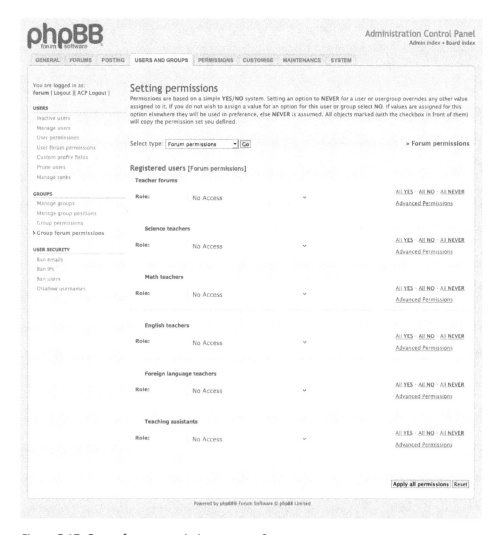

Figure 5.17: Group forum permissions, screen 3

When done setting permissions for all your groups to these special forums, you should double-check your work. One way to get a sense if your changes were done correctly is to log off the board. In my example, the restricted forums should not appear on the index because I am using the guests group's permissions. When I log back in, they should reappear because I will no longer be in the guests' group.

In Chapter 10, we will learn about how you can assume a user's permissions, which allows for more granular testing. This is also a great way to troubleshoot forum permission issues. But since there are no users created yet, except your administrator account, you can't do this now.

Add language packs

Language packs present phpBB in various languages.

Downloading language packs

If your board uses English, you don't need to add any language packs. But if your board is based in an English-speaking country in the Americas, you may prefer to install the American English language pack and use it instead of British English. British English spellings like "customisation" may be annoying to your users.

Fortunately, phpBB supports many languages. A total of 57 language packs are available. Some are variations of one language.

Figure 5.18 Language packs download link on phpbb.com

Many languages have casual and formal language versions available. For example, Spanish has both a casual and formal honorifics language packs.

You must download language packs from phpbb.com. Hover over the **Downloads** link on their menu and select the **Language Packs** link (Figure 5.18). Find the language pack of interest and click on it.

On the language pack page, you will find a green download button used to download one or more versions (Figure 5.19). Earlier versions are archived on the page, if you need them.

Figure 5.19: Language pack page, with download links

Your browser will download an archive with a .zip extension. Once downloaded, the archive needs to be expanded. The resulting language pack folder will have a name like language_name_version. For American English, the folder's name might be american_english_4.0.0.

Inside the folder are three subfolders, /ext, /language and /styles:

- The /ext folder contains a translation for the VigLink extension provided with phpBB. The folder inside it will be copied inside the /ext folder.

- The /language folder is the key folder. The name of the subfolder is the language code of the translation. For example, a /language/fr folder will be found in the French translation.

- The /styles folder contains an image that embeds text in the chosen language. Files are added to the prosilver style only. The only image needed is a translation for the icon_user_online.gif. There is also a stylesheet.css file with instructions on its styling.

Uploading and installing language packs

Appendix B discusses uploading files with FTP.

Upload the language pack files to your phpBB root folder, i.e., the folder containing your config.php file.

Figure 5.20: Adding a new language pack

Once uploaded, it's simple to install the language pack:

ACP > Customise > Language management > Language packs

Click on the **Install** link for the language pack (Figure 5.20).

Installation is almost instantaneous. You will get a link that takes you back to the same page. When refreshed, the page will show your language pack is installed.

Making the new language your board's default language

Generally, you will want to make the language pack the default language:

ACP > General > Board configuration > Board settings > Default language

Change this to the new language pack and press **Submit**.

Changing the default language for all users

A situation can arise if you add language packs after the board has been in use for a while. Users will inherit the old default language. But unless they explicitly change the language in the User Control Panel, they will always see the old default language. You would like them to use the new language pack instead.

There is a way to solve this problem: delete the old language pack by clicking the **Delete** link (Figure 5.20).

For this to work, the language pack you delete must not be the default language.

*Note: The language pack is not actually removed, just marked as uninstalled. Should you want to make it available again, click on the **Install** link for the old language pack on this screen.*

How users select a board language

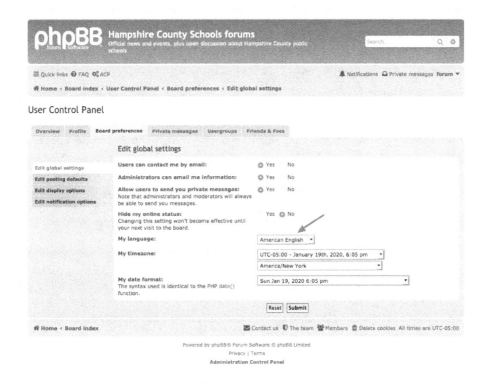

Figure 5.21: User control panel - Edit global settings

If multiple language packs are installed, a user can choose the one they want:

UCP > Board preferences > Edit global settings > My language (Figure 5.21)

However, this is option is buried so deep in the UCP that most users are unaware this option exists.

Having more than one language pack installed implies that posts can be made in more than one language. That's why enabling multiple language packs is often not a good idea because users might not be able to read each other's posts.

Disable the Contact page

phpBB has a Contact page feature. It allows anyone, including guests, to fill out a short web form to contact an administrator of the board. If enabled, a link to it is placed in the footer.

The idea of a Contact page is not bad, but in practice, it tends to attract a lot of spam emails to administrators because it has no method to discern whether a human filled out the form or not (CAPTCHA). There are extensions that can be installed that allow equivalent functionality with a CAPTCHA, but to start off, you generally want to disable the contact page.

ACP > General > Board configuration > Contact page settings > Enable contact page > Disable

Set up an effective spambot countermeasure

Spam can become a huge problem for bulletin boards, more so than for most websites because it can be easy for new users to register and then post spam. It's such a big topic that there is a whole section about dealing with it in Chapter 8.

To help avoid this issue, you want to set up an effective spambot countermeasure to be used on registration.

A number of spambot countermeasures are built into phpBB. You can disable all countermeasures if you want, but you are inviting trouble if you do. You can also set a number of fields to control the number of login and registration attempts. The defaults are generally sufficient.

ACP > General > Board configuration > Spambot countermeasures

GD Image is the default countermeasure (Figure 5.22). This embeds some numbers and letters in an image. When registering (and sometimes when posting), you must enter these number and letters. The assumption is that if you pass the test, you are a human and not a spambot.

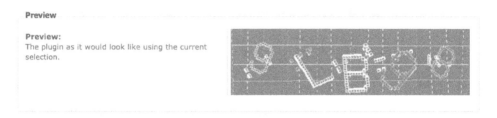

Figure 5.22: GD Image, phpBB's default spambot countermeasure

This countermeasure tends to be not very effective and if used tends to annoy users, as it is easy to type the incorrect keys. Also, it assumes the user is not colorblind or color deficient. If you tweak the image settings, it can be made more effective, but in general, it should be avoided.

You have two reasonably effective built-in spambot countermeasures:

- Q&A (Question and Answer)

- reCAPTCHA

Setting up the Q&A countermeasure

With this countermeasure, you must successfully answer one or more questions to register.

This is most effective if your board is about an obscure subject area and you expect people registering will know the answer to some questions that cannot be easily guessed with a search engine query.

To select it, even though it is greyed out, click on it in the **Installed plugins** dropdown box and select **Q&A** (Figure 5.23).

Doing this simply makes it available. The page will refresh with Q&A selected. Now press the **Configure** button. On the Questions screen, press the **Add** button.

Figure 5.23: Spambot countermeasure selection

See Figure 5.24. **Strict check** will be very picky about what the user enters: it must match the answer's letter case, punctuation and whitespace exactly.

Both the question and the answer fields must be filled out. If you have more than one correct answer for the question, then place them on separate lines in the **Answers** box. If the user enters any of these, the question will be answered successfully. Press **Submit** when done.

Add as many questions as you want using this method. One of the questions will be randomly picked for use on registration. If successful, the registration will succeed.

Note: If you have more than one language pack installed, there must be at least one question for each language pack for the countermeasure to be enabled.

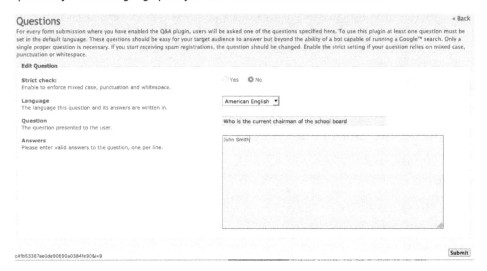

Figure 5.24: Questions screen

When done, select the **Spambot countermeasures** page link again. While the questions are available, you still haven't enabled Q&A as your spambot countermeasure. You have simply set it up. Select it again from the **Installed plugins** (Figure 5.23, it should not be greyed out now) and press **Submit**. When refreshed, the page will show a sample question in the Preview part of the page.

You can test it out by logging out, then hitting the **Register** link. After agreeing to the terms of use, you will see the question near the bottom of the Registration page (Figure 5.25).

CONFIRMATION OF REGISTRATION

Who is the current
chairman of the school
board:
This question is a means of
preventing automated form
submissions by spambots.

Reset Submit

⌂ Home ‹ Board index   ✉ Contact us 🗑 Delete cookies All times are UTC

Powered by phpBB® Forum Software © phpBB Limited
Privacy | Terms

Figure 5.25: Question on registration

Setting up the reCAPTCHA countermeasure

phpBB also supports Google's reCAPTCHA Version 2 and Version 3 spambot countermeasures. As of this writing, these are the most effective built-in countermeasures. However, it requires you to do some extra work.

There are three possible choices, depending on the version of phpBB you are using:

- On phpBB 3.3, you can choose the reCAPTCHA Version 2 invisible countermeasure or reCAPTCHA Version 3. (Version 3 was introduced in phpBB 3.3.1.) Version 3 is preferred.

- On phpBB 3.2, your only reCAPTCHA option is the Version 2 checkbox countermeasure.

First go to Google's reCAPTCHA page:

https://www.google.com/recaptcha

To use this countermeasure, you need a Google account. When you have one and are logged into it, the blue **Admin** console button at the top right corner of the page will work.

Figure 5.26: Google's reCAPTCHA add a new site page

Click the plus sign (+) on the blue toolbar to add a new site. That will take you to a web page where you'll fill out the form seen in Figure 5.26.

Here's how to fill it out:

- **Label.** Use the board's domain to make it easy to find.

- **reCAPTCHA type.** if you are using phpBB 3.3, choose **reCAPTCHA V3** or **reCAPTCHA v2 Invisible reCAPTCHA badge**. If you are using phpBB 3.2, choose **reCAPTCHA v2, "I am not a robot" Checkbox.**

- **Domains.** Use your board's domain name. You can use one set of keys across many domains if you want by adding additional domains. Do not preface this

---

with http:// or https://. It's better to leave off the www. prefix too so it will work with a broader range of URLs.

- **Owners.** This will default to the email address associated with your Google account, but you can add other email address if you want others to be able to control reCAPTCHA for these domains.

- You must accept the terms of service then press **Submit**.

- Next, you'll see a page with a site key (public) and a secret key (private). These need to be copied and pasted into the reCAPTCHA spambot countermeasure fields. Select the countermeasure similar to how you selected the Q&A countermeasure. The page will come up. Enter the keys in the appropriate fields and press **Submit** (Figure 5.27).

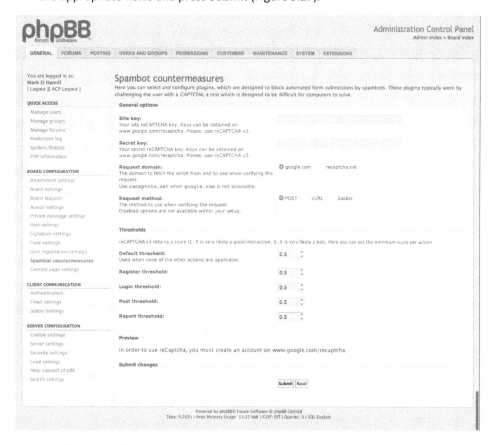

Figure 5.27: reCAPTCHA V2 and V3 key entry

While configured, this countermeasure is not yet enabled. When you get back to the Spambot countermeasures main page, select it from Installed plugins, and then press **Submit**.

The refreshed page will show the countermeasure with an image supplied by Google that indicates that reCaptcha is properly configured. It should appear in the bottom right corner of the screen.

It's important to actually test reCAPTCHA by creating a test registration. Just because the reCAPTCHA image can be seen doesn't mean that requests to the reCAPTCHA website from your server will succeed. When this happens, it's likely that you can't actually send requests from PHP outside your hosting with the default post request method. See Figure 27. First try changing the **Request method** to **cURL** and try a test registration again. If it doesn't try the **socket** method. The socket method is the least common denominator, so it will usually work.

Set the user registration settings

With a spambot countermeasure in place, it's time to consider what type of user registration procedures you want.

However, some web hosts will prohibit requests from going outside their hosting environment. So PHP may be configured to set allow_url_fopen (which gives PHP permission to access non-local URLs) to true, but a web host's firewall policy will still block these requests.

Generally, web hosts won't make exceptions, but you can ask. In this case you must revert to a non-reCAPTCHA solution. If your host won't make an exception, you will need to fallback and use a different method.

ACP > General > Board configuration > User registration settings

The **Account activation** dropdown on this screen gives you four choices (Figure 5.28):

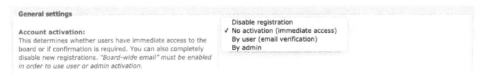

Figure 5.28: Account activation selection

- **Disable registration**. When this is enabled, no one can register. That will certainly solve the issue of spam registrations, but generally you want people to register, not to keep them out. For some private boards where the administrator creates all accounts, this might be a valid choice.

- **No activation (immediate access)**. This is the default. Having completed registration, you are also logged so you can start reading and posting. I don't recommend this approach unless you have 99% confidence that your registration process can't be hacked. If spammers can find a vulnerability, they will exploit it.

- **By user (email verification)**. This is generally the best approach. Your board sends an email to the email address entered upon registration. It contains a link that confirms registration. Until then, the account is marked as inactive. Since this step should take a human to accomplish, it gives you further confidence the registration is legitimate. However, sometimes email system slip up. Registration emails may not go out, or get flagged as possible spam and placed in a spam folder. So if you select this method, test it on a test account. We'll talk about how to reduce the likelihood that outgoing emails will be flagged as spam later in this chapter.

- **By admin**. With this, the administrator gets a notification when a user successfully registers. Most administrators find this becomes too burdensome. Also, unless you change a setting in the User Control Panel, you won't get an email notification.

There are many other fields on this screen that can be filled out. Of note, you might want to change the **New member post limit**. If a new user makes this many posts, they are removed from the Newly Registered Users group and will then have privileges for normal registered users.

By default, the first three posts must be approved by a moderator before being seen. We'll discuss setting permissions in detail in Chapter 8. Set this to **0** (zero) to disable this altogether.

Set an authentication method

Typically, anyone can try to register on a board and the password they set on registration is used for authentication. phpBB supports some alternate authentication methods.

ACP > General > Client communication > Authentication

The initial screen has only one field, with four choices (Figure 5.29).

- **Db (Database).** This is the default. phpBB's database is used to authenticate users. This means people log in using the username and password created during registration. The password entered is checked with the encrypted password stored in the phpbb_users table for the username entered. That alone suffices for authenticating a user. Based on my clients, at least 99% of boards use this authentication method.

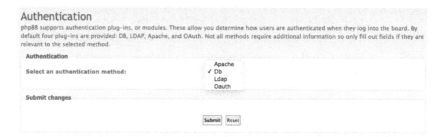

Figure 5.29: Authentication methods screen

- **Apache**. This method uses Apache web server authentication, which requires creating a .htpasswd file outside of phpBB and linking it to the board's .htaccess file. In addition, PHP's mod_php extension must be installed.

  This method prohibits you from even seeing the board until you authenticate. Instead, you generally get a white screen with a prominent nonmodal username and password dialog box you must fill out first. If you fail this authentication, you still won't even see the board as a guest. This makes it a very effective way to secure your board, if you are willing to endure the considerable hassle of setting it up and maintaining it. One big advantage to its use is that the public won't see the board at all and search indexes can't index any content.

The username and password is stored in a .htpasswd file, but the password is hashed to obscure the real password. If they don't match, further access is prohibited.

If they do match, your Apache authentication username must also be in the phpbb_users table to continue. (The password in the .htaccess file does not have to match your phpBB password.) So to use phpBB with Apache authentication, you must first establish an account on the board. This is usually done by the administrator.

Hint: Don't see the .htaccess file? In Linux, files that start with a period (.) are hidden. You can see hidden files in the current directory with this command:

```
ls -la
```

The .htpasswd file must be linked in the .htaccess file, generally the one in the phpBB root folder, by adding code to it, similar to this example:

```
AuthUserFile /usr/local/etc/.htpasswd
AuthName "Please enter your username and password"
AuthType Basic
<Limit GET POST>
require valid-user
</Limit>
```

In this case, the web server looks for a /usr/local/etc/.htpasswd file, and uses it for initial authentication. As a best practice, place the .htpasswd file outside of your web content, so it can't accidentally be accessed from a browser.

Although Apache authentication was originally a feature of the Apache web server, it's become a standard. Both the nginx and Microsoft's IIS web servers can also use Apache authentication, if they are properly set up.

One of the big costs of Apache authentication is you must put all your board's users and their password into the .htpasswd file. Here is an example of how a line in the .htpasswd file might appear:

```
johnsmith:F418zSM0k6tGI
```

In this case, F418zSM0k6tGI is a hash of the actual password and the username is johnsmith. You would have to enter both the username and the unscrambled password to access the board.

If you have SSH access you can add users to the .htpasswd file with a command. To create a .htpasswd file in the current folder and add the user abc123, a command like this would work (you will be prompted to type in a password):

```
htpasswd -c ./.htpasswd abc123
```

You will be prompted to enter the password or the username abc123, then re-prompted to ensure it is correct.

To add another user def456 to this file, omit the -c option:

```
htpasswd ./.htpasswd def456
```

Many web host control panels have a tool to handle the logistics of creating the .htpasswd file and linking it to a .htaccess file. There are also web sites that will create these files for you that you then upload to the proper directory.

- **LDAP (Lightweight Directory Access Protocol).** Many organizations use *directory services*. These directories contain authoritative information about who can access the network and what their various privileges are.

  Microsoft Active Directory is the most well-known of these directory services. It and other directory services use LDAP. If the board will be used for internal organizational use only, this is a great choice. Users authenticate against this directory and if they need a password, they use the one they use to login at the office. If successful, they are allowed to access the board. If an administrator takes away their access in the directory, they also lose their ability to log in to the board.

  However, to configure phpBB with LDAP, you will have to know a host of information about the LDAP authentication server. Generally, you will have to work with your local system administrator to fill out the many fields when you select this option.

  Note: Simply being in a directory service does not grant a user access to the board. They must still create an account with the board. Authenticating with the directory service during registration suffices for logging into phpBB.

- **OAuth.** OAuth allows users to authenticate using one or more external authorization services. At your first login from a device, you click on a button on the login page and go through a one-time authorization process with an authorization service that you belong to. OAuth is an open standard used by many websites to delegate user authorization.

phpBB supports four authorization services: Bitly, Facebook, Google and Twitter. For example, if you authorize with Facebook, you'll be taken to Facebook when you press the Facebook button on the login screen (Figure 5.30). It's assumed that you already have a Facebook account.

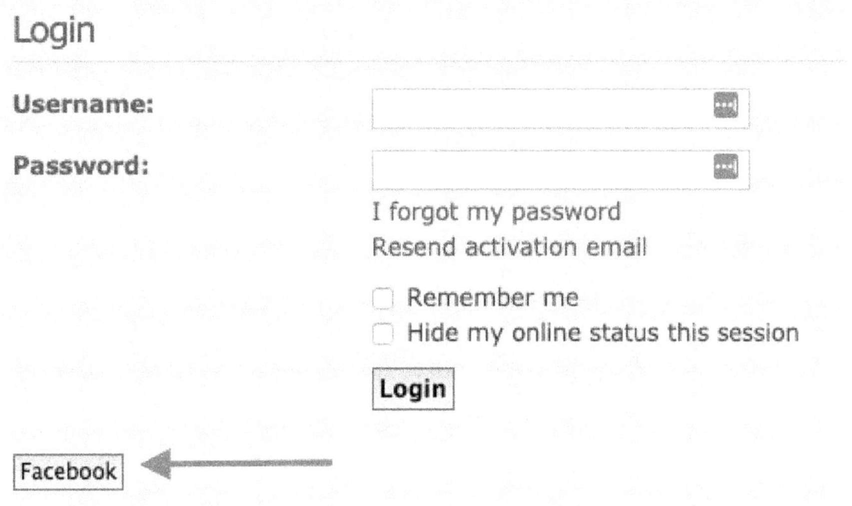

Figure 5.30: Example of logging in with OAuth authorization

If you are not already logged in there, you must login successfully login to the service. You will be prompted by the service to grant the access to the phpBB board.

After you do this, the service will redirect back to your board's login page passing a hidden token that phpBB uses to validate the service's authorization. You then do a one-time login with your username and password.

The real magic is what happens the next time you login. You just click on the authorization service button and you are logged in. There is no need to enter a username or password again, even from a different device. It just happens, and it's done securely because the external service has already vouched for you.

This one-time login process is necessary because otherwise phpBB won't know which username to associate the successful OAuth authorization with. You usually have the option to register if you don't yet have an account on the board by pressing the **Register** button (Figure 5.31).

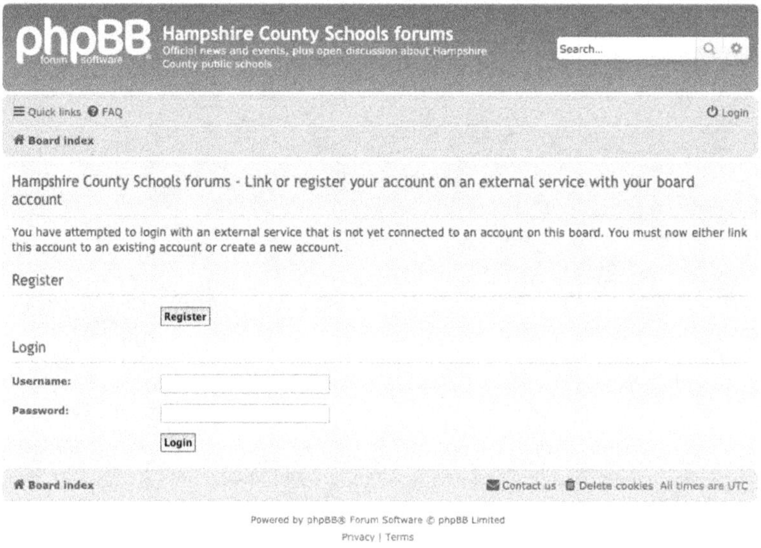

Figure 5.31: One-time database login after successful OAuth authorization

Using OAuth is optional. If enabled, you can still use the Db authentication method to login if you enter your username and password; just enter these credentials and press the **Login** button.

Making this work requires some effort from you as an administrator. **ACP > General > Client communications > Authentication**. For each service you want to enable, you must enter a key and a secret provided by the authorization service. Procedures for getting a key and secret vary depending on the provider. Bitly requires that you subscribe to a paid service to get a key and secret. Expect some confusion and hassle to figure this out. See Figure 5.32.

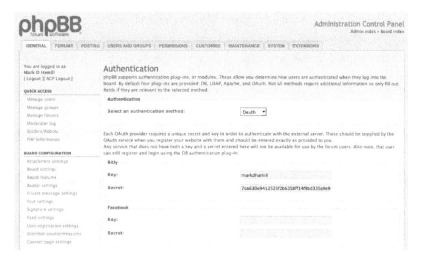

Figure 5.32: OAuth setup

If you choose Apache or LDAP authentication, you will need to create and follow some procedures outside of phpBB for handling board registrations and removing users.

Setting up and testing email notifications

phpBB depends heavily on sending emails. Unfortunately, it can't guarantee they will get delivered. You'll have to use a mail server, generally one attached to your web server, to handle that.

If you enable the option to confirm registrations via email, then phpBB requires emailing to work, or no one can complete registration. If you allow email notifications, outgoing emails need to go out flawlessly.

It's technically possible to run phpBB without it sending any emails but it's detrimental to do so. Without the nudge of email notifications, users who register may not remember to come back periodically. Without it, you can't send everyone mass emails. And it limits the options for registration.

For small boards that are not very busy, sending emails reliably is usually not a problem. It becomes problematic as the volume of email increases. This is because phpBB is usually hosted on commercial web hosts. And each web host can have different policies on how many emails may go out in a given time period.

Worse, email spam is a huge problem. Most web hosts monitor outgoing emails. They might not let any emails go out, or only some emails that don't hit some sort of spam score threshold. Most web hosts won't even bother to tell you that they are doing this, leaving you to puzzle through these issues when users start complaining.

To turn off all board emails (*not* recommended):

ACP > General > Client communications > Email settings > Enable board-wide emails > Disable

Solving emailing issues is discussed in more depth later in Chapter 6.

Create email accounts or email forwarders for your domain

To stave off email delivery issues, my best tip is to create email accounts or email forwarders for your domain. This is because outgoing email from your domain that does not use your domain in the email address is automatically suspicious. It's usually easy to create an email address using your web host's control panel. For example, cPanel has a mail group (Figure 5.33). Plesk, WebMin and other web host control panels have similar interfaces.

Figure 5.33: cPanel's mail group

You could create an email account by clicking on the **Email Accounts** link. Most administrators won't want to do this because it's hard to read email sent to the domain. You have to find the POP or SMTP server names, get a set of credentials and configure your email program to poll it. Or you need to change the domain's mail exchange (MX) records to point these accounts to a service you do use.

Creating email forwarders

After creating an email account associated with your domain, generally you will want to add an email forwarder. With a forwarder, you can have emails sent to an address like admin@myspecialdomain.com forwarded automatically to an email address you are already using. Most likely, you have a gmail.com or similar email service you are already using and will want board emails to be sent to it instead.

Figure 5.34: cPanel's email forwarding screen

In this case, click the **Forwarders** link. There is probably an **Add forwarder** button, or something similar on this page. Click on that and you will probably get a screen that looks something like Figure 5.34. Simply tell your host where to send emails for these domain email addresses.

Properly configuring email settings

Make sure the email addresses or email forwarders you created for your domain are set up for use in phpBB:

ACP > General > Client communications > Email settings > Contact email address

ACP > General > Client communications > Email settings > From email address

Doing this helps convince your web host's mail server and receiving email servers that these outgoing emails are legitimate.

Send yourself a test email

On the ACP Email settings page, toward the bottom is a button that can be used to test emailing. Unless you changed it, it will go to the email address for your phpBB account (Figure 5.35). Press it and see if it works.

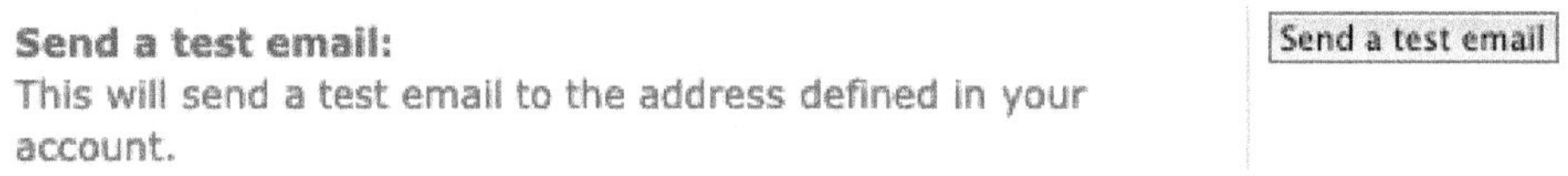

Send a test email:
This will send a test email to the address defined in your account.

Send a test email

Figure 5.35: Test email button

If you don't see an email in your inbox, wait a while. You can also check your spam folder.

If it appears in your spam folder, this suggests that most of your members will miss emails from the board. Email programs can usually be taught to direct these into an inbox, but this is not a great solution. It's better to work with your web host to find out what the issue is and correct it. This is discussed in much more detail in the next chapter.

If no emails arrive, check phpBB's error log. Often, if there are emailing issues, the problem is recorded there:

ACP > Maintenance > Forum logs > Error log

If this happens, it's usually because you set phpBB to use SMTP for emailing and the handshake with the email server is incorrect.

A successful test email, though, may give you a false sense of assurance. The test email is only a couple lines of text. Emails sent by your board could be longer, so they may get flagged as spam. If you are not using SMTP for sending outgoing emails, you should take the time to do this.

Using SMTP for outgoing emails

The default method for sending emails in phpBB is to use PHP's mail function. Email sent using PHP's mail function go to whatever email server PHP is configured to use. In most cases, these emails go out without authentication, making them inherently more suspicious. On shared hosting, it's probably a common email server used by lots of domains.

phpBB tries to get around potential issues like this by including invisible email headers that will help persuade email servers that email is going out legitimately.

It's a better to send outgoing emails through an approved email server using SMTP (Simple Mail Transport Protocol). Most web hosts provide a SMTP mail server, and you can configure the SMTP settings on the same page. The bottom of the screen has an SMTP settings block.

Why use SMTP for sending emails? It's because by using SMTP, you are usually authenticating yourself to the mail server, so it looks more legitimate.

We'll discuss setting up SMTP for your board's email in the next chapter. If you are intent on getting it set up now for SMTP, you might want to read that part of that chapter.

Chapter 6 | Advanced phpBB configuration

At this point, you can confidently unleash your board on the world. Since you've got the board set up correctly, it should work reliably and in the way you intended.

In this chapter, we get beyond the basics and into some of the fun stuff: styling, extensions and little features that can make your board look more attractive and be much more useful.

Installing styles

A style puts a pretty frame around your board's content. phpBB's default style is proSilver, but you may want some other style. The phpBB group has hundreds of free styles you can download. There are also some third-party paid styles for phpBB.

Since WordPress is such a huge platform on the web, I should note that WordPress themes are equivalent to phpBB styles. Both perform the same function. Installing a phpBB style takes more work than adding a WordPress theme, since it must be manually uploaded.

phpBB styles are not generally as sophisticated as WordPress themes. If you want to make changes to the style, you usually have to know Cascading Stylesheet syntax and have some understanding of how phpBB's templating system works.

Free styles

The easiest way to tour and download phpBB's free styles is to go to phpBB's customization database on phpbb.com. First, click on the **Customise** link on the menu. The click on the **Styles** link and then **Board styles** link (Figure 6.1).

You will want to filter the list of styles by picking those approved for your version of phpBB. Above the top of page pagination links you will see a dropdown that will allow you to pick the right style filter.

Use the pagination controls to go through the styles. Styles are arranged on the screen in tiles. Click on the link for the style in the tile to get more information on the style, download it, and to see a full sized image of the style.

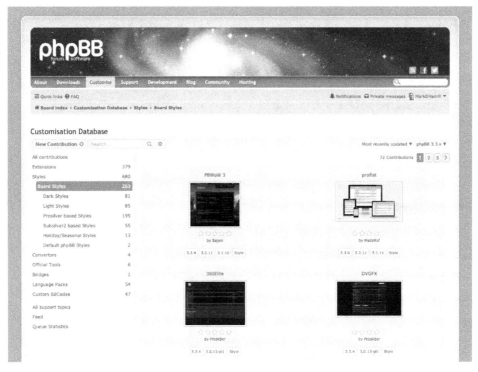

Figure 6.1: phpbb.com board styles page

Paid styles

A number of independent publishers offer paid phpBB styles. These styles cannot be downloaded from phpbb.com because they are not free. Some style publishers have free styles too, and you will often find these styles are included among the free styles on phpbb.com.

Because the phpBB Group's style team hasn't reviewed these paid styles, they might have certain deficiencies or not follow all the practices required for free phpBB styles. Many are more sophisticated than free phpBB styles and include ACP interfaces where you can fine-tune the style's attributes, such as background and font colors. Some may have switches that allow you to turn certain features on or off, such as whether to display a logo or not.

Some may have deficiencies too. For example, I've seen paid styles that did not have expected template events in their templates. In one example, this meant an ads extension could not serve an ad because the template missed a hook it needed to inject the ad.

Paid styles that include extensions for making changes to the style are also considered potentially dangerous, as these extensions bypass phpBB's approval process for extensions. In short, although not said explicitly, the phpBB Group would prefer you avoid these styles altogether and use one of their free styles instead.

A simple web search will turn up some of these sites, which include sites such as artodia.com, awesomestyles.com, rockettheme.com and themeforest.net.

If you use one of these paid styles, you can't get support for it on phpbb.com. You will need to ask for support from the vendor.

Before you buy one of these styles, make sure the style will work with your version of phpBB.

Customizing styles

A free style usually can be tweaked to make it look unique. Some administrators don't mind paying for a custom style because their board looks completely unique or needs to mimic the styling of a larger website. I don't consider myself a style artist, but I can often tailor a free style to make it look acceptable to a client with unique requirements.

Or you can pay a style artist to make a wholly unique style. In most cases, they will start with a free style or one of their own paid styles and retrofit it to meet your requirements, rather than start from scratch. Most paid style vendors offer this as a service. Such styles are usually an indulgence, as they tend to take a lot of time and thus amount to a sizable investment. But having a board that looks unique, or includes all your requirements, is often a good investment.

Perhaps a better place to inquire about customized styles is among phpBB's style artists who are available for hire. Simply post a topic in the Wanted! forum on phpbb.com's discussion forums, and you'll probably get plenty of interest.

In Appendix C, I discuss making your own customized style. This is a smart way to go if you want your style to look like an existing style, but you also want to tweak a few things. This approach lets you update the styles you depend on—because these styles evolve over time —while helping insulate your changes from these styles.

Uploading styles

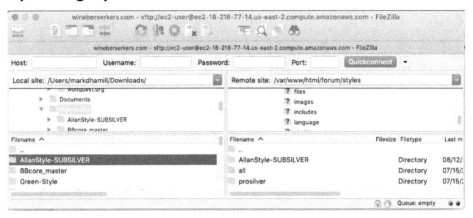

Figure 6.2: Uploading styles with FileZilla

The downloaded style will be in a .zip archive, similar to phpBB's language packs. This file must be expanded on your computer before being uploaded.

File Transfer Protocol (FTP) is used to upload the folder to your board. The folder for the style must be uploaded into the board's styles folder. (See Appendix B for details on using FTP.)

Figure 6.2 shows how this might be done using the FileZilla FTP program. In this case, I wanted to upload the AllanStyle-SUBSILVER folder in my Downloads folder. I chose to upload it to the board's style folder, which is in /var/www/html/forum/styles folder on this particular host. This shows the folder after it was successfully uploaded.

Another approach is to use your web host's file manager. Upload the .zip file for the style to the board's styles folder, then expand it with the file manager.

Installing a style

Once uploaded, the style is easily and quickly installed.

ACP > Customise > Style management > Install Styles (Figure 6.3)

Click on the **Install style** link. If you have multiple styles that could be installed, you can select the checkboxes associated with the styles and press the **Install styles** button, thus installing a number of styles at once.

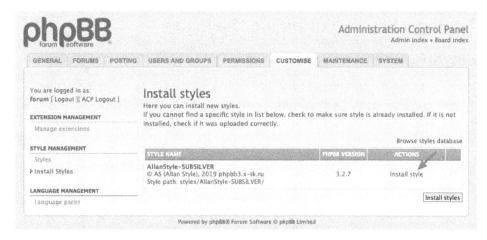

Figure 6.3: Install styles page

Installing a style doesn't mean it becomes the style everyone sees. You need to tell phpBB which style is the primary style.

ACP > General > Board configuration > Board settings > Board style

- **Default style**. This is the style that new users will use by default.

- **Guest style**. This is the style that guests will see.

- **Override user style**. If you select **Yes**, everyone will use this style, including guests. No other styles can be selected. (Figure 6.4)

Figure 6.4: Setting the board style

After installing the style and making it the default style, it is visible when you go to the board index. If there is more than one style enabled, a user can select the style they prefer: **UCP > Board preferences > Edit global settings > My board style**

Adding, changing or hiding the logo

How styles handle logos

The default prosilver style shows the phpBB logo in the top left corner of the header (Figure 6.5). Some styles don't have a logo and present only the site name and possibly the site description in the header. Some styles show only the logo and hide the site name and site description. Consequently, there is no one-size-fits-all approach to adding or changing logos. Some general approaches, though, will usually work.

Figure 6.5 phpBB logo

If you run into issues, there are resources you can turn to. For each free style, there is a discussion tab on its page on phpbb.com where you can ask questions. For paid styles, you can seek help from the publisher or see if there is an interface in the ACP for the fine-tuning the style.

Keep in mind that all approved phpBB styles are responsive. This means they intelligently "size down" for mobile devices. Some styles have two logos: one for large screens and one for small screens. Some styles hide the logo on mobile devices. A logo that looks fine on a large screen may be too big on a small screen. You should test your logo on both types of devices.

Some styles have options to present high-definition logos for screens with retinal displays. So, the general advice I supply may need quite a bit of tweaking and rework.

In some cases, it's hard to add a logo because the style doesn't support one. If you are familiar with HTML and CSS, anything is possible by editing the style's files. There's a whole course in mastering these skills. I touch on this a bit in Appendix C.

In the past, you could click on the site logo, and it would return you to the board index. That's usually not an option anymore. Most styles that support logos do what is done with the prosilver style: the logo is embedded as a background image and is thus not clickable.

In Appendix C, I discuss creating a custom style that overlays a primary style with minor changes. If you have modest HTML and CSS skills, you might want to read Appendix C now.

I will keep it simple and demonstrate how the phpBB logo for the prosilver style can be swapped for another logo. I'll also show how the site title and site description can be hidden with styling.

These same procedures will work for many styles that have logos, providing they inhabit the top left corner of the header. This approach is relatively straightforward, but has one disadvantage: if you update your style, you will need to reapply the changes. When you master Appendix C, this won't be much of an issue.

Creating a new logo

You may already have an image that you want to swap in for the default logo. Otherwise, you will need to create one.

My general advice is to keep the logo small. It should also look good with the general color scheme of your style.

If the logo will include embedded text, you might want to use a font similar to your style's primary font.

The default prosilver style logo is 149 pixels wide and 52 pixels high. The ideal prosilver style logo would be the same size, but that's often not practical.

The logo's height tends to matter more than its width, as tall logos can push the content on the page down by an unacceptable amount. Overly wide logos can be problematic as well because the site name and site description may slip under the logo, which throws off the look.

Hopefully, you have some image manipulation software on your computer that will allow you to design a logo, as well as crop or resize the image to an acceptable size. There are also websites that can do basic image manipulation like this, or you can hire someone to create a custom logo for your board.

The resulting logo image should be web ready. This means it needs to be saved in one of the following formats that browsers can display natively:

- PNG (Portable Network Graphic)

- GIF (Graphics Interchange Format)

- JPEG (Joint Photographic Experts Group)

- SVG (Scalable Vector Graphic)

- WEBP (this is fully supported starting in phpBB 3.3.7)

These use the .png, .gif, .jpg (sometimes .jpeg), .svg and .webp file suffixes. All formats support transparency, but the bleed-through color has to be selected when created. SVGs are a great choice because they scale seamlessly to fit their allotted space without losing detail. However, an SVG file is rather unique in that it instructs the browser how to render it, and creating SVG files requires a good set of tools or HTML tag knowledge that many people won't have.

Starting with phpBB 3.3, the phpBB group changed the default logo from a GIF to an SVG format. The phpBB logo is now named site_logo.svg, so to swap the old logo for a new one, you need to save your logo as an .svg file with the same name. Unless the dimensions of the image are also 149 x 52 pixels, you will have to edit a stylesheet to show the image in normal proportions. If you are not using the prosilver style, the default logo will probably have a different size and possibly a different name and image format.

Browsers usually have an **Inspect** feature that allows you to look at the properties of objects that populate a page. You can use this to figure out the existing size of the logo as well as its image format and file name. Point your mouse to the logo, then right-click on it and select the **Inspect** option. On Chrome or Chromium-based browsers, right mouse click and you will find it under **Developer Tools**. On Firefox, it appears with a right mouse click.

This option also lets you see the stylesheet file names and line numbers in those files where the styles are applied. The Inspector allows you to look through the browser's document object model (DOM) to find it. Typically, it's a background image.

The new Google-developed WEBP format tends to render the most compact images. Otherwise JPEG is a good choice. **Make a note of the image dimensions in pixels and the name of the file.**

Upload the new logo

The new image should be placed in the theme/images folder for your primary style. If you support more than one style, then it should be placed in this folder for each active style. For example, for the prosilver style, it would go in /styles/prosilver/theme/images. For the AllanStyle-SUBSILVER style, it would go in /style/AllanStyle-SUBSILVER/theme/images.

Use FTP to upload the logo to the folder, being careful to place it in the correct folder. Read Appendix B if you are unfamiliar with using FTP.

Hooking in the new logo

The easiest way to apply the new logo is to place the stylesheet commands it needs onto the end of your style's stylesheet.css file. This file can be found in the theme folder for your style. For prosilver, this would be /styles/prosilver/theme/stylesheet.css.

Note: the master stylesheet is usually stylesheet.css, but not always. If you don't find one or changes made to it don't work, examine the HTML source of your board's index page. Look through the `<link>` tags to find it. With the prosilver style installed, it should show as (all on one line):

```
<link
href="./styles/prosilver/theme/stylesheet.css?assets_versio
n=155" rel="stylesheet">
```

You can download the stylesheet, edit it with a text editor and then upload it. Or you might want to edit it with the file manager in your web host control panel, if that's an option. Save a file backup in case you make mistakes.

Assuming your new logo has a name new_logo.jpg with the dimensions of 200x75 pixels, you could add these lines to the bottom of the stylesheet.css file, past all the CSS @import statements:

```
.site_logo {
    background-image: url("./images/new_logo.jpg");
    width: 200px;
    height: 75px;
}
```

Viewing the new logo

Browsers can be a bit finicky. Generally, reloading the page should show the style changes. To be efficient, browsers will cache content on your device and try not to refresh it. If you don't see it, try holding down the SHIFT key when refreshing the page.

Sometimes you have to explicitly clear the browser's internal cache and then reload the page to see the changes. The instructions for doing this depend on the browser being used and its version. This web page has a set of instructions for clearing the cache for most browsers:

https://www.refreshyourcache.com/en/home/

Figure 6.6: SuperCacher interface

If none of this works, the image may be cached by a separate cache provided by your web host or a content delivery network. For example, many web hosts provide SuperCacher (Figure 6.6) to speed up the serving of static images. Open it and look for a control that allows you to flush the cache for the domain. Then try reloading the page.

Services like CloudFlare may also cause this problem. CloudFlare is an example of a *content delivery network* (CDN). A CDN tries to speed up the rendering of web pages by placing static images geographically close to the user, essentially putting copies of these files in many data centers around the world. Generally, the closer a file is to your computer, the faster it can be fetched. Look for a service like CloudFlare in your web host control panel and look for an option to flush its cache too.

Hiding the logo

Sometimes you don't want the logo to appear at all. In most cases, it is easily hidden. In the last example, the logo is assigned to a CSS *class* called site_logo. CSS stands for *Cascading Stylesheets* and is standard for expressing how web pages should look. CSS classes allow one set of styles to be applied to lots of HTML tags. They are distinguished by being prefaced with a period.

Your logo might use a different class name. Something like this applied to the bottom of your stylesheet.css file will hide the logo on the prosilver style:

```
.site_logo {
    display: none;
}
```

Hiding the site title and site description

Similar to hiding the logo, you can hide the site title and site description with styling commands.

Often, the logo will have the site name embedded in it, in which case placing the site title as text in the header is redundant. These CSS commands can be a bit weird to write.

In the HTML source for the header of my board, the site title is within a <h1> tag and the site description is within a <p> tag. Both are wrapped inside a <div> tag that includes the logo:

```
<div id="site-description" class="site-description">
    <a id="logo" class="logo"
href="http://www.hampshireschools.edu"
title="Home"><span class="site_logo"></span></a>
    <h1>Hampshire County schools forums</h1>    <p>A
forum for anyone interested in Hampshire county
schools</p>
    <p class="skiplink"><a href="#start_here">Skip to
content</a></p>
</div>
```

In this case, I want to display the logo but hide the rest. This can be done with CSS commands. The <div> tag encapsulating all of this can be uniquely identified because it has the ID attribute "site-description" (bolded, above). HTML tags with IDs have a unique id attribute value. Using CSS, styling can be applied to an ID, if you preface an ID with a # sign. So, with the right CSS commands, I can instruct the browser to hide <h1> and <p> tags inside the <div> tag with an ID of site-description.

At the bottom of stylesheet.css, I can add:

```
#site-description h1, #site-description p {
    display: none;
}
```

The space after `#site-description` is important because it is interpreted to mean that items after it must be inside it. Commas are used to separate multiple CSS selectors for which one set of styles will be applied.

I prefer this approach rather than removing HTML because the content is still in the page's markup, so search engines can read it.

Compiled styles

As I mentioned, many paid styles and some free styles have a user interface in the ACP that allows you to avoid writing CSS to make many changes to them. This may be a reason to prefer a paid style. Typically, there is an interface for choosing the fonts you want to use, background and foreground colors, and the margins and padding you want the major block containers to have.

These styles are actually "compiled." Normally, style changes are written to a .css file. In these compiled styles, desired changes are written to .scss files instead. SCSS stands for Syntactically Awesome Style Sheets, and it too is a standard. When changes are made, the .scss files are usually compiled by a program into one stylesheet.css file, which is used to style your board.

Some of these styles using .scss files expect you to edit these files yourself if you want to change the style. How do you compile them? You can use my extension! At the time of this writing, it is not an approved extension but I think it is safe to use. Search for "SCSS Compiler Extension" on the forums on phpbb.com.

Once installed, you can access it at: **ACP > Customise > Style management > SCSS compiler**

Installing and using extensions

phpBB is feature rich, but out-of-the-box phpBB can't do everything.

Extensions add functionality to phpBB that would not be available otherwise. There are hundreds of extensions for phpBB, and more become available every month.

If you are familiar with WordPress, extensions are a lot like WordPress plugins. Unlike WordPress plugins, phpBB extensions have to be uploaded to your board manually, and then enabled. It is likely that future versions of phpBB will simplify this process.

Extensions are relatively new to phpBB, arriving with phpBB 3.1 in October 2014. Prior to this new architecture, if you wanted to add functionality, you installed *modifications*. This often involved actual code changes to the base code of phpBB.

Figure 6.7 Extensions database, select phpBB version

Unlike modifications, extensions cleanly separate themselves from the phpBB base code, leaving phpBB's core functionality unchanged. All extensions are placed into phpBB's /ext (extensions) folder. You can update phpBB and generally not worry that your extensions will stop working. The developer of each extension asserts the versions of phpBB the extension will work with. If it won't work with your current version, the extension is automatically disabled or can't be installed.

As an extension programmer, I can assure you that the phpBB Group will only release an extension after it passes a thorough review by its extensions review team. Saying the review is thorough may actually understate these difficulty of passing a review. Getting an extension approved can feel like passing a bar exam. It can take months to get an extension approved, but in some cases, it can take years, particularly if there is a backlog of extensions to review and the extension is very complex. You can rest assured that when an extension is approved, it is safe to use.

There's a link within phpBB that takes you right to the extension database page for your version of phpBB: **ACP > Customise > Extension management > Manage extension > Browse extensions database**

A list of officially approved extensions can be found on phpbb.com. Hover over the **Customise** link in the header, and then select **Extensions DB**. You should filter the list of extensions based on the version of phpBB you are using. Open the **All branches** dropdown and select your branch (Figure 6.7).

Downloading extensions

Extension description boxes are tiled on the Extensions database page. Click the link for the extension to learn more and to be taken to the extension's page.

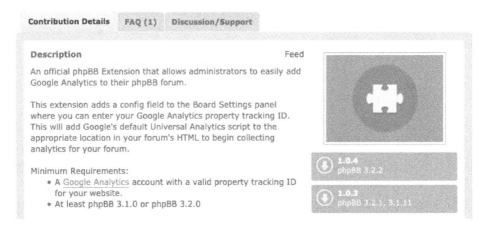

Figure 6.8: Extension summary page with download buttons

Like with styles, once downloaded, you must decompress the .zip file and then upload the files and folders using FTP.

On the extension's page, there is information about the extension, possibly a FAQ page, usually some screenshots and a discussion forum for the extension. There will be one or more green buttons that will allow you to download approved versions of the extension (Figure 6.8).

If you look at the archive for an extension, you may notice something curious: it contains a folder inside a folder; but the first folder has nothing inside it but another folder. This is because of the extension architecture. The top-level folder contains the name of the vendor that created the extension. The folder inside it is the name of the extension.

In the case of my digests extension, it ends up in a /ext/phpbbservices/digests folder. This allows my Smartfeed extension not to conflict, as it is placed in a /ext/phpbbservices/smartfeed folder. It also allows another extension writer to write a digests extension and place it in their own unique area, like /ext/vendorx/digests.

Physical separation of extension files and folders this way ensures logical separation as well, and it ensures that every extension is unique.

Uploading extensions

Upload the extension inside the /ext folder using File Transfer Protocol (FTP). If you are new to FTP, see Appendix B.

There should be one extension there already: VigLink. You will find it in the /ext/phpbb/viglink folder. VigLink is bundled in with phpBB.

If there is any confusion about where the extension should be placed, examine its composer.json file with a text editor. On Line 2 of the file, you should see something like this:

```
"name": "phpbbservices/digests",
```

This tells you that after it is uploaded, the extension's code should exist in an /ext/phpbbservices/digests folder.

Enabling extensions

Uploading an extension does not activate it; therefore, you'll need to enable it.

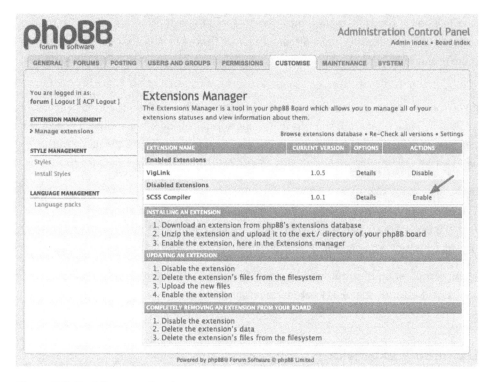

Figure 6.9: Enabling an extension

If you uploaded the extension properly, it will show up on the Manage extensions screen as a disabled extension:

ACP > Customise > Extension management > Manage extensions

You may need to refresh the page to see it.

Figure 6.9 shows the SCSS Compiler extension ready to be enabled. Click the **Enable** link to install the extension.

Extensions typically install within a few seconds, although the more complex the extension is, the longer it will take. Some extensions are so large that you may wait a minute or more for it to install.

That's because a lot of things can happen when you install an extension: changes could be made to the database, database tables could be created, columns may be added to tables, or rows may be added to various tables. Also, the extension must hook itself into various phpBB interfaces.

After enabling your first extension, you may notice a new **Extensions** tab in the ACP, on the far right. Most, but certainly not all extensions have ACP interfaces on the **Extensions** tab where you can control the overall behavior of the extension.

After enabling an extension, you may be confused as to how to use it or where to find its interface. Usually there are one or more screenshots on the extension's home page to help you out. And you can often find questions and answers on the FAQ tab for the extension too, which I highly recommend reading before you install an extension.

Sometimes there is additional work that needs to be done to use the extension properly. Some extensions only work when you assign its new permissions to various forums, groups or users.

Generally, all of an extension's data is in the database. Occasionally, the extension will create files that are saved on your board's file system. Files created should be placed in the board's /store folder, using a similar convention.

For example, my digests extension can cache digests for viewing offline by administrators, which is sometimes needed for testing and troubleshooting. For my digest extension, these can be found in the /store/phpbbservices/digests folder.

Disabling extensions and deleting their data

An extension is easily disabled on the same Manage extensions screen. Click on the **Disable** link on the extension's row to disable it. See Figure 6.10.

Disabling an extension keeps it from working and removes its interface, but it doesn't mean that its data or the extension itself is gone.

Once disabled, you can also remove all the data and settings created when the extension was enabled. Clicking on its **Delete data** link does this. This action cannot be undone! See Figure 6.10.

This process takes about as long as it took to enable the extension because all those things it did when the extension was installed must be undone. Tables may get dropped and columns and rows removed from tables. The hooks into the phpBB user interface must be removed too. If the extension creates files in the board's /store folder, they should be removed as well.

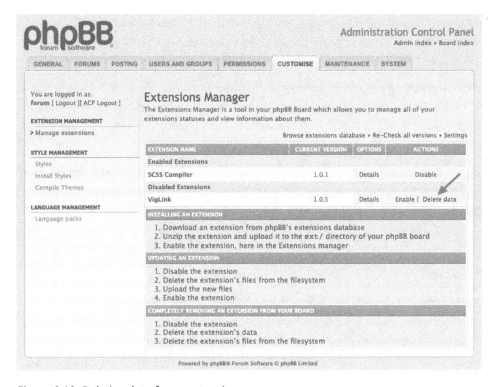

Figure 6.10: Deleting data for an extension

Deleting the extension's files

Disabling and deleting an extension's data does not remove its files, which means you can enable the extension again if you want.

To remove the files, you either need to delete them with an FTP program or use the file manager in your web host control panel. With an SSH connection, you can carefully remove these with appropriate commands too.

You should delete an extension's data before deleting its files. If you don't, this will create a database inconsistency, and when you go back to the **Manage extensions** page you should see an error.

Picking extensions

With hundreds of extensions to choose from, it might be tempting to start uploading and enabling dozens of them.

I don't recommend this approach. It's better to use the out-of-the-box phpBB for a while and get comfortable with it. Extensions are neat, but they add complexity and may slow your board's access a bit. Also, extensions can have bugs, and puzzling through these bugs and fixing them can be time consuming. Ask yourself, "Do I need this extension? Or do I just want it?" If you need it, install it. If you just want it, I suggest avoiding temptation.

However, it's a good idea to browse the extensions database just to get an idea of the breadth of extensions that are available. Most of the time now, if you want an extension that does something specific, it's available or in development.

It can't hurt to see what extensions are most popular. You can sort phpbb.com's extensions database by searching **Best rating** and **Most downloads**. Look for the dropdown arrow to the left of the **All branches** dropdown.

There are a few extensions that administrators almost always install. One of these is the Google Analytics extension because it captures the board's traffic for analysis. If you haven't used Google Analytics, you first need to create a Google Analytics account and create a project on the Google Analytics website. On the Google Analytics website, you will get a key to use for reporting traffic for your project. Then you enter this key into a field that appears in the ACP's Board settings page after you install this extension. We'll talk more about Google Analytics later in the book.

Extension support

Since each approved extension has a page on phpbb.com, it also has a discussion forum. Click on the **Discussion/Support** tab if you have questions or issues with the extension.

The instructions for installing, updating and removing extensions are also right on the **Manage extensions** page, greatly abbreviated.

Updating extensions

As you accumulate a lot of extensions, it's often helpful to know if an extension needs to be updated.

If you click on the **Re-Check all versions** link on the page, phpBB will attempt to see if new versions of your extension are available. See Figure 6.11.

- Items in red mean there is a newer version available.

- Items in green mean that you are running the most recent version.

- Items in blue mean that phpBB doesn't know if there is a new version or not. When this happens, it could mean the version check hook for the extension is not working correctly. You can't fix this. But, if you click on the **Details** link for the extension, you may be able to determine if there is a newer version or not. You can also check the extension's page on phpbb.com.

Extensions Manager

The Extensions Manager is a tool in your phpBB Board which allows you to manage all of your extensions statuses and view information about them.

Browse extensions database • Re-Check all versions • Settings

EXTENSION NAME	CURRENT VERSION	OPTIONS	ACTIONS
Enabled Extensions			
Advertisement Management	1.0.4 ❶	Details	Disable
Cron Status	3.1.2	Details	Disable
Digests	3.2.16	Details	Disable
Filter by country	1.0.8-beta	Details	Disable
Selective mass emails	1.0.8	Details	Disable
Smartfeed	3.0.12	Details	Disable
Disabled Extensions			
Advanced BBCode Box	3.1.2 ❶	Details	Enable | Delete data
Akismet Anti-Spam Extension	1.0.1 ❶	Details	Enable | Delete data
Antispam by CleanTalk	5.6.7	Details	Enable | Delete data

Figure 6.11: Extension manager after version check

While updating phpBB, the installer may attempt to update extensions automatically. I've seen mixed results in the many updates I do for clients. Sometimes it works, and sometimes it doesn't.

Regardless, if updating an extension manually, you should:

1. Disable the extension. *Don't* delete its data!

2. Remove the extension's files with FTP.

3. Upload the new version of the extension into the same file space.

4. Re-enable the extension.

As long as you don't delete the extension's data, it should retain all its previous settings.

Setting advanced board features

ACP > General > Board configuration > Board features

This page is often ignored, but its settings should be reviewed to make sure they are what you really want.

Here you can enable or disable a host of board features, such as private messaging, subscribing to forums and topics, allowing bookmarking and enabling attachments. Most of these features are turned on by default.

Note: The subscribing and private messaging features can become problematic as a board matures because they can generate a slew of emails and use a lot of resources.

Managing attachments

phpBB permits items to be attached to posts and private messages. These are called *attachments*. By default, phpBB permits attachments to posts, but not private messages.

You have complete control over the types of attachments you will allow, and even which forums can have attachments. In addition, phpBB's permission system lets you allow attachments for certain groups and disallow it for others.

General attachment management is handled in the ACP on the Posting tab:

ACP > Posting > Attachments

There is a redundant link to the Attachment settings page on the ACP's General tab.

Attaching files to posts

Before adjusting any attachment setting, let's look at how users make attachments.

If attachments are allowed, an **Attachments** tab will appear at the bottom of the posting window (Figure 6.12).

Figure 6.12: Attachments tab

Attachments can be dragged into this area if your operating system allows it, or you can press the **Add files** button and go through a dialog to attach them.

It's possible to attach more than one attachment at the same time, but by default, you can't attach more than three attachments to a post. This setting can be changed:

ACP > Posting > Attachments > Attachment settings > Maximum number of attachments per post

Once an attachment is uploaded, the Attachment tab changes, confirming the name of the attachment and its size. You can also add an optional comment to describe the attachment (Figure 6.13).

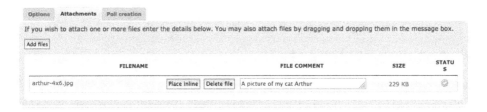

Figure 6.13: Commenting on an attachment

Typically, the attachments appear below the post's text. However, if you press the **Place inline** button, some BBCode is placed in the posting window at the location of the cursor with the attachment markup code. This will render the image at that location. This is called an *inline attachment.*

Pressing the **Submit** button will render the post with the embedded attachment (Figure 6.14). Notice that because an inline attachment was used, the picture is not below the post text, but embedded inside of it.

Most attachments are images, but if you attach a non-image, like an archive, it will show the attachment a bit differently (Figure 6.15), and will provide a download link.

Figure 6.14: Post with inline attachment

Figure 6.15: Post with non-image attachment

Changing the board's attachment settings

ACP > Posting > Attachments > Attachment settings

By default, all users cannot upload a total of more than 50 MiB of attachments, and an individual attachment may not exceed 256 KiB. 50 MiB is very small these days, so you should probably bump up this number, particularly if you want to allow uploads of photos taken off a phone's camera. In this case, I suggest changing the maximum individual attachment size to 3 or 4 MiB, because these are often stored in the camera in an uncompressed mode or at high resolutions.

To allow larger attachments, you may have to also change some PHP settings.

ACP > General > Quick access > PHP Information

Search the page for the following variables and note the values:

- **max_file_uploads**. This is the maximum number of files that can be uploaded at once.

- **post_max_size**. This is the maximum aggregate size of files uploaded together in one HTML form. It's possible to upload more than one file at once. If the combined size of all the files in an upload exceeds this value, the upload will fail and an error will occur.

- **upload_max_filesize**. No single uploaded file may exceed this value.

If you change the attachment settings to exceed any of these values, users may experience PHP errors while uploading. In this case, you should change these variables for PHP to be congruent with your attachment settings so everything goes smoothly.

Your web host control panel usually has an interface for changing variables like these. This is discussed more in Chapter 9.

How and where attachments are stored

By default, attachments are uploaded to the board's /files folder. If you go into the files folder, you will see file names that don't look the least bit like images and lack the expected file suffix (such as .jpg, .gif, .png or .webp) used to interpret the file. The file names are mostly a random hexadecimal name created by the phpBB software. Its purpose is to hide the intent of the file. They'll look like this:

```
2_09acd47ea11adef5e4d9cac2903e4ddc
```

The 2_ part of the example above tells indirectly who uploaded the file. It corresponds to the user_id column in the phpbb_users table.

If a file represents a thumbnail of a larger image, it is prefixed with thumb_.

```
thumb_2_09acd47ea11adef5e4d9cac2903e4ddc
```

A *thumbnail* is a smaller rendering of a larger image that phpBB creates automatically when needed. In the ACP's attachment settings page, you can control whether thumbnails are allowed, and the maximum size and dimensions allowed for a thumbnail. Because they are small and won't overwhelm other content on the page, thumbnails often appear in posts or private messages instead of the uploaded image. A user who wants to see the full-sized image clicks on the thumbnail for the larger view.

phpBB uses the phpbb_attachments table and a program called file.php to render the file. file.php sends information that tells the browser how to interpret the file, such as whether to render an image as a JPEG image.

This approach is quite clever—security through obscurity! Unless you are on the forum reading a topic, you have no idea what the uploaded file's name was, its file type, or who uploaded it. Moreover, you can only indirectly download it, as it is only rendered through the program /downloads/file.php.

You don't want to tamper with the contents of the /files folder, as it must be consistent with data in the phpbb_attachments table. Since uploaded files must be stored, this folder must have public write permissions.

One architectural issue with phpBB can affect the /files folder. It manifests when you have thousands of attachments. The more files in the same folder, the more the server's operating system has to manage. It can take longer to find a given file in the folder, or to add a new file to the folder when posting.

At its root, this is an operating system issue. On shared hosting, there is not much you can do about this. On other servers, changing the file system for the folder's volume, or putting the /files folder into a separate disk volume might address the issue. But this sort of task is for a qualified system administrator only!

The /files folder is essentially a data folder, so you must be careful not to change it outside of phpBB or when you are updating or upgrading phpBB.

If you want, you can tell phpBB to use a location other than the /files folder: **ACP > Posting > Attachments > Attachment settings > Upload directory**. After changing this setting, rename the files folder accordingly using FTP or your web host control panel's file manager.

Managing attachment extension groups

ACP > Posting > Attachments > Attachment settings > Manage attachment extension groups

There are five default attachment extension groups: documents, downloadable files, images, archives, and plain text (Figure 6.16). Each attachment group contains similar types of files, so they can be managed as a group. All the attachment extension groups are allowed by default except for the plain text group. This makes phpBB very flexible handling attachments.

Click on the green wheel for the attachment extension group to allow or disallow the extension group, but also to make fine adjustments to the group. You can even set some attachment permission on this page, allowing certain attachment extension groups on some forums, but not on other forums. If this isn't enough granular control for you, phpBB's permission system also lets you control whether certain groups are allowed to attach files to posts or not.

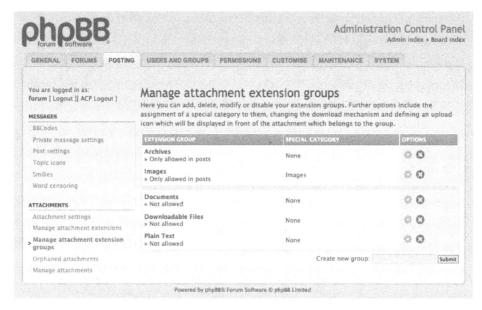

Figure 6.16: Manage attachment extension groups

If you are using phpBB 3.2, you will also see a Flash files extension group. This was removed in phpBB 3.3. Browsers stopped including Flash Shockwave support because it was considered a security vulnerability.

If you want to make a different kind of attachment group, you enter it in the **Create new group** field and press **Submit**. Then you associate the file suffixes that will be used by this group.

Managing attachment extensions

ACP > Posting > Attachments > Attachment settings > Manage attachment extensions

As you may have noticed, phpBB is all about flexibility. In addition to not allowing attachments at all, you can disallow certain types of attachments.

To delete an attachment file type, click the checkbox on the right of the extension type in the **Delete** column, and press **Submit** at the bottom of the screen.

When configuring a new board, certain other file types should probably be disallowed. For example, it's not a good idea to allow the upload of non-web-ready video files. But files with .mp4, .m4v, .ogg and .webm play natively in many browsers. In fact, .mp4 is universal across all browsers that support HTML 5, so you might want to allow these file types for videos and disallow the others. The others often require browser plugins to play. If a file type can't be rendered, browsers will usually fill the space with a message asking you to download the needed plugin. Since most users probably won't install a browser plugin to see content, why not disallow the file type?

Allowing video files of any kind has tradeoffs. Because video files tend to be large and your quota of disk space is limited, they can be "played" inside a post, but they won't necessarily stream without issues. That's because a web server is not a video streaming server. Short videos, though, usually play without issues.

Managing attachments

There are two other screens that help you manage attachments:

ACP > Posting > Attachments > Attachment settings > Manage attachments

Here you can see all the uploaded attachments and can selectively remove items, if desired. Sometimes this is necessary to save space. Some filtering of attachments that appear in the list is possible using controls at the bottom of the screen.

If phpBB thinks your attachment statistics may be inaccurate, you will be given a link to use to recalculate these statistics.

ACP > Posting > Attachments > Attachment settings > Orphaned attachments

This screen will find any attachments in the /files folder that are unattached to a post or private message. These attachments are known as *orphaned attachments*. Ideally, orphaned attachments shouldn't exist, but glitches can happen. This screen provides a simple way to find the orphaned attachments, remove them and reclaim some storage space.

Managing group and user attachment permissions

You can also allow or prohibit groups or individual users from attaching items to posts. This is surprisingly easy to do:

ACP > Users and Groups > Group permissions or

ACP > Users and Groups > User permissions

Figure 6.17: Group attachment permissions

Avoid giving permissions to users explicitly and stick with group permissions instead. The interface is similar for both approaches, so I'll show how it is done for groups.

First pick the group in the **Look up usergroup** dropdown and press **Submit**.

See Figure 6.17. Here, you may have to first click on the **Advanced permissions** link, which will lead you to a screen with the **Post** tab where the **Can attach files** permission can be easily set to **Yes**, **No**, or **Never**.

Note: If you changed permissions for an attachment extension group so that attachments are not accessible in a particular forum, but you set it to **Yes** *here, this permission will still be denied for that forum. Setting it to* **Never** *will ensure that some other group permission a user may belong to can't override a* **No** *permission.*

There's a lot more to learn about permissions that we'll get to later in this book.

Using avatars

Avatars are small cartoon-like images or icons that are used to identify individual users. You often see avatars on the View Topic page on the side of the post where the poster's information is presented. Avatars are enabled by default, but you can change this if you want. Avatars can also be actual images, although avatars are meant to be cartoon-like in nature.

Avatar settings

ACP > General > Board configuration > Avatar settings

On this page, you can set a variety of avatar settings.

Some administrators provide users with a set of default avatars to choose from, located in one or more galleries of avatars. If you'd like to do this too, be aware that the images must be uploaded first because none come installed.

You can also allow users to upload their own avatars or link to avatars offsite.

In addition, you can allow or prohibit *gravatars*. Gravatars are avatars that are globally unique, i.e., a user can use the same gravatar on your board and potentially lots of other places too. Gravatars exist only on the gravatar.com website.

Finding avatars

phpBB enthusiasts have created many sets of prebuilt avatars that you can offer on your board. The avatars are generally cartoon-like and, similar to styles and extensions, they must be downloaded, uncompressed and manually uploaded using FTP.

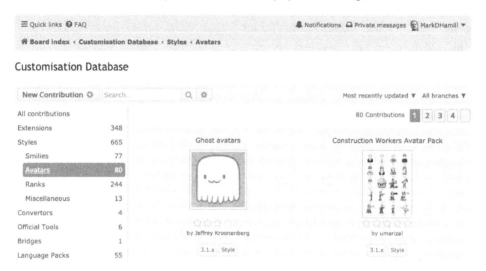

Figure 6.18: Avatars database

Avatars can be downloaded from phpbb.com's **Customisation Database**. Click on the **Styles** link and you will see an **Avatars** link (Figure 6.18). Click on that, and you will see dozens of avatar packs arranged as tiles that you can choose from.

If you click on an avatar pack, you will see previews of all the avatars in the pack and a convenient green **Download** button.

Installing avatar packs

Before uploading any avatar packs, make sure you have set the permission to allow them because they are disabled by default:

ACP > General > Board configuration > Avatar settings > Enable gallery avatars > Yes

If you are unfamiliar with using FTP to move these to your web server, read Appendix B.

Avatars must be uploaded to a folder inside the /images/avatars/gallery folder. Inside the uncompressed archive of the avatar pack, there will be a folder. You upload this folder so that the images should end up inside a folder like /images/avatars/gallery/ghosts.

You might want to change the name of this pack's folder, if it is not representative of the type of images inside it. This can be done using FileZilla and its rename command. The name of the folder is the only clue to the user as to the kind of avatars in the gallery.

You may have to purge the cache before users can see the avatars:

ACP > General > Purge the cache

Enabling avatar uploading

This feature is disabled by default. If enabled, users can upload their own avatar images from their computer onto your web server. The avatar image size must not exceed a height and width pixel size that you set. You can also set the maximum size for an uploaded avatar. Uploaded avatars are placed in the /images/avatars/upload folder, which must be publicly writeable. Fortunately, write privileges to the folder were verified when phpBB was installed.

If users are having issues uploading their avatars, it's likely a permissions issue on this folder. You can usually use FTP to change the folder's permissions. On Linux-based systems, you would set the folder permissions to 777.

To enable avatar uploading:

ACP > General > Board configuration > Avatar settings > Enable avatar uploading > Yes

Enabling remote avatars

You can also allow users to link to offsite avatar images (remote avatars):

ACP > General > Board configuration > Avatar settings > Enable remote avatars > Yes

When enabled, the user provides a URL for the image in their profile.

Allowing remote avatars is not recommended for two reasons:

- The web server containing the image may not be accessible at any given moment, meaning the image may not be served when needed. This usually results in an ugly white block where the avatar should be, and sometimes an embedded message saying the image cannot be found. In addition, some web servers prohibit hot links. *Hot links* are web content that is not server by a web page on the site. In this case, a blank space will normally appear instead of the image, throwing off the look of the page.

- If your board uses encryption (https) and the remote avatar is served insecurely (http), you have a mixture of secure and insecure content on the same page. Most browsers will call attention to this. It makes your site appear untrustworthy and may lower your site's ranking in search indexes.

Enabling gravatars

If you want, you also can allow users to link to their gravatars:

ACP > General > Board configuration > Avatar settings > Enable gravatar avatars > Yes

The user must upload a gravatar image on the gravatar.com website. Whatever image they pick becomes public across the World-Wide Web. They will need the gravatar's URL.

These images are served securely, so your browser won't flag pages with gravatars on them as insecure. The gravatar.com website is also highly available (it is managed by the people who run wordpress.com), so enabling gravatars is safe.

How users add avatars

Users add avatars in the User Control Panel: **UCP > Profile > Edit avatar**. The screen presented will look different depending on the board's avatar settings. Figure 6.19 shows one potential arrangement of the screen when the gallery and avatar uploading are all allowed.

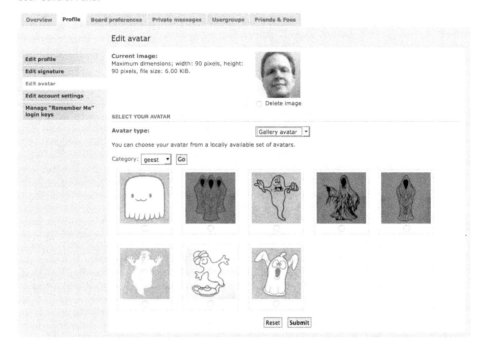

Figure 6.19: Edit avatar settings

Adding BBCodes

What are BBCodes?

We've talked a little about BBCodes already, but haven't totally explained them.

BBCodes are a special form of markup language. You enter it in a post or private message using plain text, and although it looks strange, when the post or private message is rendered, it expands into something useful.

BBCodes can range from simple to elegant. For example:

```
[b]This will be in bolded text.[/b]
```

Will render as:

This will be in bolded text.

A more complex example would be an unordered bulleted list:

```
[ul]
[*]Milk
[*]Eggs
[*]Bread
[/ul]
```

This will render:

- Milk

- Eggs

- Bread

BBCode markup syntax is very dated and a little awkward to use. But in 2000 when phpBB was created, BBCode was a standard for marking up text for display on bulletin board systems. It still is a standard, though less used than it was in its heyday. Some argue that while a bit awkward BBCode is elegant in its simplicity. You can see the full BBCode standard on the BBCode website.

BBCode *tags* enclosed in square-cornered brackets form the syntax of BBCode. The markup begins with `[tag]` and end with a `[/tag]`. The content between the tags is transformed when rendered.

Some tags allow tag attributes, similar to HTML tags. For example, you can turn text into a link like this in BBCode:

```
[url=https://www.google.com]Go to Google[/url]
```

You don't have to know the syntax of the most frequently used BBCodes, since the posting window provides some common BBCode buttons like bold and italics within the editor. But some are a bit awkward to get right without consulting a reference. It's also not necessarily intuitive to know that you must first select the text before hitting the BBCode button as a shortcut for marking up a block of text.

While old fashioned, BBCode is a fundamental technology used by phpBB and very hard to get rid of, so don't expect it to go away.

While there is a defined standard for BBCode, phpBB is flexible in that it will let you create unique BBCodes for your board. You specify the BBCode syntax and then the syntax for rendering it as HTML.

Adding a new BBCode

Here's an example of how to create a unique BBCode:

Say you want to embed a YouTube video on a web page. There is no built-in BBCode to do this, in part because YouTube did not exist in 2000 when phpBB was created. You could create the BBCode yourself. The syntax will look like this:

```
[youtube]https://youtu.be/ffHLIZh0PHg[/youtube]
```

All the user does is paste the youtu.be URL between these tags and, like magic, the following HTML would result:

```
<iframe width="560" height="315"
src="https://www.youtube.com/embed/ffHLIZh0PHg"
frameborder="0" allowfullscreen></iframe>
```

How would you do this? Go to the BBCodes page:

ACP > Posting > Messages > BBCodes

Figure 6.20: Adding a new BBCode

Click on the **Add a new BBCode** button. On the next screen, I entered the code needed to create this YouTube BBCode (Figure 6.20).

At the bottom of the page below the buttons (not shown), is an explanation for the token syntax used in these fields that contains text entered by the user, delineated with the { and } brackets.

Adding a BBCode like this takes a bit of knowledge of HTML as well as some trial and error, but once you understand it, it works well.

For this BBCode, I checked the checkbox to display it on the posting page in Figure 6.20, and now you can see it in the posting window in Figure 6.21.

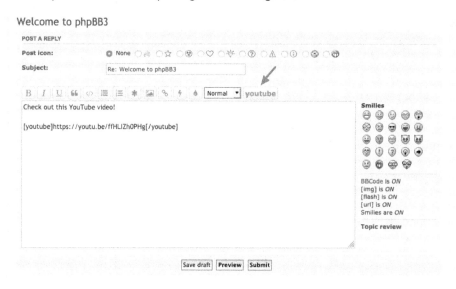

Figure 6.21: Using a custom BBCode in a post

Here's how I did it:

1. I pasted the URL in the posting window, then highlighted it by selecting all the text of the URL

2. I then clicked on the **youtube** button and pressed the **Submit** button

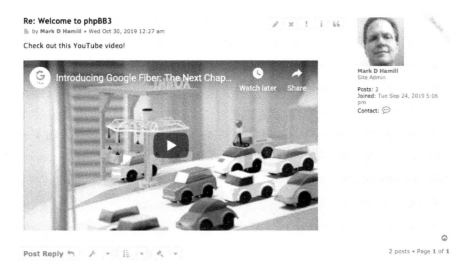

Figure 6.22: Post with rendered BBCode

Figure 6.22 shows the rendered post.

Adding new BBCodes from the Customisation Database

If the YouTube example above has you worried because it seems complicated, don't worry.

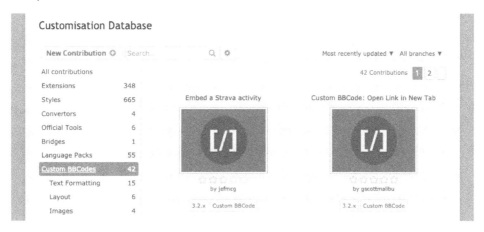

Figure 6.23: Custom BBCodes on phpbb.com

Chances are someone has already written the BBCode you need, and it's in the **Customisation Database** on phpbb.com (Figure 6.23).

You don't download these BBCodes. You simply copy and paste them from the web page on phpbb.com into the BBCodes screen on your board.

If you don't see what you are looking for and feel too intimidated to create one yourself, you can create a post in the support forum on phpbb.com describing the BBCode you want. It's likely that a number of people will provide code that will work.

There's a lot that can be done with these custom BBCodes. BBCode may be dated, but this open architecture is truly one of phpBB's strengths.

Adding smilies

Smilies are small images that are woven into posts and private messages to express various things, generally emotions. phpBB includes a small and generic set of smilies on the posting window. Smilies are sort of like a very limited set of Emoji. Arguably, Emoji evolved from common smiley images that preceded them.

Users click on the smiley they like, and the equivalent BBCode will appear at the location of the cursor in the posting field. When submitted, the smiley will be rendered in the post or private message.

Adding a smiley package

A smiley package is a set of related smilies users might like to use on your board. To add a smiley package for them, go to phpbb.com's **Customisation database**. Under the **Styles** area you will find a **Smilies** group (Figure 6.24).

Click the link in the smilies database to be taken to its page. There is a green button you can click to download the smilies archive. It's in a compressed archive (.zip file), which must be expanded.

These smilies must be uploaded to /images/smilies using FTP (Figure 6.25). If unfamiliar with using FTP, see Appendix B.

Figure 6.24: Smilies database on phpbb.com

Most smiley packages have a .pak (package) file in them. This eases the process of installing smilies in the package. The .pak file needs to be uploaded to the /images/smilies folder so it can be found.

Name	Date Modified	^	Size	Kind
orcsmiliesv3.zip	Today at 9:19 AM		69 KB	ZIP archive
▼ orcsmiliesv3	Today at 9:19 AM		--	Folder
license.txt	Jul 13, 2018 at 7:49 PM		15 KB	Plain Text
readme.md	Jul 13, 2018 at 7:49 PM		1 KB	Document
▼ orcsmilies	Today at 9:19 AM		--	Folder
o_icon_cool.gif	Jul 13, 2018 at 7:49 PM		3 KB	GIF Image
o_icon_cry.gif	Jul 13, 2018 at 7:49 PM		4 KB	GIF Image
o_icon_e_biggrin.gif	Jul 13, 2018 at 7:49 PM		3 KB	GIF Image
o_icon_e_confused.gif	Jul 13, 2018 at 7:49 PM		3 KB	GIF Image
o_icon_e_geek.gif	Jul 13, 2018 at 7:49 PM		4 KB	GIF Image
o_icon_e_sad.gif	Jul 13, 2018 at 7:49 PM		4 KB	GIF Image
o_icon_e_smile.gif	Jul 13, 2018 at 7:49 PM		3 KB	GIF Image
o_icon_e_surprised.gif	Jul 13, 2018 at 7:49 PM		3 KB	GIF Image
o_icon_e_ugeek.gif	Jul 13, 2018 at 7:49 PM		4 KB	GIF Image
o_icon_e_wink.gif	Jul 13, 2018 at 7:49 PM		3 KB	GIF Image
o_icon_eek.gif	Jul 13, 2018 at 7:49 PM		4 KB	GIF Image
o_icon_evil.gif	Jul 13, 2018 at 7:49 PM		4 KB	GIF Image
o_icon_lol.gif	Jul 13, 2018 at 7:49 PM		4 KB	GIF Image
o_icon_mad.gif	Jul 13, 2018 at 7:49 PM		3 KB	GIF Image
o_icon_mrgreen.gif	Jul 13, 2018 at 7:49 PM		4 KB	GIF Image
o_icon_neutral.gif	Jul 13, 2018 at 7:49 PM		3 KB	GIF Image
o_icon_razz.gif	Jul 13, 2018 at 7:49 PM		4 KB	GIF Image
o_icon_redface.gif	Jul 13, 2018 at 7:49 PM		4 KB	GIF Image
o_icon_rolleyes.gif	Jul 13, 2018 at 7:49 PM		3 KB	GIF Image
o_icon_twisted.gif	Jul 13, 2018 at 7:49 PM		4 KB	GIF Image
orcsmiliesv3.pak	Jul 13, 2018 at 7:49 PM		1 KB	ARC Archive

Figure 6.25: Smilies archive contents

It can be helpful to look at the .pak file in an editor. The file is essentially a CSV (comma separated values) file. A sample line might look like this:

```
'icon_e_biggrin.png', '20', '20', '1', 'Very Happy', ':D',
```

This basically says that the image file icon_e_biggrin.png is an image with a rendering size of 20x20 pixels, it should be enabled, its corresponding emotion is "Very Happy" (this will appear as a tooltip when your mouse hovers over the image) and you can use the shortcode :D in the posting window to render this image.

In this case, the image file icon_e_biggrin.png needs to be placed in the /images/smilies folder to match the image with its attributes in the .pak file, which get stored in the database. However, the line could look like this:

```
'green/icon_e_biggrin.png', '20', '20', '1', 'Very Happy',
':D',
```

In this case the image file icon_e_biggrin.png should be inside an /images/smilies/green folder.

Generally, smilies archives are consistent with the way files and folder are organized in the archive. If they are not, reading the .pak file gives you a clue on where these files should be uploaded. You could edit the .pak file if necessary to place the new smilies in the location that you desire.

Adding new smilies

To add these new smilies, go to the Smilies page in the ACP:

ACP > Posting > Messages > Smilies

If there is a .pak file in the archive, phpBB can install these more easily. You can see one in the orcsmilies folder. In this case:

1. Click on the **Install smilies package** link

2. On the next screen, select the .pak file from the dropdown list (Figure 6.26).

3. The radio buttons for **Current smilies** allow you to decide what do with smilies that are already installed. Generally, you don't want to replace all your smilies, but add them to your existing ones, which means the **Keep all** radio button should remain selected.

4. Then press the **Install smilies package** button. When you go back to the list of smilies, the new smilies will appear.

If the archive does not have a .pak file, you may be surprised to not see these new smilies in the list of smilies after they are uploaded. That's because the metadata for each new smiley is not yet entered. This becomes an extra step.

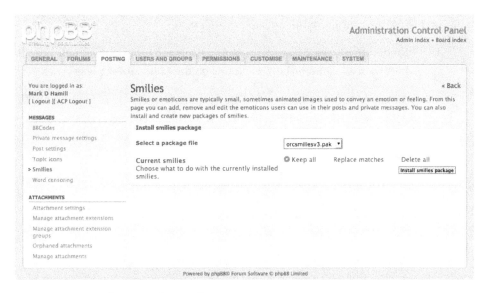

Figure 6.26: Installing a smilies package

At the bottom of the page, click on the **Add multiple smilies** button. It will show you those smilies missing their metadata (Figure 6.27).

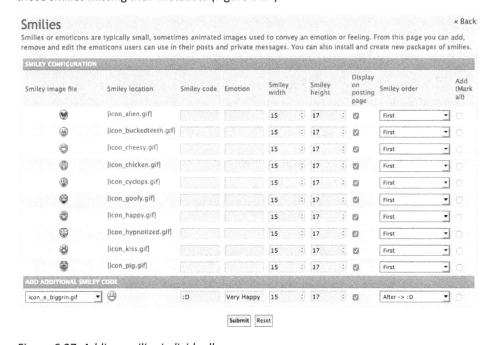

Figure 6.27: Adding smilies individually

To add one or more smilies from the package:

- The **checkbox** in the **Add** column must be checked for the smiley you want to add. To add all of them at once, clicking on the **Mark all** link saves time.

- A **Smiley code** must be entered. If this pattern is found in the post or private message text, the smiley image will be substituted. These are generally prefixed and suffixed with a colon (:), ex: :kiss:.

- The **Emotion** must be entered. This is text that explains the smiley. When you hover over the image with your mouse, this text appears.

- **Smiley width** and **Smiley height** are generally left as is. If you change these values, the smiley may appear stretched, shrunk or fuzzy.

- If **Display on posting page** is unchecked, the smiley can be used only if you enter the smiley code, such as :geek:, in the posting window.

Press **Submit** when done. Those smilies with the necessary information will appear in the list of smilies. Those without it will remain inaccessible. phpBB will give you a report on whether it successfully added each smiley you checked.

Editing, removing and rearranging smilies

Through the main ACP smilies interface, you can easily edit, remove or rearrange the order of smiley presentation on the posting page.

- To edit a smiley, click on the **Edit** icon (green wheel) for the smiley

- To delete a smiley, click on the **Delete** icon (red X) for the smiley

- To change the presentation order of the smilies, click on the **Move up** (blue up arrow) or **Move down** (blue down arrow). Drag and drop is not supported, so this is a bit tedious.

To do a mass edit of all active smilies, click on the **Edit smilies** button at the bottom of the page.

Adding and using custom profile fields

A profile is where a user shares information about themself. A capsule of this information appears next to posts on the View topic page. As the administrator, you can customize what kind of information your users can share.

ACP > Users and groups > Users > Custom profile fields

phpBB comes with ten built-in *custom profile fields*. Some of these are arguably very dated and only make sense when you realize that phpBB has been around since 2000. For example, hardly anyone uses ICQ for instant messaging anymore, but at one time it was the hot instant messaging service.

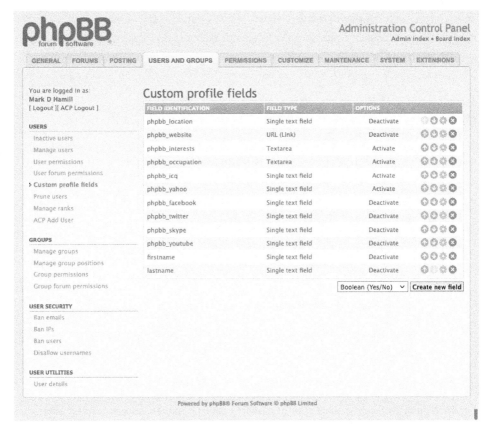

Figure 6.28: Custom profile fields screen (Google Plus was removed in phpBB 3.3.1)

By default, users can specify their location and their website's URL, but you can make it so they can add their interests and occupation just by activating those in the built-in fields. If none of these fields suffice, you can add additional custom profile fields, to which you can assign meaningful names, field types, and when they should be filled out.

Some private boards will require members to provide their real first and last names upon registration. Figure 6.28 shows the default custom profile fields with two custom profile fields (firstname and lastname) that we will discuss shortly.

Deleting legacy custom profile fields

The services associated with many of these fields are obsolete or rarely used. When configuring your board, it's better to delete fields that you don't want to allow. Use the **Delete** icon (red X).

Adding new custom profile fields

To add new fields, press the **Create new field** button at the bottom of the page. You specify the type of field before you press the button. Field types are:

- Boolean (Yes/No)

- Date

- Dropdown box. You are given a set of choices from which you pick one.

- Numbers

- Single text field. The user has one line to enter information.

- Textarea. The user gets a box to enter textual information on as many lines as desired.

- URL. A web address must be entered and it must be syntactically valid.

For each field, you'll get a host of options. Most are self-explanatory, but these aspects should be noted:

- **Field name**. The field must contain the lowercase letters a through z and one or more underscores (_) only. Why is this? It's because when you create a custom profile field, you are actually creating a new column in the phpbb_profile_fields and phpbb_profile_fields_data tables in your board's database. Database columns have requirements for their names; such as you can't use a number in the column's name. Whatever field name you choose, in the database, the column name will be prefaced by pf_. For example, the field firstname will create columns in these tables with the name pf_firstname. pf is short for profile field.

- **Required field**. When checked, the user must enter information into this field. You can require that it must be entered upon registration by checking the **Display on registration** checkbox (Figure 6.29).

Figure 6.29: Registration using custom profile fields

When you press the **Profile type specific options** button, you get another screen. This allows you to set various properties for the field. For example, for single text fields, you can specify the length of the input box, the minimum number of characters required in the field and the maximum number of characters allowed. There is also a **field validation** dropdown that can put restrictions on what can be typed into the field, such as alphabetical characters only.

If you press the **Language specific options** button and have more than one language pack installed, you must specify the language information presented to the user for each language.

There are some limitations on certain fields. For example, single text fields can contain no more than 255 characters, and text boxes are limited to the size of a text field for your database management system.

Showing custom profile fields

You can control where custom profile fields appear by editing their properties. Potential places include: in the User Control Panel (where it can be changed), on the registration screen, on the private messages screen, on the view topic screen, and on the member list screen.

The most powerful of these requires fields to be filled out upon registration. Here is an example where the custom profile fields First name and Last name must be filled out on registration (Figure 6.29).

How users change custom profile fields

Users change custom profile fields after logging in, in the User Control Panel (Figure 6.30):

UCP > Profile > Edit profile

Required fields have an asterisk (*) next to their labels.

Figure 6.30: Edit profile, with required custom profile fields

Adding and using ranks

Ranks are an optional feature enabled on some boards that denote the relative status of a user.

Ranks can either be appointed or earned.

- Earned ranks are based on the number of posts contributed.

- Administrators can grant appointed (special) ranks to those members they think deserve them. Appointed ranks can also be assigned to groups.

The user's rank is usually displayed on the View topic screen, along with other poster information. It may appear on other screens too, such as the Member list screen.

Ranks don't have to be just text. You can have rank images associated with a rank as well.

The Site Admin appointed rank is created automatically when phpBB is installed and is assigned to the founder.

Adding rank images

As with avatars and smilies, you don't have to start from scratch and create your own rank images. phpBB has plenty of rank image sets to choose from in its **Customisation database** under the **Styles** area (Figure 6.31).

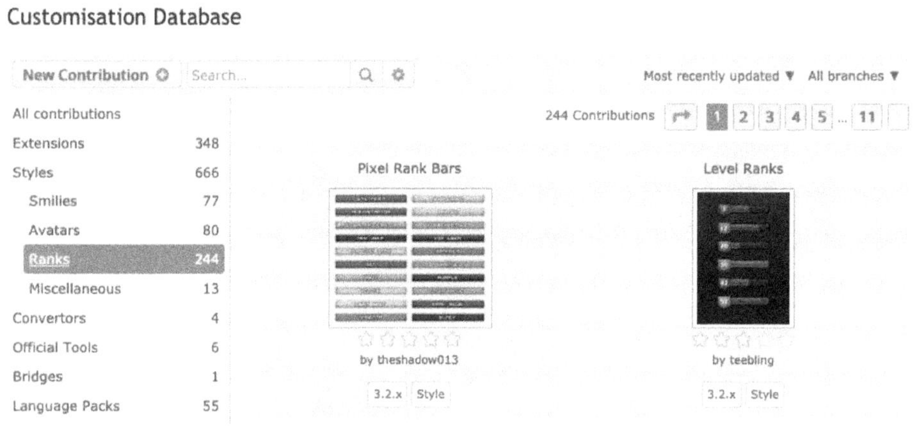

Figure 6.31: phpbb.com ranks database

Click on the link for the ranks archive of interest. Then click on the green **Download** button to download an archive of ranks in a .zip file. Decompress the file on your machine, then upload them to the /images/ranks folder for your board.

Uploading the rank images doesn't mean they can be used automatically. You can assign an image to a rank. But an image is never required for a rank.

If you want, you can create folders inside the ranks folder and place them there. This is useful if you anticipate lots of ranks of various types and categories.

Adding ranks

ACP > Users and groups > Users > Manage ranks

When you arrive at the Manage ranks page, you'll see a list of all existing ranks. Click the **Add new rank** button and you will be sent to a screen where you can add a rank (Figure 6.32).

Figure 6.32: Add a new rank

Of note:

- If you set **Set as special rank** to **Yes**, there is no number of posts requirement to earn the rank and the **Minimum posts** field will disappear. An administrator assigns special ranks.

- If not a special rank, the user must have at least the number of **Minimum posts**, a value you specify, to earn the rank.

Only one rank can be assigned to a member, unless an extension is installed to allow more than one rank. Most ranks are based the number of posts, so this is not often a problem. But if a user also has a special rank, then to see a rank based on the number of posts, you would have to remove the special rank from the user. We'll talk about how to do this shortly.

Assigning special ranks to users

Ranks based on the number of posts appear automatically when the criteria are earned. These ranks should not be inconsistent. For example, you should not have two ranks where the criteria are 1000 posts.

Special ranks must be assigned. Here's how this is done:

ACP > Users and groups > Users > Manage users

First, find the member with the **Find a member** link, or enter it in the **Enter username** field and press **Submit**.

On the next screen, select **Rank** from the **Select form** dropdown control and press **Go** (Figure 6.33).

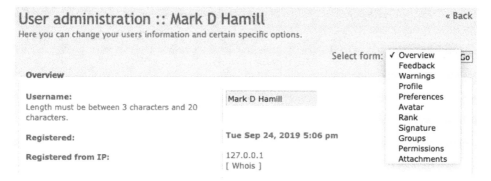

Figure 6.33: Selecting the rank function for a user

To assign a special rank, pick it from the dropdown and press **Submit**. You can also remove the special rank by selecting **No special rank assigned** from the **User rank** dropdown and then pressing **Submit**. (Figure 6.34)

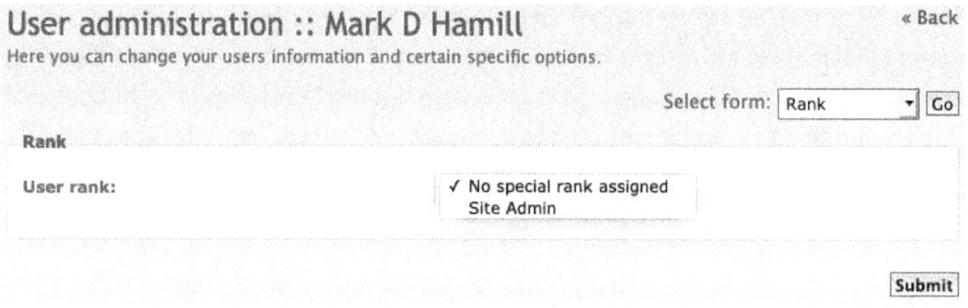

User administration :: Mark D Hamill « Back

Here you can change your users information and certain specific options.

Select form: Rank ▼ Go

Rank

User rank: ✓ No special rank assigned
Site Admin

Submit

Figure 6.34: Adding or removing a special rank for a user

Assigning special ranks to groups

ACP > Users and groups > Groups > Manage groups

For groups, the approach is a bit different compared to users. To assign a special rank to a group, you don't have to search for the group. Just find it in the list of groups then click on the **Edit** icon (green wheel).

Toward the bottom of the page, you will find a **Group wide settings** block (Figure 6.35). Open the **Group rank** dropdown and select the special rank then press **Submit**.

If you select **User default**, the special group rank is removed for the group.

Figure 6.35: Adding or removing a special group rank

Tightening security

Changing phpBB's security settings

In the last chapter, you created an effective spambot countermeasure. Here are a few more methods for making your board more secure.

ACP > General > Server configuration > Security settings

You'll notice there are many settings on this page. I will concentrate on those that have the biggest security implications:

- **Remember Me login key expiration length (in days)**. By default, there is no expiration date for how long your browser remembers your username in a cookie. You might want to set a limit for when the username cookie should be removed.

- **IP Session validation**. An Internet Service Provider (ISP) assigns an Internet Protocol (IP) address used by a device to access the Internet. These can be either IPV4 or IPV6 addresses. Most common are IPV4 addresses like 123.45.67.89. Using the default A.B.C pattern means that if your ISP changes your IP dynamically to, say, 123.45.67.90, then phpBB won't require a new session.

  When a new session is created, you may have to re-authenticate (log in).

  The A.B pattern is broader, so an IP of 123.45.99.88 would keep this session alive.

  The default A.B.C pattern is reasonable. This setting should not be loosened and should definitely not be disabled, as it invites security issues.

  Most ISPs use *Dynamic Host Configuration Protocol* (DHCP), so an IP assigned to a given device may get changed at any time. These IPs are generally changed and typically last at least a month.

  Why is this important? The idea is to prevent *session hijacking*. Once logged in, you will see the session ID in the URL. For example, the URL might look like this (session ID is in bold):

  http://forums.mydomain.com/index.php?**sid=d34018eb6f25037f6c4c446456ea 502d**

  If some malicious actor has the full URL, they could take over your session from a different location on the Internet, perhaps posting as you, reading your private messages or making spam posts. Forcing phpBB to continuously check that the IP assigned to your session hasn't changed, or hasn't changed much, prevents most session hijacking.

- **Check IP against DNS Blackhole List**. This is disabled, but if enabled, it will check the sender's IP address against a major blacklist that tracks IPs of spammers. It tends to slow things down, so it's appropriate as a last resort for dealing with spam. Even so, it's not perfect because it depends on the accuracy of the blacklist it checks, and it's possible it may block some legitimate users.

- **Force password change**. This function is disabled by default. Enabling it will improve security, but will likely upset your members, so it is normally left disabled. But if your organization has a policy on how often passwords must be changed, you should enter the number of days into this field to match the policy.

- **Maximum number of login attempts per username**. The default here is set at three attempts, and then you must go through a CAPTCHA to prove you are a human. Increasing the number is not recommended because spambots may get through before they are forced to solve a CAPTCHA. Entering zero disables this, which also invites security problems.

- **Maximum number of login attempts per IP address**. Here you can set the number of login failures allowed from a given IP address before the IP is blocked from logging in again. The default is fifty, but that's probably too high. A lower number, like twenty, is more appropriate. Also, once banned, an IP can be manually unblocked by an administrator: **ACP > Users and groups > User security > Ban IPs**

Web hosting security solutions

Outside of phpBB, your web host may offer other security features for you to use, sometimes for an extra cost. Some of these, if configured incorrectly, can cause issues with phpBB.

The spam registration issue is generally no longer a problem if you use an effective spambot countermeasure. What's more likely are denial of service attacks or denial of service-*like* attacks. These are attempts to block others from accessing your site by flooding it with requests.

Every time a phpBB program is run, a lot of PHP code is executed, which takes time and resources. If too many requests come in at once, your web server can get overloaded, potentially crashing it. Web hosts often integrate software like ModSecurity to help cope with sudden large-scale attacks like this. When configured correctly, ModSecurity is very valuable. When configured incorrectly, it can cause havoc in phpBB.

For example, some of these security solutions can be configured to disable programs they think are suspicious. Sometimes programs phpBB uses are physically removed automatically! Other times, security solutions will change file and folder permissions. I've seen the public write permissions for the cache folder turned off in some cases, which causes almost instant problems for phpBB because it cannot write to the folder.

It's a good idea to ask your web host what security software is enabled by default and if these can be disabled. If you enable security software, try it for a while and observe if there are any negative effects.

phpBB security extensions

In the last chapter, we talked about two important built-in and useful spambot countermeasures: Q&A and reCAPTCHA. Adding effective security extensions can help too.

There is a phpBB Akismet extension that can reject access from IP addresses found in its database. Akismet is most frequently used on WordPress sites, and is used to moderate blog comments. In most cases, using the Akismet service is not free, but the extension is free. You need a key from Akismet to use the extension. For noncommercial use, they ask people to chip in any amount to get a key, but you don't have to. Commercial use starts at $5 per site per month.

Similarly, there is a service called Cleantalk and a Cleantalk extension that can be installed. Cleantalk's Spam Firewall feature is very useful for keeping spam traffic away from your site, helping to offload a lot of this malicious traffic and keeping your board running smoothly for legitimate users. In case there is a false positive, Cleantalk will generate a page with a link that will take users back to the board if they click it. A bot most likely wouldn't be able to click it, so it validates real users.

Getting the Cleantalk integration to work correctly can sometimes be challenging. Like Akismet, the service itself costs some money, but is an excellent value. (Currently it is $8/year per domain, with discounts available for multiple domains.) As of this writing, the approved Cleantalk extension on phpbb.com is quite dated. If you want to enable its Spam Firewall features, download it from its Github page and make sure the software is placed in the /ext/cleantalk/antispam folder.

Neither service is going to be perfect, and it might even trigger occasional false positives. But both services, when configured properly and regularly updated, generally are 99% effective.

There are other antispam extensions you can try, including a Sortables Captcha and my Filter by country extension. With my filter by country extension, you can select the countries you want to let in or restrict.

Adjusting phpBB load settings

When a board gets inundated with traffic, adjusting phpBB's load settings can help deal with it.

ACP > General > Server configuration > Load settings

Limiting system load

If the server's central processing unit (CPU) is getting overloaded, phpBB can sometimes take action by making the board go offline. This limits the load on the system. Select **Limit system load**, the first field on the page, to enable this function.

This only works if you have control of a physical or virtual server and shouldn't work on shared hosting. You also need to know how many real or virtual CPUs you have. If you have two CPUs (real or virtual), for example, and you set this value to 2, then the board will go offline if both CPUs are around 100% utilization over the last minute. When the board is below this threshold, the board is automatically re-enabled.

As you might imagine, this approach is jarring to end users, as they may be in the middle of something like submitting a post when suddenly they cannot use the board. The good news is the error message they receive may be preferable to HTTP 500 and other error pages, which are uglier and more intrusive.

Reducing session length

Sessions are mechanisms for tracking someone's usage of a website, even if you are not logged in. You would think this would be automatic, but without sessions it's impossible.

This is because most web traffic uses the HTTP protocol, and it is stateless. To get around the issue, phpBB adds a session id (sid) parameter to the URL which allows it to track usage by an individual device.

What does it mean for a session to time out? It doesn't necessarily mean you are automatically logged off. It means that if you haven't done anything on the board for the length of a session, which is set to an hour by default, and you try to resume where you left off, phpBB should generate a new session. So, taking a long lunch break may require starting a new session. Creating a new session reduces the vulnerabilities possible with session hijacking.

You can reduce the amount of a session's time by selecting the **Session length** field and specifying a lower number of seconds, for example, 1800 seconds is a half-hour session.

Old sessions are regularly purged from the database table holding session data if the session end time is before the current time.

When used with a limit sessions number, this can give fairer access to the board, while potentially making disgruntled users too.

Limiting sessions

If you have a very active board but have limited resources (such as on a shared server), limiting sessions will keep too many people from being logged in at the same time by limiting the number of simultaneous sessions. When the limit is reached, those trying to login will get a message saying the board is too busy now and to try again later.

To limit the number of sessions, select the **Limit sessions** field. This is disabled (by setting it to zero) by default, which means potentially phpBB would have to simultaneously manage hundreds or thousands of sessions at once, probably resulting in resource limitation errors on shared hosting. This can help mitigate denial of service attacks.

Other load settings

There are a host of other load settings that are enabled by default that could slow down the board through database queries. By disabling them, you can speed things up if you need to.

For example, phpBB can show who's online, who has a birthday today, lists of moderators and administrators, etc. It takes a number of database queries to gather this information, which take both time and resources. Disabling these could speed things up because the database management system will have less work to do.

There is also a **custom profile fields** group where you can turn on or off the display of custom profile fields on various pages. We've looked at other settings that can do similar things on profile pages, but here it can be done globally with the intent of reducing the time it takes to render web pages. The default custom profile fields can be re-enabled rather easily when your board is under less stress.

The work involved in these database queries is generally quite minimal, so disabling these settings is of marginal value. When phpBB is properly configured and your database is optimized, short queries that don't return much data tend to be very fast, often taking as little as a thousandth of a second each.

Fine-tuning the search engine

In the last chapter, we covered creating and changing a search index. Typically, phpBB's built-in search engine is used because it is the default.

We talked about the MySQL and MariaDB's fulltext search engines that are also available. You can select and configure a search engine on its settings page:

ACP > General > Server configuration > Search settings

General search settings of interest

The first block of fields on the Search settings page contains common controls used for all search engines. Tuned, these settings can make your search engine more efficient and useful (Figure 6.36).

Some fields of note:

- **User search flood interval**. On busy boards, you might want to require users to wait some time before making another search. This is disabled by default. There is a separate Guest search flood interval if you want to be more restrictive of guest search queries than for members logged in.

- **Search page load limit**. As with load settings, if your server is configured correctly, you can make the search engine go offline automatically if the average one-minute load is about 100% utilized.

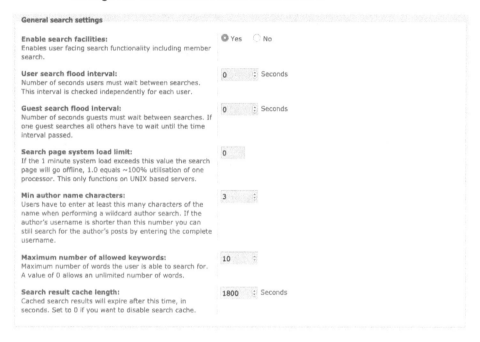

Figure 6.36: General search settings

This covers at least 95 percent of cases, but there are some lesser-known search engines that can be used.

PostgreSQL Fulltext search engine

This works only if you selected the Postgres database management system when you installed phpBB. On the search settings page, at the bottom, is a **Search backend** group. When you select a different search engine from its dropdown, the block below it dynamically changes. When changed to PostgreSQL, this block changes (see Figure 6.37) and is functionally almost identical to the MySQL fulltext search index type.

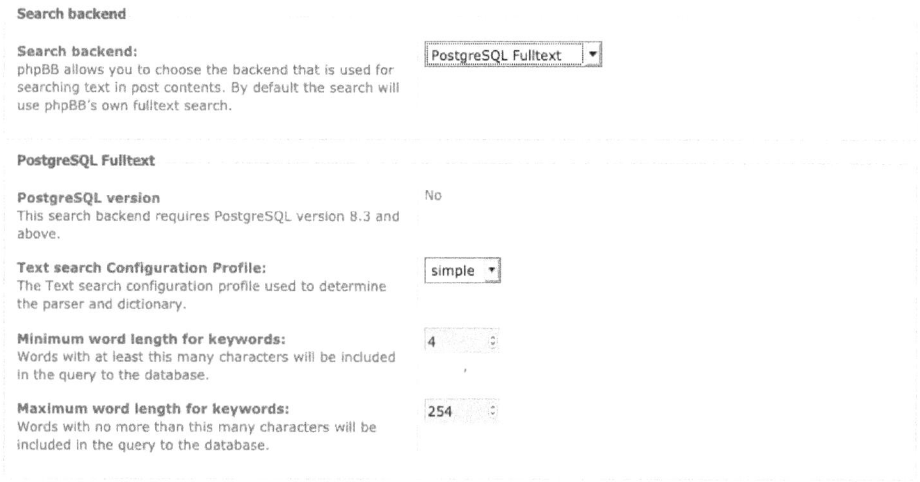

Search backend

Search backend:
phpBB allows you to choose the backend that is used for searching text in post contents. By default the search will use phpBB's own fulltext search.

PostgreSQL Fulltext ▼

PostgreSQL Fulltext

PostgreSQL version
This search backend requires PostgreSQL version 8.3 and above.

No

Text search Configuration Profile:
The Text search configuration profile used to determine the parser and dictionary.

simple ▼

Minimum word length for keywords:
Words with at least this many characters will be included in the query to the database.

4

Maximum word length for keywords:
Words with no more than this many characters will be included in the query to the database.

254

Figure 6.37: Postgres SQL search settings

Sphinx Fulltext search engine

The open-source Sphinx Fulltext search engine is also selectable from the **Search backend** dropdown (Figure 6.38). This search engine requires MySQL, MariaDB or Postgres to be your board's database management system. The Sphinx Fulltext search engine must be installed on your web server, which generally makes it an option only for dedicated, cloud or virtual private servers, since generally you will have to install it using a package manager.

Once installed, you can use this interface to connect it to phpBB. It's not a trivial exercise because a number of folders, plus a sphinx.conf file must be created. This interface will help with this, but some steps must be done manually outside of phpBB.

First, you need to create a table in your database. In addition, you need to create a process than runs every five minutes to update the index, called a cron job. This means that the search index may be up to five minutes behind what has been posted. We'll talk about cron jobs shortly.

It's a lot of hassle, but on very large or highly trafficked board, it has a big payoff in that it's considerably faster than any of the other search engines.

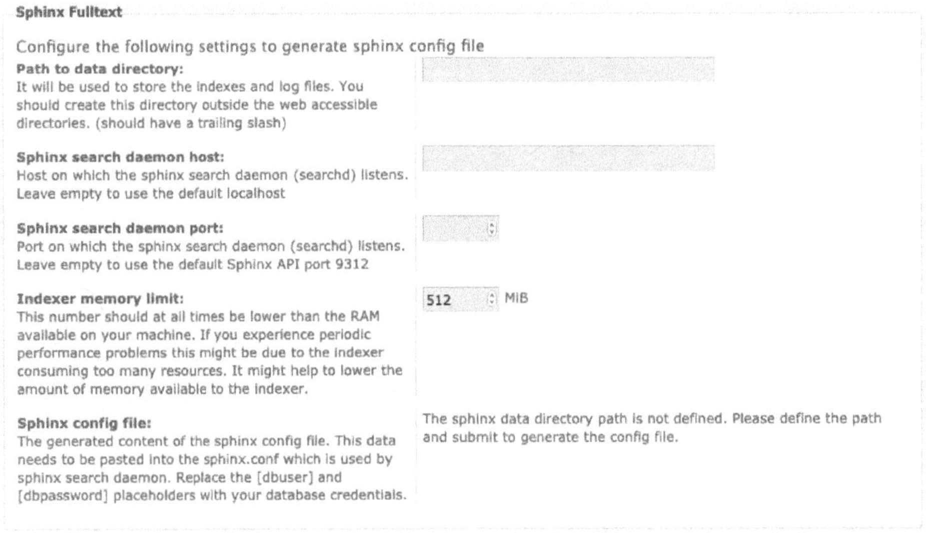

Figure 6.38: Sphinx Fulltext search settings

Are special search features available with Oracle, SQLite and SQL Server?

These database management systems are supported by phpBB, but phpBB cannot use any of their native text pattern-matching search capabilities. Your must use the phpBB Native search index.

Minimum and maximum keyword lengths

With the phpBB Native and PostgreSQL Fulltext search engines, you can control the minimum and maximum length of words in the search index. The default is 3 and 14 for phpBB Native, and 4 and 254 for PostgreSQL fulltext. In the case of phpBB Native, this means a word must be at least three characters but no more than 14 to go in the search index.

As mentioned, search indexes can get huge: fifty percent or more of the overall size of your board's database. Changing the minimum word length to five or six characters might save a lot of space in the database. Of course, the penalty is that words with smaller sizes can't be found in the search index.

Common word threshold

The phpBB Native search index has an interesting feature: it can remove words that are "too common" from the index.

For example, if you have a board that discusses vinyl records, "vinyl" might exceed five percent of all the total words in the index. In that case, it meets the criteria for being too common; so, all references to the term in the search engine will be removed, saving lots of space. You can change this value. Setting it to zero effectively disable this feature.

Understanding and using phpBB and system crons

The term *cron* comes from the world of Linux and similar Unix operating systems. It's a feature built into the operating system that regularly forces the operating system to wake up and check if it has any special tasks to complete. If so, cron will do this as an automatic service.

phpBB's mail queue

On the ACP's system settings page (**ACP > General > Server configuration > Server settings**), there is this innocuous looking setting (Figure 6.39):

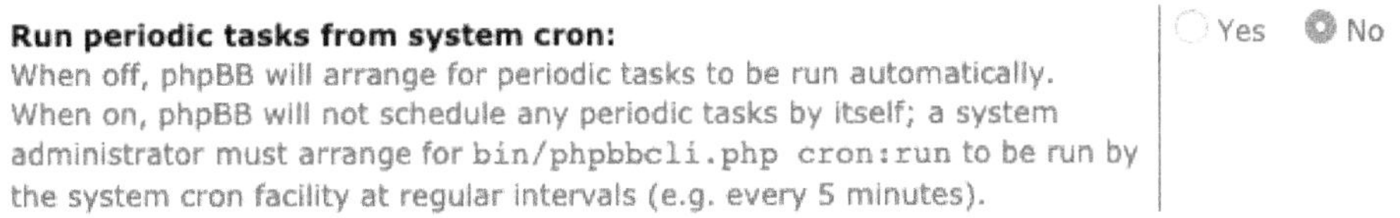

Run periodic tasks from system cron: ○ Yes ● No
When off, phpBB will arrange for periodic tasks to be run automatically.
When on, phpBB will not schedule any periodic tasks by itself; a system
administrator must arrange for `bin/phpbbcli.php cron:run` to be run by
the system cron facility at regular intervals (e.g. every 5 minutes).

Figure 6.39: System cron setting

It's easily ignored, in part, because it talks about a "cron." Non-technical people have no idea what this means, but phpBB's "cron" capability has a lot of implications.

phpBB allows members to subscribe to forums and topics. These subscriptions can notify users if there are new posts in a forum or topic via email. This means there could be hundreds of email notifications going out each time a new post occurs. That's a lot of emails, and some web hosts may not allow that many emails to go out in so short a time.

phpBB tries to get around this by using its mail queue. When someone makes a post, some email notifications may go into this queue for processing a bit later.

phpBB's email settings allow you to control how many emails go out in one batch. The default is twenty emails, which can be seen on the email settings page:

ACP > General > Client communication > Email settings (Figure 6.40).

Email package size:
This is the number of maximum emails sent out in one package. This setting is applied to the internal message queue; set this value to 0 if you have problems with non-delivered notification emails.

6.40: Email package size setting

If you set this value to a positive number greater than zero, phpBB won't keep the poster waiting when the **Submit** button is pressed on the posting page. Instead, it will place these email notifications in the email queue. How and when do these emails get sent?

System crons

What phpBB calls a *system cron* is what the rest of the world simply calls a cron. It's a periodic event run automatically by the server's operating system that *you* must set up. With a bit of off-board configuration, phpBB can work with system crons. We'll cover how to do this shortly.

phpBB crons

Creating system crons is a task for system administrators and geeks. Realizing this, the developers of phpBB thought, "Let's create our own cron!" They did, and you will see it referred to as a *phpBB cron*. But it has one problem: it's not really a cron because by definition a cron happens at fixed intervals. A phpBB cron depends entirely on someone doing something on the board. This means because you can't count on board traffic happening with any regularity, you can't depend on emails or other phpBB actions occurring at a particular time.

Let me give an example. If you have a hundred email notifications in phpBB's email queue and your board gets no traffic for a whole day, these email notifications will arrive a day later, or possibly even later! This avoids the messy business of creating a real cron, but it has the downside of depending entirely on humans accessing your board with a browser to push these email notifications out. The emails will go out, but if your board is lightly trafficked perhaps later rather than sooner.

Crons and Windows hosting

phpBB boards are usually hosted on servers running Linux, but it's not an absolute requirement. Web servers can run on Windows too, or other variants of Unix.

Since Windows is definitely not Linux, it doesn't have a command called cron. But it does have something similar called *Windows scheduled tasks*. It is largely functionally identical to a cron, but the interface is completely different, and it is arguably easier to use. In Windows, administrators usually have a nice desktop application for creating scheduled tasks. On Linux, you often have to do it from the Linux command prompt.

We won't get into creating a Windows scheduled task. The information is easily found online.

Creating a system cron

If it's unacceptable to wait for board traffic to send email notifications in a timely manner, you'll need to create a real cron (or on Windows, a scheduled task). You'll also need to decide how often you want to wake up the server's operating system to see if there are any phpBB tasks that need doing, and if there are, to go do them. How often to wake up the server depends on what you specify.

If you go with this approach, you have to tell phpBB not to do this work when someone hits the board and that you'll use a real cron instead. See Figure 6.39.

ACP > General > Server configuration > Server settings > Run periodic tasks from system cron > Yes

If you do this, you *must* create a real cron on your operating system instead or no cron processing can happen in phpBB.

Web host control panels like cPanel make it easier to create crons through a web interface. The popular cPanel control panel usually has a cron interface available. Just search for "Cron," which is usually in a cPanel Advanced group (Figure 6.41). Almost all web host control panels come with some sort of cron interface. In the Plesk control panel, it's called Scheduled tasks.

Warning: a cron is run by executing a program in phpBB's /bin directory called phpbbcli.php. This program must be publicly executable. Check the file's permissions with an FTP tool like FileZilla. If it is set to 644, change it to 755.

Opening the **Common settings** dropdown allows you to tell the server's operating system how often you want this cron to run. You can run it as often as once a minute, but I recommend once every five minutes, just make sure it's set to run every day and hour.

Below that is the **Command** field, which can be intimidating because it's hard to know what command to type in.

Here are the two commands you'll need:

1. Change to the directory (folder) containing phpBB on your server.

2. Run a special program. It will look something like this:

```
cd /path/to/board && ./bin/phpbbcli.php cron:run
```

or possibly:

```
cd /path/to/board; ./bin/phpbbcli.php cron:run
```

If you are wondering what */path/to/board* is, it is a path that is typically hidden unless you have command line access to the server. Because it has to be an absolute path, it *must* start with a slash (/). (In the case of Windows, it starts with a backslash character \. Windows uses this character to delineate paths.)

The && in the command is used on POSIX-type systems, which includes Linux. It executes the command to the right of the && if and only if the command to its left is executed successfully.

On cheap, shared web hosting the real absolute path to your board is not often shared. You would think the file manager in your web host control panel would have it, but it probably won't show the real full absolute path. An inquiry with your web host's technical support may provide it.

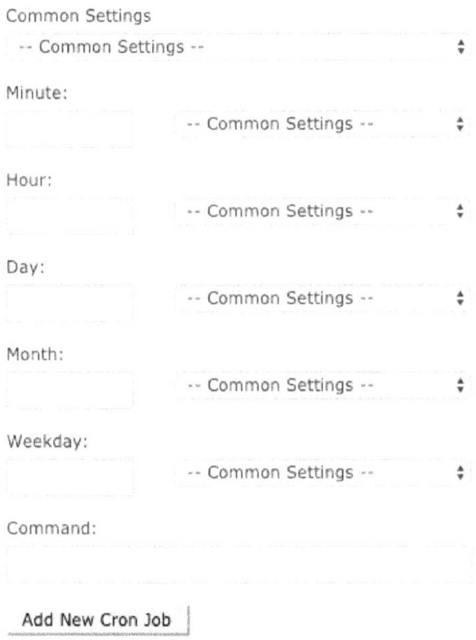

Common Settings
-- Common Settings --   ‡

Minute:
                    -- Common Settings --   ‡

Hour:
                    -- Common Settings --   ‡

Day:
                    -- Common Settings --   ‡

Month:
                    -- Common Settings --   ‡

Weekday:
                    -- Common Settings --   ‡

Command:

Add New Cron Job

Figure 6.41: cPanel add new cron job page

Once programmed though, you have to test it to see if it works. It helps to have it send you an email until any bugs get worked out. The email should help troubleshoot the issue. Afterward, you usually want to turn off the emails. This can be done like this (all on one line):

```
cd /path/to/board && ./bin/phpbbcli.php cron:run /dev/null 2>&1
```

There is one other issue with this system cron worth noting. The above will work only if the default version of PHP on your server is one supported by phpBB, generally PHP 7.1.3 or higher if running phpBB 3.3. Sometimes the default version of PHP on your web server is too old, such as PHP 5.6. If you can trap an error message from the cron, it will generally tell you that the version of PHP is unsupported.

To fix this, first find out the version of PHP that you need:

ACP > General > Quick links > PHP Information

Note your version of PHP. Your web host should be able to provide the correct path to this version of PHP. Assuming it is /usr/local/bin, the following cron would work on Linux-based operating systems (all on one line):

```
export PATH=/usr/local/bin:$PATH && cd /path/to/board
&& ./bin/phpbbcli.php cron:run
```

If all this doesn't work, you need a Plan B. I have a Plan B and a Plan C.

Using curl in a system cron

One approach is to use curl. curl is a Linux command that lets you fetch something over the web from the command line. You can use it to run the cron as a URL while pretending to be a browser, identifying the browser with the −A (agent) argument. The cron ends up looking something like this (all on one line):

```
curl -A='Mozilla/5.0'
http://www.yourforum.com/forum/app.php/cron/cron.task.cron_
task
```

With this approach, though, you have set **Run periodic tasks from system cron** to **No**. This approach also takes some trial and error to get right. For example, you may need to specify the path to curl.

If for some reason curl isn't available, `wget` is also usually installed, so you might want to try that instead. Often `lynx` is available too.

If your forum uses HTTPS, you generally will want to tell cron not to validate the site's certificate because this takes time. The −k argument tells curl to skip certificate validation. In this case, this variant should work (all on one line):

```
curl -k -A='Mozilla/5.0'
http://www.yourforum.com/forum/app.php/cron/cron.task.cron_
task
```

Using a site monitoring service

If you don't have a cron interface or none of the above works, there is another approach: use a site monitoring service. Free and paid site monitoring services are used to independently test if a web site is alive and notifies you when it's down.

With this approach, you don't need to call cron.php directly. You just need to regularly hit the board using the site monitoring service. You need an HTTP test, not a ping test, however. So, set up a site monitor to periodically poll any page on your website, like the index, and a phpBB cron will be triggered if there was no recent site traffic. If your board uses https, make sure the URL you call is using https too.

You are still using a phpBB cron, just indirectly through an external robot acting like a human being using a browser. However, it will act *like* a system cron because it should happen at the regular intervals you specify.

Real crons are coming!

When released, phpBB 4.0 should have a real cron interface, presumably making a lot of this discussion obsolete.

If phpBB 4.0 is the current version when you read this, look into how cron handling in phpBB is to be handled.

Reliably sending emails

We touched on sending out emails in the last chapter where I hinted there was a lot more to this topic. Now it's time to tackle emailing issues that often arise over time.

Getting emailing to work reliably and to continue working reliably can be surprisingly difficult. I offer insights and solutions that typically work, but don't be surprised if you have to work closely with your web host to resolve emailing issues. Sending emails has lots of moving parts, and phpBB won't necessarily know if errors occur.

Unfortunately, emailing issues just seem to crop up from time to time, and you usually don't know about it until someone complains. Fixing these problems can be time consuming and painful.

Outgoing email filtering

Web hosts don't want to send any spam emails. If they do, their email servers can end up on email blacklists. That's a mark of shame, but more importantly, it can lead to a loss of business. Consequently, before they allow emails to go out, they will examine each email and make a judgment on whether it contains spam or not.

There's no human making these judgments. Instead, they use software, or they contract with a service that makes the judgment for them. They have every incentive to be overly paranoid, so they generally are extra paranoid.

Worse, most web hosts won't bother to tell you if they are blocking outgoing emails. If you find out at all, it's usually when a user of your board complains and you dig into the issue.

This is why in the last chapter we discussed using a SMTP server with account credentials for sending out emails. These emails at least look authorized, which helps reduce the likelihood they will be flagged as spam.

There are no messages passed between phpBB and these email filtering services. phpBB may be able to detect if an email did not go out, but it usually has no idea if some spam filter on the email server stopped an email from being sent. It depends on what (if anything) the email server passes back to phpBB.

Email blacklists

When this filtering software flags what it thinks is spam, it may report your domain to one or more email blacklists. Typically, if your domain ends up on a blacklist, few of your emails will reach their intended recipients because your web host will block them from ever being sent. If they are sent, your web host will probably add an email header that indicates its spam probability, and these emails usually wind up in a spam folder.

phpBB contributes to the problem by using email templates. Templates largely say the same thing, but might plug in a different link or username in the body or subject field. Templates amount to a pattern, and when email patterns are detected across lots of emails, they become inherently suspicious.

But your board's content may contribute to the problem too. The content of the post is usually not in these emails, but the subject of the post or title of the topic may be. If these contain words that are often found in spam emails, they are likelier to get flagged. So, the less controversial your board's content is, the less likely these emails will be flagged as spam. This is also why getting legitimate users and preventing spam registrations is a must, along with actively moderating forums.

A sensible approach to dealing with these blacklists is to periodically check if your domain or the IP of your domain is on email blacklists. There are services that can do this for you, and some are free. I subscribe to one free service that sends me a weekly email to let me know if my domain is blacklisted.

Using Sender Policy Framework

Sometimes emails can be sent purporting to be from your domain. We all get the spoofed emails trying to coax you into giving out private information by pretending to come from a legitimate site.

You can tell the world, "These are the only authorized outgoing email gateways for my domain." By doing this, you are implying that emails sent from other email gateways are spam. This is done with *Sender Policy Framework* (SPF), a standard for broadcasting this information.

You have to know two things:

- **The name and/or IP address of the mail server that sends out emails for your board.** There are a number of ways to figure this out. You can ask your web host. Or if you have a sample email notification from phpBB from your board, you can often find it in the email's header. The email's header contains a lot of meta information and is rarely seen, but can usually be read if you look for an option in your email program. When phpbb.com's board sends me an email notification, and I look in the email's header, I can see information on the email server used:

  ```
  Received: from fraxinus.osuosl.org
  (smtp4.osuosl.org. [140.211.166.137])
  ```

  So, I now have both the outgoing email server's name and its IP address: smtp4.osuosl.org and 140.211.166.137.

- **The email servers you use to send personal emails for your domain**. This is done through an SMTP mail server. Unless you create an email account on your web host and send emails through its SMTP server, this is likely a SMTP server provided by your ISP, like comcast.net. If you use a web mail interface, like Gmail, it's their SMTP server.

  If you are using an email client program like Outlook or Thunderbird, somewhere inside it is the configuration information for the program. With web mail, a simple search query will usually turn up the SMTP server settings.

Send yourself an email. Looking at its hidden mail headers can also show you this information.

With this information, you can take advantage of SPF. This involves adding a MX (mail exchanger) record to your domain. Your web host may have an interface for doing this, or it may need to be done on your domain registrar. You need to add an SPF record to the domain. Here's an example (all on one line):

```
v=spf1 a mx ip4:69.64.153.131 include:_spf.google.com
~all
```

This record essentially says that emails sent from a server with the IP address 69.64.153.131 and any Gmail SMTP server represent legitimate emails sent by the domain. It also implies that emails sent from other locations are illegitimate.

This is a very effective solution, but you have to keep the record updated when information changes, such as when you rehost or if your host moves you to a different server. You also have to assume that spam-filtering software is checking SPF records. Most do.

Using DomainKeys Identified Mail (DKIM)

Another method provides a way to verify if the email was sent from your domain. This is done with a DomainKeys Identified Mail (DKIM) public key that is sent in the email header. Public key encryption works with two sets of keys: a private key that is not shared, and a public one that anyone can access. Using the protocol, the receiving email server can verify the public key given in the email header with a separate query to your domain. Your domain essentially sends back replies of either "Yes, the public key is valid for this domain" or "No, this public key is invalid for this domain." This does not necessarily provide assurance that the email is not spam, but it does indicate it was legitimately sent by your domain.

Most web host control panels have an easy-to-use interface for creating these public and private DKIM keys and for managing queries from receiving email servers. They are often created automatically. If you think about it, this approach likely can't be used for sending emails from your domain with email clients like Microsoft Outlook, which is why a set of SPF records is highly desirable.

Email quotas

There is another potential issue with sending emails: your web host may have quotas on how many emails can be sent over a given unit of time. If you exceed these quotas, generally excess emails are unceremoniously discarded rather than placed into a queue.

There is no way for phpBB to take action if an outgoing email fails to go out due to a quota issue. The email server would have to send back an applicable error message, and most won't, but even if sent it would show in phpBB's error log only. If you don't know if you have a quota on outgoing emails, you should check to see if this is the case. It's unusual to be allowed to send unlimited emails. Ask your web host:

- Is there a limit on the number of emails that can go on in one hour? One day?

- When does the count reset? (It's probably at the start of the hour.)

- Is there a limit to the number of email addresses that can be in any one email?

The easiest way to find out is to file a support ticket. This information is rarely in a web host's knowledge base.

You essentially have three tools in phpBB to try to deal with any quotas:

- **Your email package size** (see Figure 6.40). This is the number of emails that phpBB will try to send out at one time. This at least can help stagger the number of outgoing emails.

- **The use of a system cron** (see Figure 6.39). This lets you send out emails regularly, rather than depending on board traffic to do it.

- **A phpBB configuration variable called queue_interval**. This is not easily changed.

If your email package size is twenty (the default) and you are using a system cron that runs every five minutes, then phpBB can send a maximum of 240 emails per hour. Note that if your board is part of a larger website, other parts of your website may be sending out emails too.

In most cases, you want to send an identical email to as many people as possible. phpBB will do this if the outgoing emails in one batch are identical, such as with mass emails. These should be bundled into one or more emails by phpBB. To set the number of distinct addresses allowed in one email:

ACP > General > Client communications > Email settings > Maximum allowed email recipients

Enter the value given by your web host.

Make sure to do this because the default phpBB setting is up to fifty email addresses per email, which may be more than is allowed. It could keep some recipients from getting emails.

Understanding the queue_interval

The queue_interval value represents the number of seconds phpBB must wait before more emails in the email queue can be sent. It is stored as a configuration variable, which is to say it's a row in the phpbb_config table in your database. That table is where phpBB records information on how your board is configured.

It is set to 60, for sixty seconds. So, if at 12:00:00 someone hits the board, a phpBB email cron process will start, if at least sixty seconds have elapsed since emails were last sent.

If someone else hits your board at 12:00:30, the email process will not start because the full sixty seconds has not elapsed. But, at 12:01:15, if someone hits the board, a phpBB cron to process emails will run because more than sixty seconds has elapsed since emails were sent.

When the cron completes, its completion time is recorded in phpBB's database. That timestamp is used to determine whether the next cron is run or not.

phpBB has no interface for changing queue_interval, but it can be changed inside the database using a tool like phpMyAdmin. This is a web interface to the MySQL or MariaDB database management systems.

Be aware, this is dangerous if you don't know what you are doing. You should backup your board's phpbb_config table, just in case you make a big mistake.

For example, to change this interval to five minutes, it must be changed to 300. So, a Structured Query Language (SQL) statement similar to this would work:

```
UPDATE phpbb_config SET config_value = 300 WHERE
config_name = 'queue_interval';
```

If you do this, make sure to commit the change to the database, then purge your board's cache:

ACP > General > Purge the cache

Configuring phpBB to work with email quotas

The truth is it's hard to achieve one hundred percent efficiency sending out emails. That's because phpBB can't control when people will use your board. It's their actions that kick off email processing.

Let's assume that your web host allows a maximum of 400 emails per hour, and the count resets at the top of the hour. It's possible that from minutes 00 to 55 there will be no traffic on your board, and in minutes 56 to 59, someone will post on the board, which will initiate an action to send 400 emails.

With a board default of 20 emails in a batch, and with the requirement that at least one minute must elapse (queue_interval = 60) before more are sent out, we can get an idea of how email will be sent out. In the four minutes left in the hour, no more than 80 of the 400 emails could go out. In a sense, this means you have "wasted" the opportunity to send out 320 emails. If the board's traffic had been evenly staggered throughout the hour, it might have been possible. So, you must live with this limitation.

You can certainly tune phpBB to try to send out any emails in its queue regularly or you could create a system cron that tries every minute. If your quota is 400 emails per hour, an email package size of six would let up to 360 emails go out. That's fewer than 400. If the size is seven, phpBB would try to send out up to 420 emails, but it's possible the 20 over quota would be lost and never actually sent.

What this amounts to is:

- If you want emails to be sent by a phpBB cron less or more frequently than once a minute, you will have to change the queue_interval configuration variable.

- You will need to set up a system cron (see last section), create a pseudo-system cron to hit your board as if a browser were hitting it, or use a site-monitoring service to ensure emails are staggered throughout an hour.

- If the queue_interval was changed, the cron should reflect that change. So, if the queue_interval is changed to 300, make sure the cron runs every five minutes. Otherwise, it can be run every minute.

- You need to figure out an email package size that will keep you under quota and enter that. Divide the hourly quota by the number of times emails will go out per hour, and then round the number down to the nearest whole number. **ACP > General > Client communications > Email settings > Email package size**

- It's a good idea to periodically check phpBB's error log. If there are emailing issues, they may show up there: **ACP > Maintenance > Forum logs > Error log**

Using a third-party emailing service

One clever but somewhat problematic way of getting around these email quotas is to use a third-party email service. The most widely known one is Amazon Web Services' Simple Email Service (SES). You have to pay a fee to Amazon Web Services based on the number of emails sent. The costs are very modest.

However, my experience is that integrating it is problematic for several reasons:

- Your web server must allow outgoing emails to be sent outside its local environment. Many don't, so check with your web host to see if it's allowed before doing anything else. The PHP allow_url_fopen setting must be set to On. You can check this: **ACP > General > PHP Information.** But even if this is set, your web server may have a firewall setting prohibiting outgoing SMTP connections.

- These services don't want to send out spam either, so you must go through a process to convince them that you won't do this. This takes time and effort.

- Lastly, you need to configure phpBB to use SMTP with these services. These services will provide a SMTP server and credentials to use. Expect a lot of trial and error to get it right. **ACP > General > Client communications > Email settings**

If you can get it to work, it's a sweet solution at generally very affordable costs.

Managing bots

We discussed bots a bit in the last chapter. You are probably aware that search engine robots, or bots (sometimes called crawlers or spiders) are constantly looking through the web for content to index. These bots will find your board soon after you make it available, assuming the domain can be read publicly.

Generally, bots are good because they help people find your board. Sometimes though, bots can be bad, particularly if you don't want your board's content indexed or a bot's intent is malicious.

phpBB allows you to control bots it knows about. You can see a list of these bots:

ACP > System > General Tasks > Spiders/Robots

There are over fifty popular search engine bots phpBB tracks.

Adding bots

If you become aware of a new bot you want to start tracking, it can be added:

ACP > System > General Tasks > Spiders/Robots > Add bot

For example, DuckDuckGo is a popular search engine that was only recently added to phpBB's list of known bots. Figure 6.42 shows how you might add this bot to phpBB. Once added, these same rules would apply to managing it as it would to any of the other bots that phpBB knows about.

Note: You can instruct phpBB to present a language and a style for the bot to use when indexing. Most boards use a single language pack and a single style, so the default language tends to be fine.

When adding a bot, you need to know its *user agent*. The agent is a text string that should uniquely identify the bot. Sometimes these strings can be long and will identify the version of the bot, a URL, and other information, which is why a partial match for the most relevant part of the string is what you need. A simple search query should reveal the User Agent string to use.

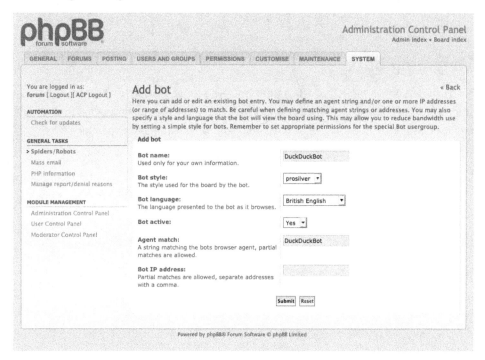

Figure 6.42: Add bot screen

For DuckDuckGo, the user agent string is:

```
DuckDuckBot/1.0;
(+http://duckduckgo.com/duckduckbot.html)
```

From this, you can infer the part of the string to match, which is simply DuckDuckBot, and enter that in the **Agent Match** field.

Denying or allowing all bots

There is a web standard you can use that instructs bots what sites or parts of sites should be indexed. Simply create a text file called robots.txt. If you want it to apply only to the board, place it in your board's main folder. If you want it to apply to your entire website, place it in your web root folder.

To deny all robots, the robots.txt file should have:

```
User-agent: *
Disallow: /
```

Allowing all bots is implied if there is no robots.txt file, but you can specify it explicitly:

```
User-agent: *
Allow: /
```

Well-behaved bots will follow instructions in this file. But it's just a text file, so malicious bots could certainly choose to ignore it and index anything they can read.

How to ensure your board cannot be indexed

If you want to ensure that no bots can index your board, then you need to disallow guest and bot access to all your forums:

ACP > Users and groups > Groups > Group forum permissions

Do this for both the **Guests** and the **Bots** group. Make sure you select the **No Access** role. This way, only registered users to the board can read any of its content.

This has a big downside: it will appear to guests that you don't have any forums on your board. phpBB will show what is arguably a misleading message instead: "This board has no forums." In short, you have to complete a registration process to see any content.

If you don't mind guests and bots seeing only the names of your forums, after selecting the **No Access** role for each forum, go back into each forum for the **Guests** and **Bots** groups, select **Advanced Permissions**, click on the **Actions** tab, then select **Yes** for **Can see forum.** If a guest or bot tries to access the forum, they get a message saying they lack the necessary permissions.

Controlling private messages

Private messages allow users to send notes to each other. It's somewhat like text messaging, except that users must be logged into the board to read private messages.

This feature is enabled by default. Of course, there are plenty of settings that allow you to control their behavior.

ACP > General > Board configuration > Private message settings

Perhaps the biggest decision is whether to allow them or not. After that, you'll have to decide whether to allow attachments in private messages, which is disabled by default.

You can also control the number of mail folders that members can create and the maximum number of messages in their private messages box.

Are private messages truly private?

Just how private are private messages? For example, can you as an administrator read these private messages intended for others?

The answer is generally no. As a general rule, the phpBB Group seems uncomfortable allowing this sort of functionality. They did allow it for my Spam remover extension, but presumably only because it lets you determine if the private message text marked as spam is really spam or not. My extension won't show private message text not flagged as spam.

If you can read the database, you can sort of read these private messages. phpMyAdmin is usually provided by web hosts for manipulating the database. If you can read the phpbb_privmsg table, the content can be read in the message_text column.

Warning: These tools are very powerful. Inexperienced users can easily perform catastrophic actions, like dropping tables or entire databases.

The content will look a little strange because it contains markup language, and it can be hard to know who the sender and receiver are because this information is contained in other tables.

Private message text is not encrypted in the database. Someone with modest programming skills could create a script to read them.

Some boards contain sensitive content. Private messaging may allow members of the board to exchange legally dubious information. If you run a board like this and are worried about your legal liability, this might be reason to disable private messaging, as well as carefully moderate your board.

Reading private messages

Users create and read private messages from a **Private messages** link on the navigation bar of the board that only appears when logged in, or from the User Control Panel: **UCP > Private messages**.

Most boards enable notifications, so new or unread private message counts will appear on the navigation bar when a user is logged into the board.

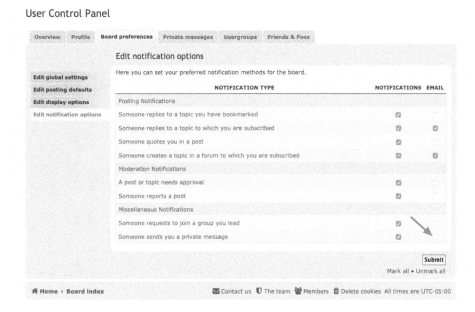

Figure 6.43: Setting for getting email notifications for private messages

Users can also opt to get emails when someone sends them a new private message: **UCP > Board preferences > Edit notification options > Miscellaneous notifications > Someone sends you a private message** (Figure 6.43). Curiously, this is disabled by default.

Chapter 7 | Growing your board

Your board should now be all set up: shiny and new, and ready for active use. If you've followed all my suggestions, you've done what I would have done had I set up your board for you, minus my fees.

It's great to have a board that your whole community can use, but it won't be of much use without a community that visits it regularly and contributes their insights in your forums. Naturally, I get a lot of questions on how to make a board successful.

Attributes of successful boards

- **It's a group project from its inception.** Ideally, a group of enthusiasts in a topical area who already know each will other pool their time and resources to stand up a board. If so, part of your planning should be to figure out and follow a marketing strategy, doling out responsibilities between various members, including creating a board. This fosters a spirit of shared collaboration and commitment.

- **They grow organically**. Almost no board is quickly successful. It tends to be an organic process. Like everything else, it requires effort. In a sense, you are planting a garden that you must tend with care. In the beginning, you should fuss over it, do your best to promote it and encourage your members to bring in other members. By choosing phpBB as your forum solution, you've picked great software. You might say you planted the seed in good soil. Now you hope for regular rain and sunshine and see if it takes off.

- **Their content is unique**. If there's another board out there serving similar content already, that board will likely retain most of the traffic, unless your board has compelling content the other one doesn't have.

- **Its owners keep their expectations modest**. Most phpBB boards do not cover highly topical areas, and those that do are well established. Rather, forum solutions like phpBB excel at filling in niche areas.

  I don't run my own board anymore, but when I did, it was hardly a huge success. Over about eight years, it got about 58,000 posts. This actually is pretty good. Based on my consulting, it's pretty typical for most boards. For the most part, I didn't have to recruit members because we were already an electronic community from the days of dialup electronic bulletin boards, which preceded the World-wide Web. In time, my board became obsolete too, and was effectively replaced with social media sites like Facebook. But also, one primary member passed away. Without his presence, members came less frequently. In 2009, I shut it down.

- **Its owners know that quality is its own reward**. My board with 58,000 posts over eight years wasn't a failure. That's thousands of posts a year. Early on, we had over 10,000 posts a year. Those of us who participated regularly enjoyed our participation. We loved interacting with each other and debating topical issues. If it was a bit isolated, at least it was collegial. We didn't have the trolls that other sites typically get. It was a fun place to hang out online. Smaller can be better.

  Most phpBB boards are like this. It's not really how many thousands of posts you have, but the quality of the content and the meaning it gives to those who participate that matters. Hopefully, phpBB makes these online conversations easier to manage.

Growing your membership

Growing your membership starts by inviting a core set of users you probably already know who are willing to join and post on your board.

It's pretty rare to work with a client who puts up a board without knowing anyone who might want to be a member of the board. Most of those boards fail; either from lack of attention or the market they were hoping for failed to materialize.

You could certainly spend money to advertise your board and hope for the best. Starting off though, you would do well to attract a dozen or so members and just get commitment from them to post regularly, several times a week hopefully. Search engines will notice sites where the content is regularly updated and possibly boost your search ranking because of its activity.

With a small and core group of posters, you may find some modest success just by hanging out there regularly and posting.

As an administrator, you should post to the board too. When someone replies, quote their reply to highlight their ideas, and add follow up questions and comments. This kind of attention encourages members to become habitual posters. Encourage them to post pictures where appropriate, and to comment their pictures. Search engines like pages that contain relevant pictures.

Search engine optimization strategies

Search engine optimization (SEO) is a set of methods that help boost the ranking of web pages in search engines.

Most board administrators want their board to rank highly in relevant search queries. It brings traffic to the site and makes finding members easier.

Unfortunately, search engines like Google don't give out much information about how they rank content. Since search-indexing methods are proprietary, there is no way to know for sure if someone's SEO strategies will work for your board.

Bulletin boards, though, are structurally different than most web sites, which tend to host relatively static content. The content on a board changes dynamically as posts are added, edited and moderated. Moreover, you only indirectly control what is posted. Posters contribute the content. So, the content in a search engine for your board is going to be somewhat dated.

General SEO rules

I don't consider SEO one of my specialties. To do SEO right pretty much becomes a career and a subject of endless study. I do have a few friends in the SEO community and have discerned some general rules on what matters in search engine ranking:

- **URLs don't matter.** phpBB generates URLs that don't embed the topic title or other relevant information in the URL. Not having this doesn't matter in the least. Ten years ago, putting this in the URL was considered a great strategy, and there were SEO versions of phpBB that did just this.

- **Content matters the most.** Search engines will read a page and decide its placement in the search index based on its content. The more relevant it is to a search query, the higher it will rank.

- **Concise content is better than lengthy content.** Search engines rank higher those pages that offer succinct responses to questions asked or implied in the search queries they receive. Your posters decide what to post, so there's not much you can do about this.

- **Recent content is best.** Search engines rank fresh content higher, which appears to be the most important factor in deciding its relevancy. Pages with older content are likely to be way down in search index, if they appear at all. So, the more your board is focused on topical information, the higher it is likely to rank in search indexes.

- **Page titles can matter.** In phpBB, a topic's page title (the content inside the <title> tag) is typically a mash up of the topic name plus the board name. These words get some weight in determining the importance of the page because it explains succinctly what the page is about. It's basically metadata. It's possible that changing a topic title to something more relevant will make it more SEO-friendly. Of course, it's hard to know what to change it to which would make it more SEO-friendly. In general though, it's the content of the posts in a topic that matter much more than the topic's title.

- **HTML heading tags can matter**. Search engines assume that markup for <h1> tags is relatively more important than <h2>, and the same is true down to the <h6> tag. The <h1> tag is usually in a larger font than the <h2> tag. The HTML specification also indicates that these tags should be used to show relative prominence within a page.

  That's not to say your content will rank higher if you stuff its content inside of <h1> tags, but that search engines will assume that content inside a <h1> tag is intended to get more prominence within a page than content inside a <h2> tag or a <p> tag, all things being equal.

- **Moderation matters**. Removing clearly offensive, irrelevant, vulgar and obscene posts in a timely manner can help because it makes the topic more relevant and concise. It may upset posters, however.

- **<meta> tags with keyword attributes don't matter.** In the early days of SEO, adding relevant keywords in HTML <meta> tags was considered smart. Today, however, it appears as if search engines totally ignore these keywords, and figure out the keywords that matter from studying a page's content. They likely don't hurt, but they don't help in your search ranking like they used to. The general consensus is that taking the time to set keywords is better spent elsewhere.

- **Styling doesn't generally matter**. Search engines parse text, so they don't see styling at all. Styling might matter to you or your members who like a site to look bright and inviting, but search engines can't tell a pretty style from an ugly one. But, if a page requires horizonal scrolling on mobile devices, or pinching and zooming to see content, search engines will notice and probably rank the page lower in the index. There is some evidence that colors may matter. If the colors suggest it may be hard to read, such as dark green letters on a black background, this may cause your pages to rank lower, as it affects accessibility to certain people with color impairments.

- **Too much unrelated stuff on a page may matter.** The presence of too much ancillary content, like widgets on sidebars, ads, or links to sites of dubious reputation may matter.

- **Mobile matters**. Most web pages are read from mobile devices. Google has figured out if your content flows well on mobile devices, and it cares more about how it flows on mobile devices than it does on desktop devices. Since all phpBB styles are responsive (intelligently size down page content for mobile devices), you should be covered.

- **Pictures can matter.** Pictures break up text so it is less monotonous. The adage that a picture is worth a thousand words is true. Particularly if your board is focused on some sort of product, like small boats, pictures can also be a great way to engage users.

  Ideally, pictures will be highly compressed. The smaller in size, the faster they can be downloaded and rendered. Search engines may give some small preference to optimized pictures on a page, particularly if they have a relevant caption, title, description and alternate text, which make them more useful and accessible.

- **Page loading speed matters**. People will naturally tend to drift away from sites that slowly populate web pages. Search engines study the time it takes, not just to load the page itself, but all its associated pictures and embedded content, including content on remote sites. All things being equal, faster loading pages are preferred over slower ones. Consequently, the quality of your hosting matters.

phpBB does a good job of speeding things up where it can. The whole point of its cache folder is to speed up the delivery of its dynamic content. Ultimately, it's how well your web and database servers are tuned that matters more because board content is in posts, and they are pulled from a database. On shared servers, too many others using the same server can slow page load speeds.

Ideally a page will be fully drawn within five seconds or less. Many web hosts offer services like Cloudflare to help. These content delivery networks push static content (like images) geographically closer to the user, so they take less time to download. So much of phpBB's content must be created dynamically that having an efficiently running server tends to be the most important factor.

Sites like pingdom.com can help give you an idea of how fast your pages load. Also, the Inspector built into your browser usually has a **Network** tab where you can see how long it takes for individual content segments to download, and the order of their download. These tools can suggest pragmatic ways to speed up the loading of pages on your site.

- **https matters**. In 2014, Google announced that sites that send and receive data encrypted using https would rank higher than those that don't.

- **A sitemap.xml file can help**. This file won't necessarily help your content rank higher, but since it contains a definitive list of your board's content, it can help search engines find and index all your content, and do it efficiently. There is a phpBB SEO SiteMap extension that could be installed to help out search engines. Search engines will look for this file, and if they find it, they will parse it and probably systematically go through all the links inside of it. There is a specific format for this file, so it needs to be created by software, especially since board content changes so frequently.

These rules are generally true today, but no one can ever say definitively that they will remain true. Search engines will continually refine their algorithms in hopes that they can provide a better set of relevant results to search queries than their competitors.

If you have a niche board, that's not necessarily bad. It helps make your content unique. Topics should be topical, relevant, concise and contain information likely not easily available anywhere else. That other posters chime in with related posts is generally good, as the presence of related information in close proximity on a page can increase its relevance.

Today, search engines are all about discerning relevant content. So, if you have a board that is mostly whimsical rather than topical, search engines will probably mostly ignore it. That doesn't mean your board can't be successful, but it does mean that members will come principally from members recruiting other members.

SEO services

There are many people and companies that will sell you their SEO services. They can help implement strategies to get your board more traffic, show you your site's popular search queries and show you trends over time as you implement their strategies.

You can do a lot of the basic analysis yourself if your board is connected to services like Google Analytics. You might want to try this approach before spending money on SEO services. For example, if you notice a certain topic is getting a lot of page views, it suggests more similar topics will help bring in more readers and members.

Good SEO services can certainly improve your search rankings. Just be forewarned: there are many bogus or poor SEO services out there. Also, unless you are monetizing your board, search ranking may not matter that much as most searchers are looking for an answer to a particular question, so are unlikely to repeatedly visit or register.

Membership engagement strategies

As I mentioned, the best boards tend to grow organically; core sets of members will use it regularly and their enthusiasm will promote your board to others in the community, who then will do the same.

General engagement strategies

Search engines can certainly help others find your board. But search engines are oriented around answering particular questions. Once searchers get what they are looking for, they usually don't hang around.

Good boards will pique the interest of like-minded people. The topics will be interesting, insightful and invite others to chime in.

Good boards will also be active. You don't have to have hundreds of posts per day, but good boards will generally get some posts every day.

Don't be shy to ask your members to recruit other members. Show appreciation when they do post by replying to their posts and trying to further expand on the topic. You can also create and use ranks to show appreciation for the content they contribute.

Also encourage members to attach pictures, as appropriate. Pictures that are relevant to the topic naturally make a page more interesting to look at.

Typically, certain forums on a board will get the bulk of the traffic. That's one reason I suggested keeping the number of forums manageable when setting up a board. As it grows, you will get a sense of when it makes sense to create more related forums.

I don't recommend putting forums inside of forums because they become hard to find. They should all be on the index if possible. Ideally, the number of forums should be a dozen or less, with an upper limit of about two-dozen on the index.

I suggest putting your most trafficked forums near the top of the index because lots of users are lazy and won't bother to scroll down the page. Fortunately, forum order on the index is easily repositioned in the ACP.

Extensions that help engage users

phpBB has hundreds of extensions. Some may help engage your users. I list some of the more useful ones below, based on my work with clients and my own opinions. Doubtless these will change with time:

- **phpBB Media Embed Plugin.** This is an official extension created and maintained by the phpBB Group. By using a `[media]` BBCode, it allows media content hosted on many websites to be easily embedded within topics.

- **Topic preview**. This extension displays a short excerpt of text from the first post in a tooltip while the mouse hovers over a topic's title.

- **phpBB Sitemaker**. This extension creates a portal-like landing page for your board using a drag and drop editor.

- **Digests**. This is one of my extensions. It sends periodic emails to users containing the latest posts. Users can select forums of interest, the hour of arrival, and the frequency of the digest: daily, weekly or monthly. Links in the digest allow easy access to topics and posts if a subscriber wants to reply. Private messages can also appear in the digest. While neat, it can be complex to set up. And because digests are wordy, they can sometimes be flagged as spam.

- **Pages**. This extension allows static pages to be created that use your board's style.

- **mChat**. This provides a real-time chat outside of the topic and post framework for people on your board. The chat window appears on the index and users will hear a chirp when a new chat message is posted.

- **ShareOn**. This allows easy sharing of posts and topics with dozens of popular social networks, including Facebook.

- **Large Font**. This extension provides controls for users to easily change the font size. This is great for boards with lots of older users.

- **Thanks for Posts.** With this, you press a thumbs-up button if you like a post. The number of times a post is thanked is tracked, and you can see statistics on most which members thank others most frequently and which members get the most thanks. *Note: This does not cause any Facebook Likes and only has meaning inside a board.*

- **Knowledge Base**. This allows you and others to create a knowledge base for your board. This is not exactly Wiki software, but it serves a similar purpose and works in a phpBB environment.

- **Recent Topics**. This highlights on the index the most recently active topics.

- **Selective mass emails**. This is another extension of mine. This expands the ability of an administrator to send mass emails in the ACP. It seems to be used primarily to reach hard to reach sets of users, such as inactive users, or those who haven't contributed many posts.

Moderating posts

In the beginning, administrators usually perform the double duty of moderating content. As you find members who show both passion and good judgment, ask them if they are willing to become moderators. By moderating, there is an implied commitment to visit regularly.

Once they've committed, put them to work. Explain how moderation is done and encourage them to keep topics relevant, removing garbage or spam posts, and police users when they break board rules or the rules of common decency. You will probably find that the more you trust and empower your moderators, the more vested and valued they feel in their work on the board.

Global moderators

Figure 7.1: Adding a global moderator

A global moderator cannot moderate all forums unless they have access to all forums on the board. If their forum permissions do not allow them access to certain forums, they won't be able to moderate those forums. This makes sense, if you think about it.

Here is a link to a moderator's guide that can be useful:

https://www.phpbb.com/support/docs/en/3.3/ug/moderatorguide/

It's easy to add a global moderator:

ACP > Users and groups > Groups > Manage groups > Global moderators > Members (Figure 7.1)

Forum-specific moderators

You can also have moderators for specific forums only. The best way to do this is to set up a forum-specific moderators' group. This way, you can add or remove moderators to these forums as needed.

For a forum-specific moderation group, the best practices are to:

1. Create the moderation group: **ACP > Users and groups > Manage groups > Create new group.** Generally, the group name should reflect the forum or forums these moderators will moderate.

2. On the Manage groups page, in the **Copy permissions from** dropdown, select **Global moderators.**

3. Next, place any members you want to be forum-specific moderators into the group by clicking on the **Members** link for the newly created group.

4. Assign the new group to one or more forums. **ACP > Permissions > Forum based permissions > Forum moderators.**

5. Select the forums wanted for these forum-specific moderators and press **Submit.**

6. Under **Add Groups**, select the group that you created and press **Add permissions.**

7. For the role, select the type of moderator role, such as Full Moderator and press **Apply All Permissions.**

Note: You can assign different moderator roles for different forums to the same moderator. For example, the moderator can be a full moderator for one forum and a queue moderator for another forum.

Forum moderation can also be assigned to a specific user, instead of to a group. As a best practice, avoid assigning permissions outside of a group because it's hard to remember or determine exactly who was given these privileges.

Using feeds

Feeds (sometimes called *newsfeeds*) make it relatively easy to grab a board's content for the general public to read or use offsite. In fact, some websites are little more than a collection of feeds containing content from other websites.

There are two protocols for feeds: Atom and RSS. RSS (Really Simple Syndication or Rich Site Summary) is the older one, and comes in two versions: RSS1 and RSS2. RSS2 is the more popular version.

phpBB provides a built-in Atom feed, which can be used to highlight your topics and posts on other websites or other parts of your website outside of phpBB.

Whether you use RSS or Atom, from the perspective of the user, the differences don't generally matter. Both provide the content in a relatively simple XML (Extensible Markup Language) format, making it easy to transform it into something else, like to embed in a web page elsewhere.

How feeds are used

Feeds tend to be public, so they are designed to spread information. Lots of popular software, like phpBB and WordPress, has built-in feed capabilities.

Figure 7.2 shows an example of reading phpbb.com's support forum with phpBB's feed URL and using feedly.com.

The real value of a feed is that you don't have to visit a site to read its content. That may not be ideal from your perspective, as you want people to visit your board and read it there. But if someone wants to read lots of sites, it's a pain to visit each one in their browser. Rather, they can bundle the sites they are interested in inside one application, scan them all, and if they find an article of interest in their feed, they can click on it to read the full article on the site of origin.

Feedly.com is one of many websites that do this. I can tell you that feeds make my time online much more efficient because I don't have to wait for pages to load to see content I don't care about. I also don't have to spend time scrolling through pages or navigating among a site's pages.

You can also read feeds with desktop programs. Both the Outlook and Thunderbird email programs support feeds, in addition to acting as an email program.

Figure 7.2: Reading phpBB's support forum on feedly.com

You can also find browser extensions to read and aggregate RSS feeds too, such as Chrome's RSS Feed Reader extension.

Controlling feeds

By default, phpBB enables feeds.

ACP > General > Board configuration > Feed settings

As an administrator, you have a lot of granular control about what shows up in your default feed, such as which forums to include or exclude. There is also a master **Enable feeds** switch that can turn feeds on and off easily. Generally, only forums that are open for guests to read can be placed in phpBB's built-in feed. phpBB's feeds can support HTTP authentication if you enable that feature, but it requires some extra work on your part. In this case, to get the private content the user must add an `&auth=http` parameter to the feed's URL manually.

Advertising feeds

You don't have to tell the world your board has feeds. It is broadcast in the HTML markup for a page automatically. The HTML markup will look similar to this:

```
<link rel="alternate" type="application/atom+xml"
title="Feed - phpBB Services Extensions Development
Forum" href="/phpbb/app.php/feed">
<link rel="alternate" type="application/atom+xml"
title="Feed - New Topics"
href="/phpbb/app.php/feed/topics">
```

Essentially, the first line says, "Here's a feed for a list of recent posts on this board," and the second one says "Here's a feed of recent topics."

I wrote a Smartfeed extension for phpBB. Unlike phpBB's built-in feed, it supports the RSS protocol. More interesting perhaps is that it supports database authentication, so users can read content in private forums they can access with it. It also has additional options and filtering beyond phpBB's Atom feed.

With additional parameters in the URL, you can get a feed for a particular forum on a board, limit the number of items in the feed, and ask for active topics only. More information is available on phpbb.com or on my website.

Integrating a phpBB feed into a website

Often a board exists as part of a larger website. On the larger website, you might want to highlight current posts and topics on your board.

Because of phpBB's feeds, this can be quite simple to do, particularly if you are familiar with WordPress, a popular content management system. This can help drive traffic to your board too.

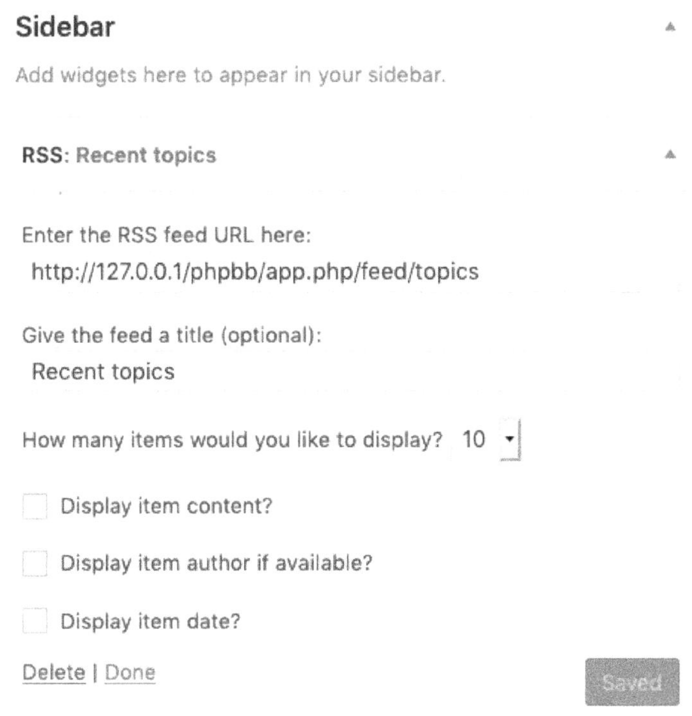

Sidebar ▲

Add widgets here to appear in your sidebar.

RSS: Recent topics ▲

Enter the RSS feed URL here:
http://127.0.0.1/phpbb/app.php/feed/topics

Give the feed a title (optional):
Recent topics

How many items would you like to display? 10 ▾

☐ Display item content?

☐ Display item author if available?

☐ Display item date?

Delete | Done   Saved

Figure 7.3: WordPress RSS widget connecting to a phpBB feed

I'll demonstrate this with WordPress, since WordPress dominates the market. In this example, you want to get a list of recent topics on your board to show up in a WordPress sidebar, with the most recent topics showing first.

1. Login to WordPress as an administrator. The WordPress dashboard should appear, but if not click on the **Dashboard** link.

2. WordPress comes with an RSS Widget that also can be used for ATOM feeds. You can find it off the dashboard: **Dashboard > Appearance > Widgets**

3. Click on the **RSS Widget**, and then press the **Add Widget** button which by default appears on the sidebar.

4. In the sidebar, click on the RSS Widget that was added (Figure 7.3). Enter the absolute URL for the feed. To get a list of topics, the URL must end with /app.php/feed/topics. I also gave the feed a title "Recent topics." Then press **Save**.

5. I dragged the widget to the top of the sidebar so it would appear first on the sidebar. Of course, you can place it anywhere on the sidebar that you like.

6. Go to your WordPress site and find it on the sidebar. See Figure 7.4 to see how it might be placed in WordPress.

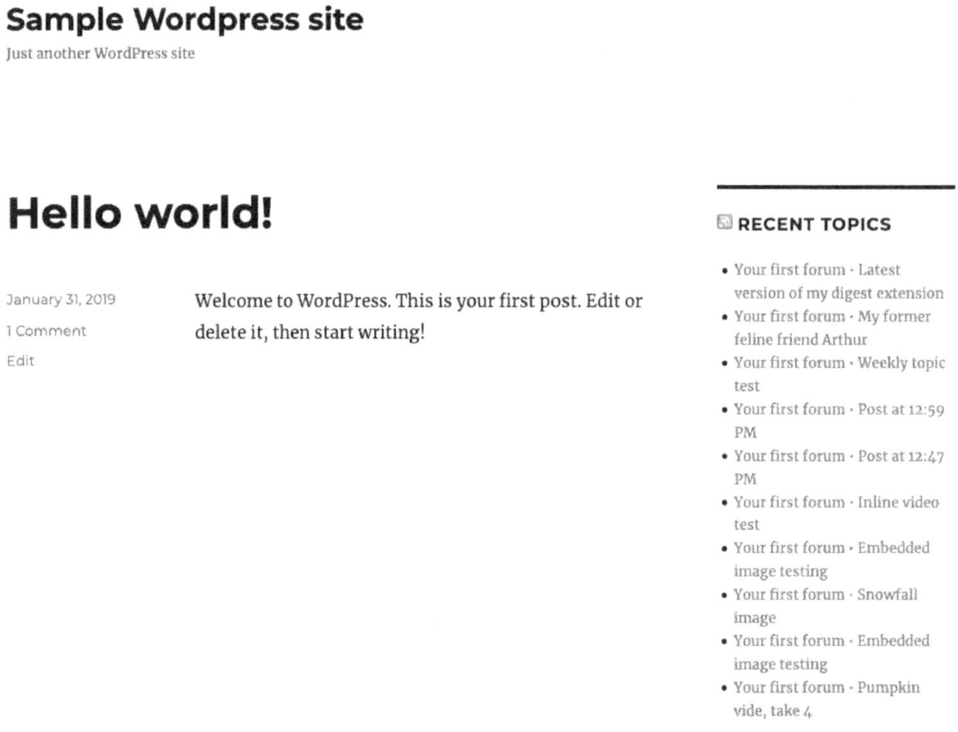

Sample Wordpress site

Just another WordPress site

Hello world!

January 31, 2019

1 Comment

Edit

Welcome to WordPress. This is your first post. Edit or delete it, then start writing!

RECENT TOPICS

- Your first forum · Latest version of my digest extension
- Your first forum · My former feline friend Arthur
- Your first forum · Weekly topic test
- Your first forum · Post at 12:59 PM
- Your first forum · Post at 12:47 PM
- Your first forum · Inline video test
- Your first forum · Embedded image testing
- Your first forum · Snowfall image
- Your first forum · Embedded image testing
- Your first forum · Pumpkin vide, take 4

Figure 7.4: WordPress site with recent board topics

People on the page simply click on the topic-of-interest link to view it.

This approach will work for any WordPress site, so you should encourage others with WordPress to highlight your topics and posts on their sites using this method.

My Smartfeed extension offers more options for presentation, if you want them. The URL syntax is different, however.

Since the Atom and RSS feed formats are open standards, there are other ways to integrate this content if WordPress is not used. For example, if you are familiar with jQuery, there are several jQuery feed libraries that would work. The PHP SimpleXML library is one way you can do it in PHP with a short PHP program.

Monitoring trends

You should pay regular attention to who is using your board and what they are posting.

Out of the box, phpBB won't provide much in the way of information about who is accessing the board and how many page views you are getting. If it's enabled, you can see who is online and basic information about usage of the board, like when a post was last made in a forum. Within a forum, you can see the most recent topics at the top of the page, which is a default setting. And within the ACP, right on the main page, you can get some general statistics like the number of posts and users you have.

For some administrators, this is enough. Going to the board regularly will also give them a sense of who is posting and what the hot topics are.

Using Google Analytics with phpBB

My experience is that administrators want to know a whole lot more than phpBB's basic information. I already mentioned the Google Analytics extension. This makes it easy to tie your board into Google Analytics.

On the Google Analytics website, you can easily see overall visits, page requests and a mind-boggling array of information. In fact, it tends to be way too much for most administrators (Figure 7.5).

You can discern plenty of information if you search for it, such as popular pages, most frequent visitor paths and even some advanced information about your board's viewers, such as their age ranges, gender percentages and occupations. You can see where visitors came from and what social networks are linking to your sites. And, you can get statistics on mobile vs. desktop usage, browsers used, devices used and hot spots on your pages. It may feel overwhelming, but it's worth exploring.

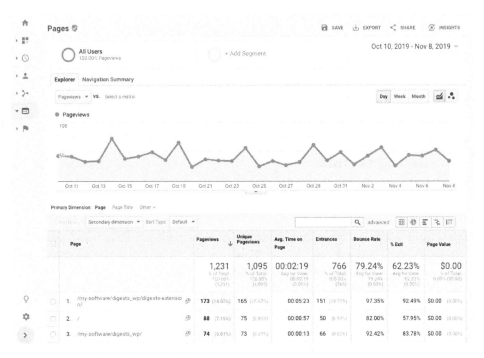

Figure 7.5: Google Analytics dashboard

Integrating other analytics packages

It's possible to integrate other analytics packages. But as of this writing, Google Analytics is the only one with an extension available for phpBB that integrates a web analytics package.

Generally, you have to include some Javascript on your board's pages to report to other analytic services. This usually means editing overall_footer.html for your style. If you want to use this approach, consider creating a custom style (Appendix C) to minimize the styling impacts.

I will demonstrate integrating the tracking code for Statcounter, a lightweight and rather basic analytics tool.

First you need to set up a project on Statcounter's website. Under **Project Config** in the sidebar, there is an option to get the code needed to be placed on your website. It looks something like this:

```
<!-- Default Statcounter code for My domain
http://mydomain.com -->
<script type="text/javascript">
var sc_project=9999999;
var sc_invisible=1;
var sc_security="997d312b";
</script>
<script type="text/javascript"
src="https://www.statcounter.com/counter/counter.js"
async></script>
<noscript><div class="statcounter"><a title="Web
Analytics"
href="https://statcounter.com/" target="_blank"><img
class="statcounter"
src="https://c.statcounter.com/9999999/0/997d312b/1/"
alt="Web Analytics"></a></div></noscript>
<!-- End of Statcounter Code -->
```

The instructions say to place it immediately before the ending </body> tag on the web page. The ending </body> tag is contained in the template overall_footer.html for your style. For the default prosilver style, you will need to edit /styles/prosilver/template/overall_footer.html.

This is easiest to do in your web host's file manager, if you have one. Otherwise, you must download this file, make the changes with a text editor and upload it, replacing the original file. Then purge the cache: **ACP > General > Purge the cache**. Make a backup of the original file before you begin, in case you make an error.

Near the bottom of this file you will see:

```
<!-- EVENT overall_footer_body_after -->
</body>
```

Consequently, when edited, this block of code will become (added lines are bolded):

```
<!-- EVENT overall_footer_body_after -->

<!-- Default Statcounter code for My domain
http://mydomain.com -->
<script type="text/javascript">
```

```
var sc_project=9999999;
var sc_invisible=1;
var sc_security="997d312b";
</script>
<script type="text/javascript"
src="https://www.statcounter.com/counter/counter.js"
async></script>
<noscript><div class="statcounter"><a title="Web
Analytics"
href="https://statcounter.com/" target="_blank"><img
class="statcounter"
src="https://c.statcounter.com/9999999/0/997d312b/1/"
alt="Web Analytics"></a></div></noscript>
<!-- End of Statcounter Code -->
</body>
```

This will not capture traffic in the Administration Control Panel. If you want to capture this too, you need to do something similar to /adm/style/overall_footer.html.

Hopefully, there will be phpBB extensions developed to track a wider array of statistics, so that much of the basic analysis can be done inside phpBB.

Chapter 8 | Administrative chores

Managing backups

It would be nice if computers were perfectly reliable. Since they are not, you will need to keep your board regularly backed up.

phpBB's content is logically split into two parts: files and the database. Both should be regularly and concurrently backed up.

Automatic backups

Your web host may be doing backups automatically for you. Often this is done for an extra cost, but it depends on your hosting plan. If you have a virtual, cloud or dedicated server, backing up generally becomes your duty to manage.

Web host backups, though, may lag what's on your board by some days, or a week or more. These backups tend to back up the whole site, so to recover your board to a point in time, you may have to roll back your whole site to a point in time, which may not be what you want. If you have multiple domains on your hosting, then you may be recovering all domains back to that point in time too. Sometimes you can back up a domain to a point in time, or specify a folder to recover to a point in time. It all depends on what backup features your web host offers.

If your web host backs up your site, you should find out how often it is backed up. This can often be found in your web host control panel in a backups group. I most often see weekly backups. Sometimes you will see daily backups. You generally get a few weeks of backups. If their backup interval will meet your needs, this will generally suffice. Just make sure that the backup includes your databases too. This may require a ticket with your web host's technical support department to find out.

Your web host control panel often has an interface where you can set the backup intervals or do a snapshot backup if you just want to save the state of your hosting before making a big change.

Making database backups in phpBB

You can manually make a backup of your database in phpBB at any time:

ACP > Maintenance > Database > Backup

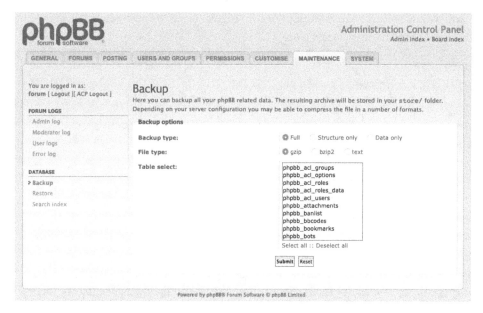

Figure 8.1: Database backup in phpBB

See Figure 8.1 and use these procedures:

1. **Disable the board: ACP > General > Board configuration > Board settings > Disable board > Yes**. You do this to avoid the possibility of an inconsistent database while the backup is occurring. Backups can take many minutes or longer, depending on the size of your board.

2. **Choose the Backup type**. **Full** is the default, which will back up both the structure of your tables and their content, which is generally what you want. It doesn't take much extra space to back up the structure of your tables too. **Structure only** will not back up any data in your tables, but will allow them to be re-created without any data. This is never useful. You may not see this option as it was removed in more recent versions of phpBB 3.3. **Data only** will not back up the structure, but will back up the data.

3. **Choose the File type**. The options that appear here depend on how PHP is configured on your web server. The likely compression file types include **zip**, **gzip** and **bzip2**. Typically, a compressed file will be about thirty percent the size of the uncompressed text option.

4. **Select the tables to backup.** To back up all tables, click on the **Select all** link. You must select at least one table for the backup to occur. When we discuss updating phpBB, you will learn that you only need to backup tables that will change their structures with the update.

5. **Press Submit**.

6. **Verify the backup is complete**. This is discussed shortly.

7. **For consistency, make a file backup now.** This is discussed shortly as well.

8. **Download the backups.** Typically you will want to download the backups you created as part of a disaster recovery process.

9. **Upon completion, re-enable the board: ACP > General > Board configuration > Board settings > Disable board > No**

The larger your database, the more time it will take to make the backup. You should get a successful green dialog box saying the database is backed up.

The backup is just a file, and can be found in your board's /store folder. The file will have a name like backup_1573415798_kgpkxsr5nci01bri.sql.gz. In this case, the 1573415798 in the file name specifies a Unix timestamp from which you can infer the actual backup date and time, if necessary. kgpkxsr5nci01bri is a random unique string assigned by phpBB.

You can use FTP to download the file to your computer.

Mostly on shared hosting and on large boards, you may get an ugly error page after a while. This is usually some variation of a "not enough resources are available" error. It usually means the backup is incomplete because you exceeded your quota of database resources. Time will eventually allow you to try again, but if it happened once, it's likely to recur. We'll shortly discuss other ways to back up your database in these situations.

Verifying the database backup

Sometimes when backing up the database, phpBB will say the database was backed up successfully, when it wasn't *fully* backed up.

This happens with larger boards, mostly on shared hosting when you exceed your quota of database resources. phpBB often will not detect this event. The only way to know for sure is to check it manually:

1. Use FTP to download the backup file from your board's /store folder. There are often multiple backups in this folder, so make sure you get the right one. The file's last modified date should be the current date.

2. If this is an archive, expand the archive. If expanding the archive triggers an error, you know you have an incomplete complete backup. This is because while writing the file, it was abruptly stopped when the process ran out of resources, so the checksum used to verify the archive is consistent is missing.

    On a local computer running MacOS or Linux, you can use the **gunzip** command to extract a .gz file. On Windows computers, there are a number of options. 7-Zip is a frequently recommended program that allows you to extract a variety of compressed files on Windows.

3. Look at the end of the extracted file, which will have a .sql suffix. You can do this in a text editor, but sometimes it will crash your text editor because it is too big. On Linux or a Mac, you can use the **tail** command in the terminal program to easily see the end of the resulting .sql file.

    The last file backed up is the phpbb_zebra table. You should see a reference to the table at the end of the file.

    Note: The last character of the file must be a semicolon.

    If all this is true, you have a complete backup:

```
sh-3.2# tail
backup_1573415798_kgpkxsr5nci01bri.sql

# Table: phpbb_zebra
DROP TABLE IF EXISTS phpbb_zebra;
CREATE TABLE `phpbb_zebra` (
  `user_id` int(10) unsigned NOT NULL DEFAULT
'0',
```

```
  `zebra_id` int(10) unsigned NOT NULL DEFAULT
'0',
  `friend` tinyint(1) unsigned NOT NULL DEFAULT
'0',
  `foe` tinyint(1) unsigned NOT NULL DEFAULT '0',
  PRIMARY KEY (`user_id`,`zebra_id`)
) ENGINE=InnoDB DEFAULT CHARSET=utf8
COLLATE=utf8_bin;
```

Automatically backing up the database

If you think it would be great for phpBB to automatically backup your database, a clever extension author wrote an extension that does just this.

https://www.phpbb.com/customise/db/extension/auto_database_backup_2

This approach uses phpBB's cron process to create these backups, so it might not back up your entire databases when a particular cron is run. Subsequent invocations should backup the rest of the database. This means that the content may be inconsistent if recovered. It's possible that there will be topics for which there are no posts, because the posts table was backed up before the topics table.

If you database is relatively small this is generally not a concern, but can become a concern as your board grows.

Restoring phpBB database backups

phpBB also can restore a database backed up inside of phpBB:

ACP > Maintenance > Database > Restore

Warning: if you had issues making a complete backup in phpBB, it's possible there will be a timeout or resource issue restoring the database too. This is typically only a potential problem for larger sized databases.

1. As with backing up, you should disable the board first: **ACP > General > Board configuration > Board settings > Disable board > Yes**

2. If you stored the backup offline, you may need to upload it to your board's /store folder first. Select the backup from your board's /store folder that you want to restore, and then press **Start restore**.

3. Hopefully you made a files backup at the same time as the database backup. This should also be restored after the database is successfully restored.

   If you skip restoring the files, there could be unattached attachments. These *orphaned attachments* can be removed: **ACP > Posting > Attachments > Orphaned attachments**

   It's possible there will be other inconsistencies as well. For example, if you uploaded a smilies pack since the database was backed up, the smilies pack may need to be reinstalled. Generally, these aren't issues unless you are recovering a much older database backup. But it's always better to restore files from a backup of the same date and time as the database backup.

4. Re-enable your board: **ACP > General > Board configuration > Board settings > Disable board > No**

You can use this interface to delete old backups too.

You can use a program like phpMyAdmin to do a visual inspection to see if the restoration was successful. All seventy-plus tables should be there, and most of those tables will be populated. The phpbb_zebra table should be the last table. If you get errors when using the board, it's a sign that the restoration failed.

We will talk about other ways to restore backups shortly.

Making file backups

Backing up your database is not enough. Unless you don't allow any attachments, you also need to back up your files. That's because some folders contain related data that isn't placed in the board's database. Most of these are attachments to posts. So, for consistency, a backup of relevant files should be done when you back up your database.

If you are making an ad-hoc backup, do this too before re-enabling your board, to ensure that your board is consistent.

Since phpBB has over 4500 files, it's impractical to download all of them. Almost all of these files are software programs, so they can be recovered, if necessary, from a phpBB archive.

At the very least, download or copy elsewhere the following folders because they contain data:

- **/files.** This contains all attachments to posts and private messages made by users.

- **/images.** This contains avatars, smilies and ranks that may have been uploaded.

- **/store.** This contains database backups and other occasionally files that may be needed by phpBB or an extension.

While not required, it's a good idea to also download:

- **config.php**. This file contains information on how to connect phpBB to your database.

- **The /ext folder**. All your extensions are here. If you don't have the files, reinstalling extensions is time consuming, plus you will get errors going to the Manage extensions page until these are fixed.

- **The /styles folder**. If you made any changes to phpBB's styles, such as adding a style other than prosilver, uploading a logo, or stylesheet (CSS) changes, you want to back up these too. Otherwise not only will the board look different after it is recovered, but there may be database issues. One issue could be that the database references a style that won't be installed.

Make sure to keep these files in a folder somewhere with the database backup, so you know they go together.

There are some real dangers to backing up only data files. If you later recover the files, it may be that phpBB was updated or upgraded after the data files backup was made. In this case, you may have a lot of missing data files. Posts with attachments and pictures could have blank spaces because these attachment files are missing.

We'll get more into this when we discuss updating and upgrading phpBB.

Making a database backup using phpMyAdmin

phpMyAdmin is typically available in your web host control panel. If your database management system is MySQL or MariaDB, you can use it to make a backup of your database. You'll generally find it in a databases group (Figure 8.2). phpMyAdmin may also be available as a separate URL provided by your web host. Click the icon or link to invoke phpMyAdmin.

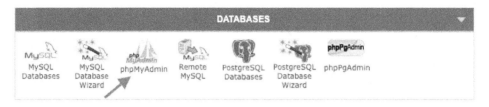

Figure 8.2: phpMyAdmin interface in cPanel

Note: You may be asked to provide a database host name, database user name and database password to get into phpMyAdmin. Entering the credentials in your board's config.php should work.

If your database management system is Postgres, there is probably a phpPgAdmin program in your web host control panel. It is functionally very similar to phpMyAdmin, so the instructions for phpMyAdmin should be similar to what you would do in phpPgAdmin.

Warning: phpMyAdmin is a very powerful tool. You could make serious or permanent changes to your database if you use it incorrectly! Proceed with caution!

1. Even though you are doing this outside of the database, to ensure consistency, you should disable your board first: **ACP > General > Board configuration > Board settings > Disable board > Yes**

2. Start phpMyAdmin.

3. Click the **Databases** tab.

4. Click the link corresponding to the database for your board. If you don't know the name of your database, you will find it in your board's config.php file.

5. Click the **Export** tab.

6. Scroll until you see the **Export method** section. If you select **Quick,** the export will not be compressed. I recommend clicking the **Custom** export method. In the **Output** block, you can choose a **Compression**. The compression types you will see depend on your PHP configuration. See Figure 8.3.

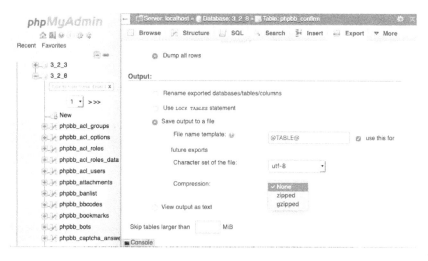

Figure 8.3: phpMyAdmin database export

7. Scroll to the bottom of the screen and press **Go**. If you don't choose a compression type, the download will start right away. If you choose a compression type, there will be a lag before the download starts because the extract must be written to a .gz or .zip file first.

8. If there is an issue like insufficient database resources, you will generally see the error.

9. Always check the integrity of the database using the methods discussed earlier.

10. For consistency, make a file backup at this time. This was discussed in the last section.

11. After successful completion, re-enable your board: **ACP > General > Board configuration > Board settings > Disable board > No**

Using phpMyAdmin is usually not any faster than using phpBB. It also won't store the file in your board's /store folder. It only permits exports to be downloaded. You can also specify a name for the downloaded file, which defaults to the database name.

It's possible that you will get errors exporting using phpMyAdmin too, because limits on system resources apply even in a web hosting control panel environment. If this happens, you can try exporting sets of tables, such as table names from a-m in one batch, and n-z in another. Sometimes it makes sense to download the largest tables, like phpbb_posts, separately. There are even ways to download portions of a table using phpMyAdmin, but this requires advanced skills.

In some extreme cases I have opted not to back up the search tables (any tables meeting the pattern phpbb_search_*), or opted to download their structure only. The search index can be re-created if necessary. I've often adopted this approach when I've had to rehost clients, as it was easier to re-create the search index than successfully export and reimport the massive search tables.

Restoring a database backup using phpMyAdmin

Warning: Recovering a database backed up using phpMyAdmin is a risky, multi-step process. You could end up with a board that doesn't work if you cannot successfully re-create all your tables.

1. Disable your board first: **ACP > General > Board configuration > Board settings > Disable board > Yes**

2. Start phpMyAdmin. *Note: You may be asked to provide a database host name, database user name and database password to get into phpMyAdmin. The credentials in your board's config.php should work.*

3. Click on the **Databases** tab.

4. Click on the link corresponding to the database for your board. If you don't know the name of your database, you will find it in your board's config.php file. You should see a list of tables in your board's database, but if not click on the **Structure** tab.

5. This is the scary part. You need to drop all the tables phpBB uses in your database. **Only drop tables that start with your $table_prefix variable.** You can see your $table_prefix variable in the config.php file in your board's root folder. If your database contains only tables for your board, there is a relatively easy way to drop them all: scroll to the bottom of the page, click on the **Check all** checkbox, then select **Drop** from the **With selected** dropdown box. Then press **Go**.

6. Click on the **Import** tab for your database.

7. Look for the **Browse** button. Next to it will be text showing the maximum size allowed for an uploaded database. Make sure your copy of the database is smaller than this size. If you downloaded an uncompressed extract of the database, you can compress it to a .sql.zip or sql.gz file on your machine. If it is smaller than the maximum size, you could upload that instead.

   If the size is too big to upload, you may be able to change some PHP configuration variables to allow it to upload. There is usually a web host control panel interface for making these changes. Sometimes a php.ini file with these commands in your board's root folder will work too.

   Here is an example of changes to a php.ini file to allow files of up to 120 MiB to be uploaded. It also allows 200 seconds of execution time and upload time.

   ```
   php_value upload_max_filesize 120M //file size
   php_value post_max_size 120M
   php_value max_execution_time 200
   php_value max_input_time 200
   ```

8. Link your copy of the exported database with the **Browse** button. Then press the **Go** button on the **Import** tab.

   Wait. Hopefully, it will all restore properly.

   One nice thing about phpMyAdmin is that if it fails there is an option to let you try again, and it will attempt to pick up where it left off. Select that option if it presents itself and press **Go** again.

9. Scan the list of tables and see how many rows are in each table. The last table should be the phpbb_zebra table.

10. For consistency, upload the files you backed up at the same time after successful completion to the same folders they were downloaded from. This was discussed in the last section.

11. Re-enable your board: **ACP > General > Board configuration > Board settings > Disable board > No**

Making a database backup from the command line using SSH

In Chapter 4, I discussed creating a database for your board using SSH and the mysql prompt.

Backing up the database with SSH has one big advantage: it will either do no damage to the database if it doesn't work, or it will do it completely and correctly. So even if your database is huge, it should back it up completely, although you may have to wait a long time to get a new command prompt. There is a term for this: *idempotency*.

Since most boards use MySQL or MariaDB, I will demonstrate this approach.

Both MySQL and MariaDB come with the mysqldump command. In one command, you can export an entire database or part of a database.

Consult a reference for the full syntax needed. The basic command is:

```
mysqldump [options] db_name
```

If mysqldump is not in the path, you have to preface it with the path. You should be able to use the database name and database password in your board's config.php file.

1. **Disable your board first: ACP > General > Board configuration > Board settings > Disable board > Yes**

2. **Dump the database to files.** I will assume your server's operating system is Linux, the database username is "forums," the database name is "forums" and the database username password is "abc123." In this example, mysqldump will export the database to a file called backup.sql, which is written to the home directory of whoever is logged in. (~ represents the home directory of the logged in user.) This would all appear on one line.

   ```
   mysqldump -u forums -pabc123 forums > ~/backup.sql
   ```

   > is used by Linux-based systems to say, "Take the output provided by the command and output it to a file instead of to the screen." In this case, the file name is backup.sql, which consists of a lot of SQL statements in plain text.

   You may want to compress the file at the same time. This can be done with a Linux (|) pipe command. This basically says, "take the output as uncompressed text, compress it with gzip compression and place the compressed version of the backup in a file name backup.sql.gz in my home directory". This would all appear on one line.

```
mysqldump -u forums -pabc123 forums | gzip >
~/backup.sql.gz
```

It can take quite a while to make a full backup of the database. If you have a very large database, it could take an hour or more. You will get a new line and a command prompt when it finishes.

3. **Download the database for safekeeping.** You might want to download the file with FTP. Unless you see an error message, you should not have to worry about whether the backup is complete.

4. **Make a files backup too.** For consistency, make a files backup at this time. This was discussed in the last section.

5. **Re-enable the board**. After successful completion, re-enable your board:
   ACP > General > Board configuration > Board settings > Disable board > No

You might want to automate this process with a cron so it happens at intervals you specify. If you have a choice, then save these backups on a different physical volume than the one containing the database. Crons were discussed in some detail in Chapter 6. The cron command you need is the mysqldump command you used to make a backup.

Restoring a database backup from the command line using SSH

Databases can be repopulated from the extract you created from the command line too. The tables first have to be dropped, i.e. destroyed. **Dropping all your tables makes your board dysfunctional until all tables are re-created and restored properly.**

Strangely, the fastest way to do this is to drop the entire database and grant it the same credentials that are in your config.php file. Otherwise, you must issue a lot of DROP TABLE commands, and there are more than seventy tables, so it's tedious.

1. **Drop the board's database.** *You should only do this if the database contains tables only for your board.* Assuming the database for your board is called

forums and you are logged in to mysql on the command line with the proper credentials, the command is:

```
DROP DATABASE forums;
```

2. **Create your board's database again.**

```
CREATE DATABASE forums;
```

3. **Grant database user permissions to the database again.** Since the database is new again, privileges to the database matching the information in your board's config.php file must be granted again. Assuming the database name is "forums," the database username is "forums" and the database exists on localhost, these commands would work. This would all appear on one line.

```
GRANT ALL PRIVILEGES ON forums.* TO
'forums'@'localhost';
```

Type **quit** or **exit** and press **Enter** or **Return** to exit the MySQL command line.

4. **Decompress the archive, if the backup is in an archive.** For example, a backup called backup.sql.gz can be decompressed if it is in the current directory:

```
gunzip backup.sql.gz
```

5. **Restore the database's data.** Assuming the above, your server is using Linux for the operating system, the database username's password is "abc123," and the file backup.sql is in the user's home directory, this command will work:

```
mysql -u forums -pabc123 forums < ~/backup.sql
```

The < tells the mysql command to use the contents of the file backup.sql in the user's home directory for input. MySQL will be smart enough to see it as a lot of SQL statements and process them one by one.

Restoring files

Files are easier to restore than the database, but still require some hassle.

If you backed up the /files and /images folders only:

1. **Delete the files and images folders.** The easiest way to do this is to do it carefully with your web host file manager. I prefer this method because the deleted files generally go into the digital trash can, so they can be recovered easily if needed.

2. **Upload these folders and the files inside of them using FTP.** Make sure they are being uploaded into the root folder of your board.

3. **Make sure there are 777 (public write) permissions to the /files and /images/avatars/uploads folders.**

4. **Upload other folders and files, if desired.** You may also want to upload other folders and files you backed up, although this should not be necessary.

If your files are archives, you may find it easier to upload the archives and decompress them using your web host's file manager. Make sure the files are placed in the appropriate folders.

Managing users

Ideally, your board is a nice and harmonious place where civility among your board's users is the norm. But you obviously can't guarantee this.

That's where moderators come in handy. If you don't have moderators, then you will assume that chore too, or at least take action when users get unruly.

A good set of board rules specifying the expected behavior of users can help. You might want to install the Board rules extension to set these expectations. Your moderators can refer users to them as needed. Stickies (sticky topics) can be created within forums to indicate the decorum expected by users of a forum.

In this section, we look at handling users, both the good and the not so good kinds. But, let's first look at how users can handle them.

Creating friends and foes

phpBB has a friends and foes feature. Users can mark other users they appreciate as friends and users who grate their nerves as foes.

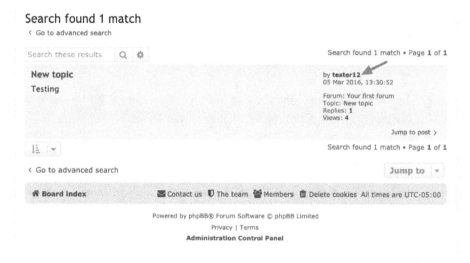

Figure 8.4: Poster profile link on view topic page

Posts from foes are not fully visible by default. Using the prosilver style, online friends have their usernames bolded, and offline friends' usernames are in italics (Figure 8.4).

While this feature exists, in my experience it is rarely used, mainly because phpBB does not call it to your attention. But, let's look at how users mark other users as friends or foes.

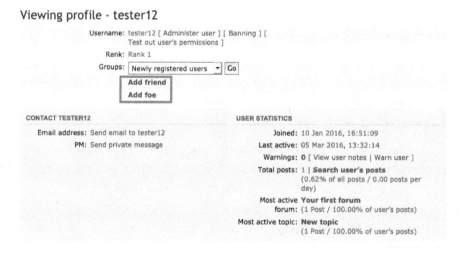

Figure 8.5: View profile page

You can declare a friend or foe in the User Control Panel (Figure 8.5):

UCP > Friends & Foes > Friends

UCP > Friends & Foes > Foes

On this tab, you can also decide to remove friends and foes from your lists.

A more natural way is to click the poster's username, which is next to each post.

This takes you to the poster's profile page. From there, two links make it easy to add the user as a friend or foe.

Managing inactive users

Handling a queue of inactive users is another chore that administrators need to do regularly. Inactive users are users that have not completed registration. You can also deliberately make a user inactive.

If you have set your user account activation to *by admin*, then you or another administrator with the privilege must approve new users. phpBB makes this easy.

- By default, administrators don't get emails when new users require activation. If you want to get these emails: **UCP > Board preferences > Edit notification option > User requiring activation > Email** (Figure 8.6). This only appears if you specify administrators must approve all new users.

Figure 8.6: Setting to get emails on users requiring activation

- In the emails, you will get a link that makes it easy to view a new user profile and decide if they should be approved.

- If you visit the board, there should also be a notification on the navigation bar, providing the notification checkbox is checked.

- If you go into the Administration Control Panel, the latest ten inactive users appear at the bottom of the default page (Figure 8.7).

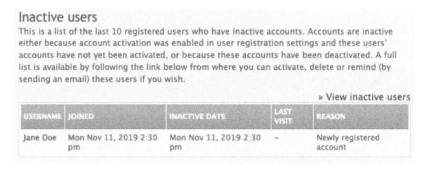

Figure 8.7: Inactive users at the bottom of the Administration Control Panel's main page

The link for the username takes you to a page that will show you details about the user. Toward the bottom of the page is a **Quick tools** dropdown. Selecting **Activate account** then pressing **Submit** will allow the user to use the board (Figure 8.8). The new user should get a confirmation email.

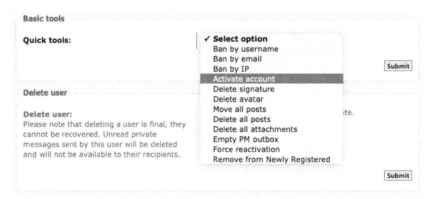

Figure 8.8: Activating a new user

- An easier way to do these in bulk is to go to the Inactive users page:

ACP > Users and Groups > Users > Inactive users (Figure 8.9)

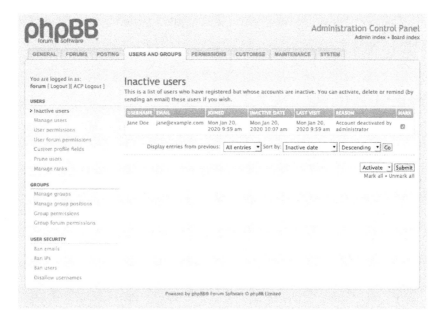

Figure 8.9: Inactive users page

Click the checkbox on the rows for those users you want to activate, or click on the **Mark all** link to easily check them all.

Next to the **Submit** button, make sure the dropdown selects **Activate**, then press **Submit**.

If you have set account activation by user (email verification), the new user should get an email. When they click on the link in the email, the account is activated. Then they can log in with the username and password they set upon registration.

If this email doesn't arrive, or ends up in a spam folder, or gets ignored, the user remains inactive. You can periodically send reminder emails to these users. An easy way to do this in bulk is to select **Remind** rather than **Activate** from the dropdown shown in Figure 8.9, then press **Submit**.

Sometimes users will never complete their registration. In this case, you can also use the Inactive users page to permanently delete these accounts. Select **Delete** instead of **Activate** from the dropdown shown in Figure 8.9, then press **Submit**.

My selective mass emails extension makes it easy to send a mass email to inactive users, perhaps to remind them to activate their account. Once installed, the additional fields can be found on the regular mass email screen: **ACP > System > General tasks > Mass email**.

Banning users

In extreme cases, you may have to ban a user. A ban can be temporary or permanent. In either case, if one of these users tried to login, they will get a banned message and posting will be prohibited.

You can ban users by username, IP or email address. Banning by IP is the most useful since it makes it difficult for the user to register again under a different username.

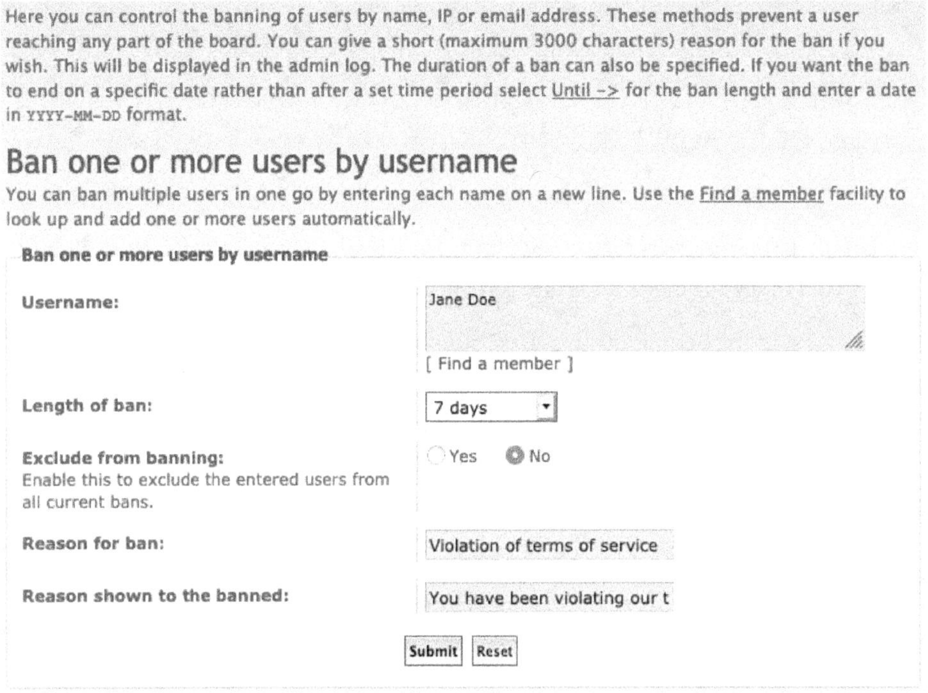

Here you can control the banning of users by name, IP or email address. These methods prevent a user reaching any part of the board. You can give a short (maximum 3000 characters) reason for the ban if you wish. This will be displayed in the admin log. The duration of a ban can also be specified. If you want the ban to end on a specific date rather than after a set time period select Until -> for the ban length and enter a date in YYYY-MM-DD format.

Ban one or more users by username

You can ban multiple users in one go by entering each name on a new line. Use the Find a member facility to look up and add one or more users automatically.

Ban one or more users by username

Username:	Jane Doe [Find a member]
Length of ban:	7 days
Exclude from banning: Enable this to exclude the entered users from all current bans.	○ Yes ◉ No
Reason for ban:	Violation of terms of service
Reason shown to the banned:	You have been violating our t

Submit Reset

Figure 8.10: Banning by username

When banning by IP or email address, you can ban a pattern or range, such as a range of IPs, or domains like hotmail.com.

ACP > Users and groups > User security > Ban emails

ACP > Users and groups > User security > Ban IPs

ACP > Users and groups > User security > Ban users

Users with full moderator privileges can also ban users: **MCP > Banning**. The interface is like the one used by administrators.

The interface is virtually the same for each type of ban. Figure 8.10 shows the interface for banning by username.

When you enter a reason for a ban, it is retained for future use. You can add, delete or edit the text for these banning reasons in the ACP: **ACP > System > General tasks > Manage report/denial reasons**.

Pruning forums

It used to be that database space was precious. This is generally not a problem anymore, but when it was, it was sometimes necessary to prune old topics.

Your web host usually has some sort of limit on the overall size of your databases. For example, as of this writing Siteground's shared hosting limits databases to 1 GiB with their GoGeek plan. This limit applies to all your databases, but some hosts may have limits on how big one database can get.

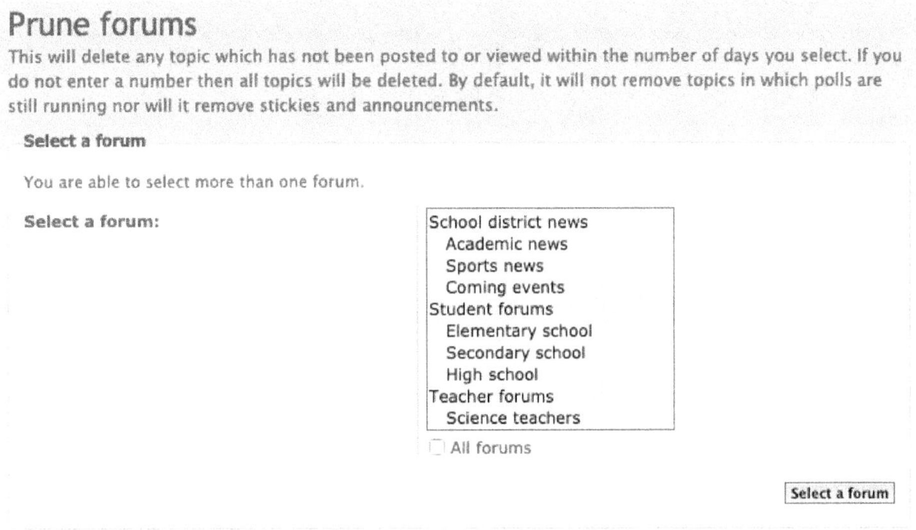

Figure 8.11: Prune forums, part one

A highly trafficked and active board can use up its quota of database space sooner than you think. As mentioned earlier, a search index is a huge factor in a database's size. Disabling searching and removing the search index can free up a lot of database space, but at the cost of losing this functionality.

ACP > Forums > Manage forums > Prune forums

I recommend disabling the board before pruning forums and re-enabling it afterward. This is because pruning can involve a fair amount of database work. It generally goes okay, but on shared hosting, you might hit a resource limitation, abruptly cutting off the work with an error message. **Consequently, it's a good idea to back up the database before pruning.** If it happens, you are generally able to try it again to finish the process.

Another way to reduce the likelihood of a timeout and other issues while pruning is to prune multiple times. For example, if your board has eight years of content, you might want to remove posts more than 2555 days old (seven years), then 2190 days old (six years), etc.

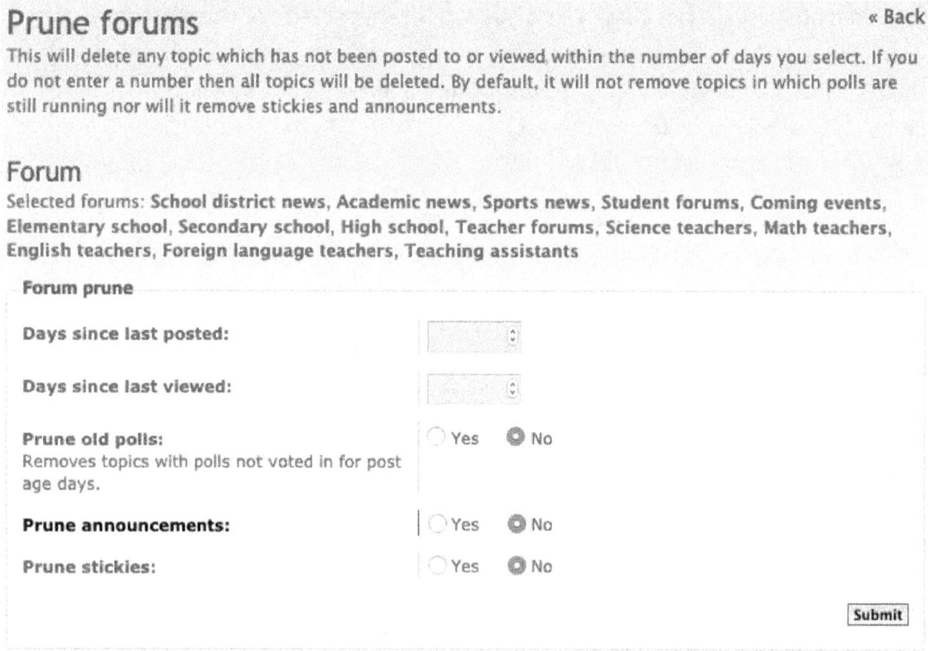

Figure 8.12: Prune forums, part two

Pruning forums is a two-step process. First you pick the forums you want to prune (Figure 8.11). If you want to prune all forums, click on the **All forums** checkbox. Then press **Select a forum**.

The next screen lets you select how to prune these forums. You have two choices:

- Remove topics that haven't had a post in X days

- Remove topics that haven't been viewed in X days

See Figure 8.12. You have the option to prune old polls, announcements and stickies in the selected forums too.

Pruning users

You can also prune users, but unless you delete their posts while doing this, it doesn't save a whole lot of space.

Of course, you might simply like to keep a tidy board and remove users who haven't posted in five years on the assumption they won't be coming back. If you opt to delete their accounts and you choose to retain their posts, their posts appear as guest posts. Their username is retained in the post, but cannot be linked to their profile because the account no longer exists.

To get rid of spam users and their posts, you need to know the usernames they created and enter them in the user interface in the **Prune Users** block (Figure 8.13). Reviewing the **Memberlist** on the **Quick Links** dropdown on the navigation bar can help identify these users easily, especially if you sort on join date. These "users" tend to stand out like sore thumbs. If you see a block of these starting, say, August 1, you can enter that in the **Joined after** field.

Other ways for handling spam are coming right up!

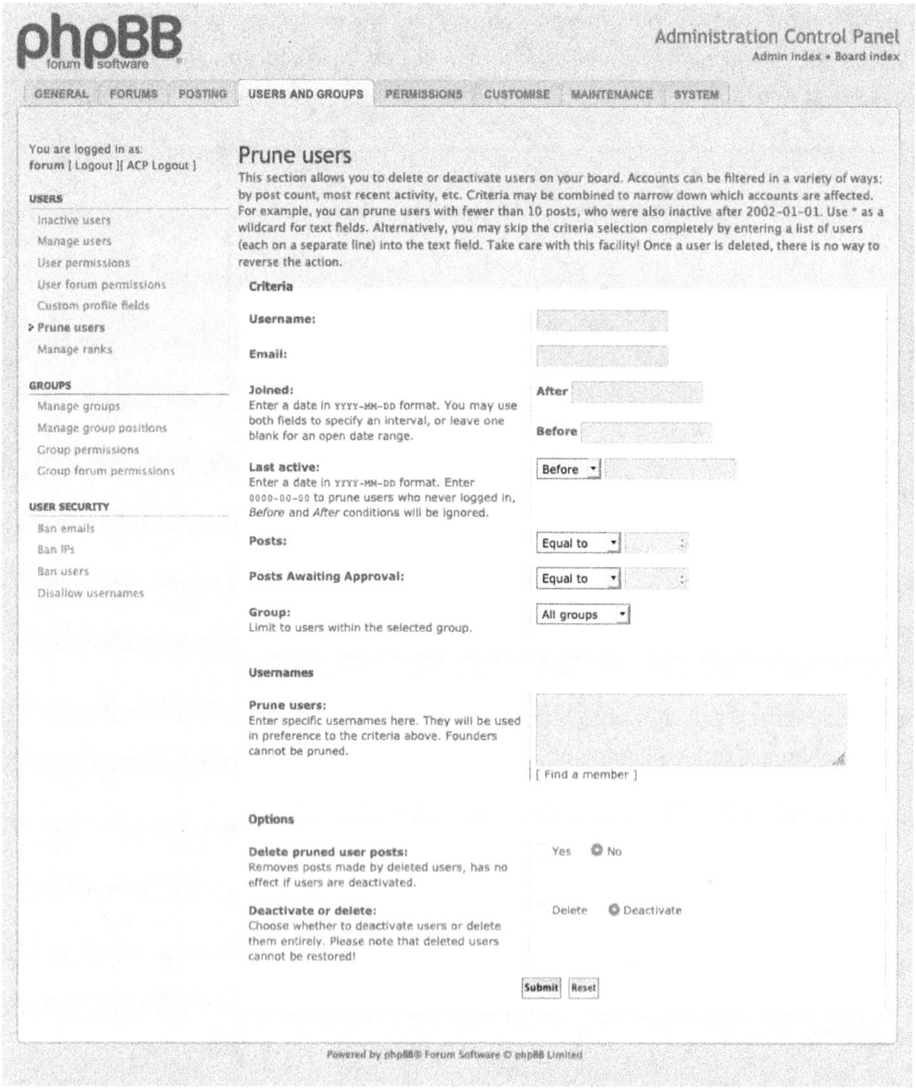

Figure 8.13: Prune users

Handling spam

As I've noted, bulletin boards make inviting places for posting spam. Boards tend to be highly read, so spam can be posted then quickly seen by lots of people, perhaps before you or a moderator can take action.

A large spam attack can leave hundreds of bogus users and hundreds of bogus posts, and possibly bogus private messages as well. It can be challenging and, in some cases, almost impossible to remove all the spam.

Consequently, throughout this book, I have been recommending a proactive approach by using effective spambot countermeasures. Active moderation helps too, so if a spam event occurs, moderators can deal with it before it becomes a major issue. Users can help too. They can mark posts as spam, allowing moderators to focus on these posts and take action.

When spam events happen, it's an indication that something has broken through your defenses. So, in addition to removing the spam, you also need to up your defenses.

Don't allow guests to post

phpBB allows guests to post, but only if this is explicitly enabled. Allowing guests to post just creates problems and can make it very easy for spammers to post without the hassle of creating an account, if they can bypass any CAPTCHA. So just say no to guest posting.

If you must give guests permission to post, at least require them to go through a CAPTCHA with every post. Fortunately, this is enabled by default:

ACP > General > Board configuration > Post settings > Enable spambot countermeasures for guest postings > Yes

To allow guests to post, you must also give the group posting permissions to applicable forums:

ACP > Users and groups > Groups > Group forum permissions > Guests

Select the forums where you want guests to post. On the next screen, change the role from **Read Only Access** role to something else, perhaps **Limited Access**.

When guests post, at the time of posting, they create a pseudo-username. No account is created.

Handling contact page spam

We've discussed this briefly already. The most frequent entryway for spam is if you enable the contact page feature in phpBB:

ACP > General > Board configuration > Contact page settings

Contact Administration

Please use this ONLY if there is no other way to contact us

Your name: Length must be between 3 end 20.	
Your email address: Please enter a valid email address, so we can contact you.	
Reason:	General Question ▾
Message body:	

What does a car need to work? Please drag the options to the correct list, to avoid automated registrations.	To Use	Not needed
	Gas	
	Motor Oil	
	Keyboard	
	Driver	
	Computer	
	Printer	

Submit

Figure 8.14: Contact admin extension

There is no CAPTCHA on the form, so anyone can access it. The contact page is enabled by default, so it's typical for administrators to get spam emails, not understanding that it's because the contact page is enabled.

The good news is that the contact page sends emails only to administrators. So, while you get spam, they do not end up as posts or get stored in your board's database. Only administrators are bothered, and no bogus accounts are created.

The simplest was to handle this is to disable the contact page:

ACP > General > Board configuration > Contact page settings > Enable contact page > Disabled

If you definitely want a contact page, still disable the contact page, but use an extension that has equivalent functionality as well as a CAPTCHA. The Contact Admin extension does this. Guests must puzzle through a simple CAPTCHA to submit the form. See Figure 8.14.

Letting moderators handle spam

If you have active moderators, you can have them remove spam and spam users for you. However, they need full moderator privileges to remove users. You might also need to train them in how to do this:

MCP > Banning

You should still keep a spambot countermeasure enabled. Moderators usually have enough to do and don't need the extra hassle of deleting spam entered by robots. Spam they catch is likely to be deliberately introduced by a malicious user.

Change your spambot countermeasure

Many boards use the Q & A (Question & Answer) spambot countermeasure. To register, a user must correctly answer one or more questions.

This works if the question is unusually specific and would only be known by someone with specialized knowledge of your topic area.

If the question is too broad, it should be avoided. For example, a question like "Who is the President of the United States?" is too broad. Any question that can be answered from a Google "I'm feeling lucky" search is a bad one.

Anyone willing to spend the time can usually figure out the answer. Once answered, it's possible to set up all sorts of bogus accounts and start creating spam posts. It rarely happens, but it is possible.

Consequently, the most effective out-of-the-box spambot countermeasure is the reCAPTCHA Version 3 countermeasure, which takes some setting up. This is discussed in Chapter 5.

There are a number of other anti-spam extensions available as well. Akismet and Cleantalk were discussed earlier, but these are best as a second layer of defense. The Sortables Captcha Plugin extension forces users to place items into logical columns, which require physical movement. This is quite effective. See Figure 8.15.

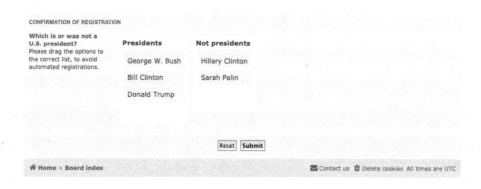

Figure 8.15: Sortables Captcha Plugin extension

Change account activation to: by admin

If you want to stop registration spam, it's impossible to beat this approach. It requires an administrator to approve all new users manually. However, it's time consuming for administrators. So, most administrators avoid it.

ACP > General > Board configuration > User registration settings > Account activation > By admin

Disallowing new registrations

If you have a closed community, it is better to disallow all registrations:

ACP > General > Board configuration > User registration settings > Account activation > Disable registration

With this approach, you may want to install the ACP Add User extension to create accounts for new members and send them their board access credentials. After the extension is enabled, the interface can be found on the Users and Groups tab:

ACP > Users and Groups > Users > ACP Add User

Removing spam users and posts

Either an administrator or a moderator can remove individual spam posts manually. A full moderator can also ban them, either temporarily or permanently. If the spam attack is not too large, this may be a way to go. The marked posts are hidden, so the spam is no longer visible.

Administrators can delete their accounts in the Administration Control Panel, where you can choose an option to delete all their posts too:

ACP > Users and Groups > Users > Manage users

In the case of large, recent attacks that are quickly noticed, the **Prune Users** function discussed in the last section is effective at removing both spam users and their spam posts, providing the problem is detected within a reasonable time frame and you can identify a date when these were started. If you've got years of spam on your board, you've got a much bigger problem.

ACP > Users and groups > Users > Prune users

You would specify a value in the **Joined after** field. See Figure 8.13.

However, doing this catches all, so any legitimate users and their posts would get deleted too. However, legitimate users could re-register.

As mentioned, the Cleantalk extension, in combination with its paid service, has a feature that finds likely spam users. As of this writing, its interface is not well integrated as it doesn't allow pagination and seems slow. Cleantalk seems to make all its judgments based solely on the IP address of the user, not the content of the post. IP addresses on their list may get "cleared" from time to time, and when this happens, it won't catch these spam users and their posts. It's also possible it will generate some false positives.

In Cleantalk, look for a **Check users for spam** button on its interface page. If you don't see it, it's likely because you need a newer version of the extension than phpBB has, so search for it on GitHub. If installed, it is at:

ACP > Extensions > Antispam by Cleantalk > Spam protection settings

Cleantalk, though, is much better at preventing users from registering in the first place than cleaning up the messes they leave behind.

There is an Akismet extension for phpBB that can also be installed to prevent new spam posts and users. It requires a subscription to the service, which is not usually free. Generally, the Cleantalk service is a better value.

Removing large volumes of spam

In some extreme cases, just to get rid of it, administrators have restored their board to a point in time before the spam started. Of course, doing this also removes any legitimate posts and new topics posted after the recovery date.

Sometimes, spam attacks are too large or went unnoticed for too long to make this usable. If you have to remove only a dozen spam users, it's a viable process. If it's hundreds of spam users in a short period of time and thousands of posts, or old spam posts that were neglected, it will be time consuming and tedious.

Fortunately, my spam remover extension is now approved by the phpBB Group. It uses the Akismet service (used principally to moderate comments on WordPress sites) to find and remove spam posts and private messages. The Akismet service is not necessarily free, but the extension is free. To deal with a one-time problem, you might want to pay for month of Akismet service.

Understanding permission roles

Roles are one of phpBB's most useful but most obscure features. They can be a little hard to understand.

Roles essentially are a collection of enabled permissions with a name. This collection of permissions can be assigned broadly to individual users and groups.

What's neat about roles is that you can change their properties at any time. Make one change on one screen, save it, and the changes instantly affect everyone that uses the role.

Types of Roles

Four categories of roles exist:

- **User roles.** These are broad permissions that apply to any user of your board.

- **Administrator roles**

- **Moderator roles**

- **Forum roles**. These allow permissions to be finely tuned for individual forums. They are applied after any user-role permissions and may override some user role permissions.

User roles

User roles bundle sets of permissions that apply to what users can do on your board. They do not include setting permissions for particular forums but do include some broad forum permissions that are applied where none may exist on a particular forum.

Pre-defined user roles

There are six built-in user roles:

- **Standard Features**. Users can access most, but not all, user features. Users cannot change their user name or ignore the flood limit, for instance.

- **Limited Features**. Users can access some of the user features. Attachments, emails or instant messages are not allowed.

- **All Features**. Users can use all available forum features for users, including changing the user name or ignoring the flood limit. Not recommended.

- **No Private Messages**. This has a limited feature set, and is not allowed to use private messages.

- **No Avatar**. This has a limited feature set and is not allowed to use the avatar feature.

- **Newly Registered User Features.** A role for members of the special newly registered users' group; contains NEVER permissions to lock features for new users.

Changing user roles

The permissions for user roles are easily changed. For example, the Standard Features user role describes the privileges users with this role have.

You can view and change the permissions for this role:

ACP > Permissions > Permission roles > User roles > Standard Features > Edit

Setting	Yes	No	Never
Can attach files	●	○	○
Can disable word censors	●	○	○
Can download files	●	○	○
Can save drafts	●	○	○
Can use signature	●	○	○

Figure 8.16: User role permissions

Figure 8.16 shows some of the user permissions for the Standard Features role. The permissions come in four sets, represented by a tab. Here, the Post permissions for the role are shown.

This tab has a green square because all permissions are set to **Yes**. Change just one of these to **No** or **Never**, and after the permissions are saved, the green turns to blue. The squares on the **Profile**, **Misc** and **Private messages** tabs are blue, letting you know that at least one of the permissions on these tabs is not **Yes**. If the square color is red, all the permissions on the tab are either **No** or **Never**.

Since these are user permissions, any user granted the **Standard Features** role will get these permissions, such as the ability to attach files. These are the default user permissions. Forum permissions may override these settings.

Creating user roles

If you want to create a new user role, there is nothing stopping you.

ACP > Permissions > Permission roles > User roles > Create role

Select the role you want to inherit the permissions from in the **Use settings from** dropdown. Then press **Submit**.

The role details group lets you change the role name, plus add a description to the role, if desired.

Change the permissions as desired for each tab.

Once a new role is created, you generally want to assign groups or users to that role. Use one of the following paths:

ACP > Users and groups > Groups > Manage groups

ACP > Users and groups > Users > Manage users

Moderator roles

In addition to having global versus forum-specific moderators, phpBB allows you to place moderators into various roles. The permissions of the role determine how much power a moderator has.

Moderation uses a term *moderation queue*. This is a list of post actions needing moderation and can be seen in the Moderator Control Panel, accessed on the navigation bar. One moderator role doesn't allow access to the moderation queue.

Pre-defined moderator roles

These moderator roles come out of the box:

- **Standard moderator**. This type of moderator can use most moderating tools, but cannot ban users or change the post author.

- **Simple moderator**. This type of moderator can only use basic topic actions. They cannot send warnings or use the moderation queue.

- **Full moderator**. This type of moderator can use all moderating features, including banning.

- **Queue moderator**. This type of moderator can use the Moderation Queue to validate and edit posts, but nothing else.

Changing moderator roles

Editing the role's permissions easily changes moderator role permissions. The process is similar to changing user roles. For example, to change the permissions for the Standard Moderator role:

ACP > Permissions > Permission roles > Moderator roles > Standard Moderator > Edit

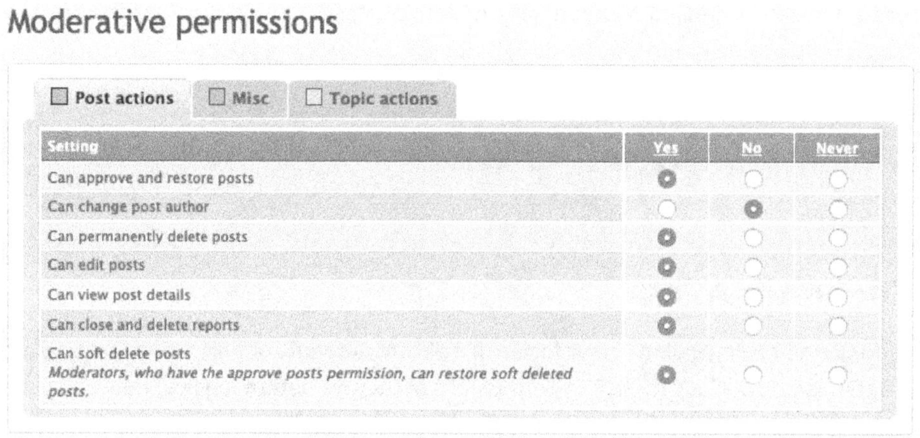

Figure 8.17: Moderator role permissions

See Figure 8.17. Change any settings on any of the tabs, then press **Submit**. Anyone using that role will have the role's permissions immediately take effect.

Creating moderator roles

Let's say you have a popular and busy board with a lot of topics that are frequently out of place. You want to keep the primary moderator for handling the bigger duties, but delegate moving topics, splitting topics, merging topics and locking topics to another type of moderator via a newly defined moderator role. You can do this by creating new moderator roles.

In Figure 8.18, I first create the role called Special Moderator. Since a Full Moderator has all permissions, I'll start with its permissions and take away permissions I don't want the role to have.

ACP > Permissions > Permission Roles > Moderator roles

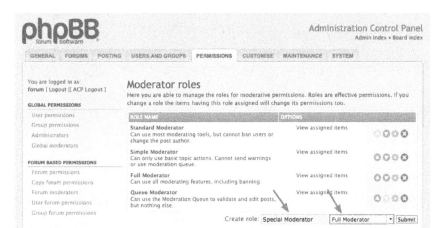

Figure 8.18: Create new moderator role, part one

I enter "Special Moderator" in the **Create role** field and select **Full Moderator** from the **Use settings from** dropdown, then press **Submit**.

Figure 8.19: Create new moderator role, part two

On the next screen, I first went to the **Post actions** tab and clicked on the **No** column to disallow all those privileges. I did the same on the **Misc tab**. On the **Topic actions** tab, I left these as is. See Figure 8.19. Pressing **Submit** created the role.

Figure 8.20: Assigning moderators, part one

With the role now defined, I can select moderators to have this role. Since I want these moderators to do this for any forum, it's easiest to make them global moderators, but with the Special Moderator user role I created.

ACP > Permissions > Global permissions > Global moderators

See Figure 8.20. The first step is to add the users to get this role in the **Add users** block, and then press the **Add permissions** button below the field. The **Find a member** link makes it easy to find the usernames, if you don't know them.

The next step is to assign the newly created moderator role to these users. In the **Role** dropdown, I selected the Special Moderator role I created, then pressed the **Apply all permissions** button. See Figure 8.21. Done!

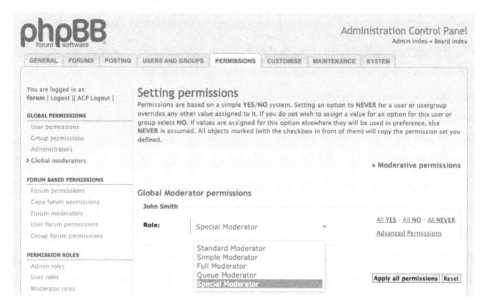

Figure 8.21: Assigning moderators, part two

Administrator roles

It's tempting to think of administrators as one size fits all, but you can have various kinds of administrators too. The kinds of administrators are based on the roles they are given.

Pre-defined administrator roles

There are four pre-defined administrator roles:

- **Standard Admin**. This role has access to most administrative features but is not allowed to use server or system related tools.

- **Full Admin**. This role has access to all administrative functions of this board. Not recommended.

- **Forum Admin**. This role can access the forum management and forum permission settings.

- **User and Groups Admin**. This role can manage groups and users and has the ability to change permissions, settings, manage bans, and manage ranks.

The main role to worry about is the **Full Admin** role, because if you grant it, then you are giving the administrators virtually complete control of the board.

Large and busy boards might need to assign people to the Forum Admin and User and Group Admin roles. In that case, these new administrators get into the Administration Control Panel the same way you do: by selecting the link in the navigation bar or from the link that appears in the footer. However, they won't necessarily see all the tabs and options in the sidebar that a founder would see.

Quickly creating administrators

If you don't want to be granular about administrator privileges, simply add the user to the administrator's group:

Figure 8.22: Adding an administrator

ACP > Users and groups > Groups > Manage groups > Administrators > Members

In the **Add Users** block, enter the usernames on separate lines that you want to make administrators. Use the **Find a member** link if needed, and press **Submit** when done. See Figure 8.22. These new administrators will inherit the Standard Admin role's privileges.

Creating founders

Founders are a special kind of administrator with special privileges. Founders can never be banned, deleted or altered by any other administrators unless they are also founders.

If your board would eventually die if you died or were incapacitated for a long period of time, then you should grant this permission to one or more highly trusted users. Remember: these users can do anything, including removing all forums, effectively destroying all your board's content! You should also consider giving these users other keys too: like web host control panel access, so they can handle issues affecting your board outside of phpBB.

An administrator with the Full Admin role is not technically a founder, but might as well be since they can do pretty much anything a founder can do too except make themselves a founder or create additional administrators.

If you want to make someone a founder, you first must already have founder privileges.

ACP > Users and Groups > Manage users

Enter the user's name and press **Submit**. In the **Founder** field, select **Yes** and press **Submit**.

Tip: if you need to be a founder but can't find someone to make you a founder, and you can access the database using a tool like phpMyAdmin, you can make yourself one by *carefully* changing the database. Find your row in the phpbb_users table and change the value of the user_type column for your user to 3. This will give you founder privileges.

Tip: If you made yourself a founder this way, and still cannot access the ACP because the link does not appear, this means that while you have founder privileges you don't have any administrator permissions assigned. Use phpMyAdmin or a similar tool to change the user_permissions column for your row in the phpbb_users table. Just empty out the field for your account only, which is possible if you double-click on the field in browse mode. You may need to manually purge the cache by deleting the content inside the /cache/production folder with the file manager or FTP.

Creating new admin roles

You can also create a new administrator role if you want using procedures similar to creating new moderator and user roles:

ACP > Permissions > Permission roles > Admin roles > Create role

As a practical matter, the pre-defined admin roles should meet the needs of ninety-nine percent of boards.

Forum roles

As the name implies, forum roles control the privileges to what can be done inside forums. Forums are the key structure in phpBB and are where most of the conversation happens, so there should be a lot of ways to finely tune privileges and access to forums.

Forum roles are most typically used to control forum privileges because they simplify the process. I will also demonstrate a way of circumventing these roles to set more granular user forum permissions.

We've touched on using forum roles in Chapter 5, in the context of setting up your board. If you skipped that chapter, you might want to review that section. It's critically important that your groups have the correct permissions set so that content is hidden where necessary and posters can't take actions that exceed their intended authority.

User roles provide broad sets of permissions, many of which extend to work users do in forums. Allowing attachments to posts is one example. Since roles are bundles of permissions, permissions in forum roles may override some user role permissions to selected forums.

Pre-defined forum roles

The following forum roles come built-in to phpBB:

- **No Access**. Users can neither see nor access the forum. This should be applied when you want to hide a forum from appropriate groups and users. You most typically use it to hide forums from guests and bots.

- **Read Only Access**. Users can read the forum but cannot create new topics or reply to posts. You often see this role applied to guests.

- **Limited Access**. Users can use some forum features but cannot attach files or use post icons. This role is often applied to newly registered users.

- **Limited Access + Polls**. Users have limited access but can create polls. This role is also often applied to newly registered users.

- **Standard Access**. Users can use most forum features, including attachments and deleting their own topics, but cannot lock their own topics, and cannot create polls.

- **Standard Access + Polls**. This is like Standard Access but can also create polls.

- **Full Access**. Users can use all forum features, including posting of announcements and stickies. They can also ignore the flood limit. This is not recommended for normal users, and is often applied to more privileged users, such as moderators and administrators.

- **On Moderation Queue**. Users can use most forum features, including attachments, but posts and topics need to be approved by a moderator. This role can be applied to a problematic poster known for making inflammatory posts or breaking board rules.

- **Bot Access**. This role is recommended for bots and search spiders. It does allow bots to read the forum, so if you don't want bots to read the forum, the bots groups should use the No Access role.

- **Newly Registered User Access**. This is a role for members of the newly registered users group and contains **NEVER** permissions to lock features for new users. This gets around a quirk in phpBB where newly registered users can start new topics (which have to go through moderation) only because they are also in the registered users group. It's strange that phpBB is not configured this way by default.

There is one other implied role: **No role assigned**. It doesn't necessarily mean no permissions exist, but no collection of privileges (a role) has been assigned. Other permissions may be applied, such as permissions granted explicitly to a user.

Creating new forum roles

You can define a forum role using similar procedures for user, moderator and admin roles:

ACP > Permissions > Permission roles > Forum roles > Create role

In general, the existing roles make it unlikely that you will need to create other forum roles.

Overriding role permissions

While not a good idea generally, I should point out that you could override forum role permissions for groups and users. Use either:

ACP > Users and groups > Users > User forum permissions

ACP > Users and groups > Groups > Group forum permissions

Figure 8.23: User forum permissions, pick a user

Here's an example of how it can be done for a user's forum permissions.

In this example, Jane Doe is a teacher and is in the teacher's group, so she has **Standard Access** role's permissions to the teachers' forums. This means she cannot post sticky topics, i.e. posts that stick near the top of the list of topics in a forum.

I would like to allow her to post stickies but don't want to change her permissions otherwise.

First, I enter her name by in the **Find a member** field and press **Submit** (Figure 8.23).

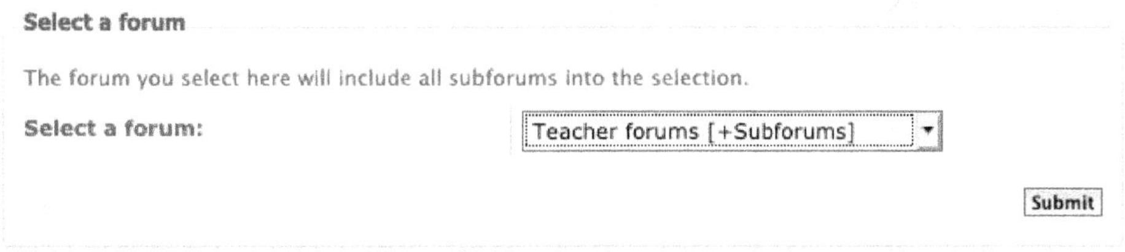

Select a forum

The forum you select here will include all subforums into the selection.

Select a forum: Teacher forums [+Subforums]   ▼

Submit

Figure 8.24: User forum permissions, select a forum

Then I pick the forums where I want the permissions applied. In this case, it makes sense to select the Teacher forums category and the forums inside it. Once selected, I press **Submit**. See Figure 8.24.

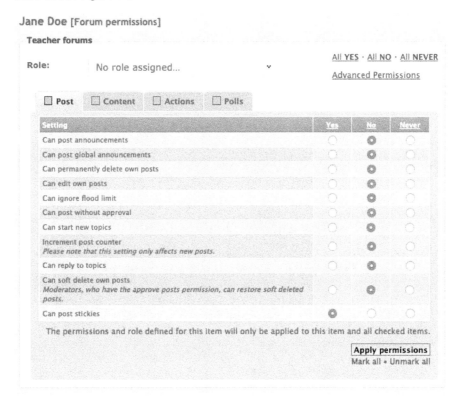

Figure 8.25: User forum permissions, advanced permissions

On the next screen, the role shows no role assigned because no *user* forum role has been applied. The user still has a group forum role applied, so I click on the **Advanced permissions** link.

You can select any permission you want to grant. In this case, I granted the **Can post stickies** permission by changing it to **Yes**. Since multiple forums should be shown on the screen, do this for each forum in the category. See Figure 8.25, which shows only the permissions for the Teacher forums category.

Clicking the **Apply permissions** button will make the permission stick for this category, or click all of them and press the **Apply all permissions** button at the bottom of the page. Now Jane Doe has the necessary added permission, but it was done outside of the forum role.

Chapter 9 | Handling versioning

Like all good software, phpBB evolves over time. Due to its rich feature set, phpBB tends to evolve slowly. However, board administrators still should keep phpBB software up-to-date, principally so any security issues that are found can be promptly addressed.

Handling versioning is addressed in two ways: updating and upgrading. We'll discuss each in detail.

Understanding phpBB's versioning nomenclature

phpBB adopted Composer's versioning system, which is widely used in open source software.

phpBB consists of *major versions*, *minor versions* and *micro versions*, where each is a number separated by a period: major-version.minor-version.micro-version, ex: 3.3.1.

In this case:

- 3 is the major version

- 3.3 is the minor version

- 3.3.1 is the micro version

Version 3.3 is a minor version of version 3, and 3.3.1 is a micro version of minor version 3.3.

Micro versions are small changes principally to fix bugs and newly-found security issues. Occasionally, a new feature will be introduced in a micro version, but it's unusual. For example, phpBB 3.0.6 added a feed capability.

Updating vs. upgrading

Going from one micro version to another, such as 3.3.0 to 3.3.1, uses an *update* process. The work involved is relatively straightforward.

An *upgrade* is when you move from minor versions, like 3.0 to 3.3, which tends to involve more work and risk. An upgrade process should also apply to moving from version 3.3 to 4.0, when 4.0 is released.

Minor version upgrades don't tend to introduce a lot of new features. As a result, a lot of board administrators wonder why they should upgrade to the next minor version. Most minor releases are focused on keeping phpBB current with the PHP programming language as it evolves. phpBB 3.2 was released in part to ensure compatibility with PHP 7.3 and 7.4, which had become widely available. phpBB 3.3 is compatible with PHP 8. New versions of PHP include new features that phpBB can use, and optimizations designed to let programs run faster.

phpBB also supports *conversions*, allowing you to potentially migrate to phpBB from another forum solution. Migrating from phpBB 2.0 to 3.x is such a major change that it is considered a conversion.

In this chapter, we discuss handling updates and upgrades. Conversions are rare, so they are discussed in Appendix D.

Generally, at least a few times a year, the phpBB Group will release an update. Every few years, the software will get an upgrade. There are no scheduled release dates. However, you should see a notice in the ACP if a new version is available (Figure 9.1).

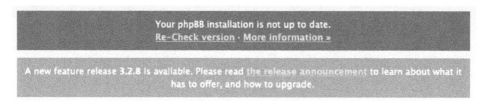

Figure 9.1: New version dialog boxes

Styling, language and extension considerations

Going from one version of phpBB to another often involves more than updating phpBB.

You should also update your style, if a new version of your style is available. This is because new *template events* can be introduced. Newer extensions and phpBB could use these new events, so if your style can't hook into these events, certain features of these extensions potentially can't be used.

Fortunately, the default prosilver style always includes the most recent template events, and all styles inherit these templates from the prosilver style unless a style has their own version of a template.

The British English language pack is also updated with every release. But if you use another language pack, it should be updated, if a newer version is available.

During an upgrade or update, it's also a good time to update any extensions that may have a newer version available. Official extensions are reviewed by the phpBB Group before being included in their Customisation Database, but it's always possible that a security or performance issue will be discovered, or that there are some bugs that need to be fixed. There may be new features in your extensions as well. Sometimes if there is a new version of an extension, phpBB will update it as part of an update.

Updating phpBB

If an update is available to phpBB, you will see a notice when you enter the Administration Control Panel (Figure 9.1).

Note: You can get a more expanded page of information by clicking on the **More information** link, which takes you to: **ACP > System > Automation > Check for updates**. The page contains a list of steps we will cover in more detail.

Updating methods

phpBB supports four ways of updating documented on its Downloads page:

- **Update (previously Full package)**

- **Advanced Update (previously Automatic update)**

- **Patch Files**

- **Changed Files**

Generally, you should only use the Update method. The Advanced Update and Patch Files methods are only used if you made changes to phpBB's source code that you need to retain in a newer version of phpBB. This requires PHP programming skills that most people don't have. If you have these skills, you shouldn't find the Advanced Update or Patch Files updating methods intimidating.

All methods have a number of manual steps, and all ask you to back up your board's database and files as a precaution before updating.

Updating phpBB is not computationally intensive, so it generally takes only a few seconds to run the update script. The exception is if you use the Advanced Update or Patch Files methods, where you may have to decide how to incorporate your custom changes.

The general steps for updating are:

1. Disable the board

2. Back up the database

3. Back up the files

4. Perform the update using your chosen updating method

5. Update styles, language packs and extensions if needed

6. Re-enable the board

Why you should disable the board before updating

The official instructions don't include this step, but I always do this when I update a board for my clients.

Unless you disable the board, it's possible (but unlikely) that while the updated files are uploading that users will notice some inconsistencies, triggering errors or warnings that might alarm them. Some of these can't be avoided. By disabling the board, most likely all the user is likely to see is a message saying the board is disabled.

Also, when backing up a database, you want it to be consistent in case you have to recover it should the update fail. For example, if your database is very large, the phpbb_posts table may be backed up ten minutes before the phpbb_topics table. If you have to recover the database later on, there may be database inconsistencies: topics may be in the database for posts that don't exist.

So, by disabling the board, users cannot make any changes to the database, so this potential problem can't occur.

As soon as the install folder is uploaded, phpBB will detect it and effectively disable the board.

Back up the database

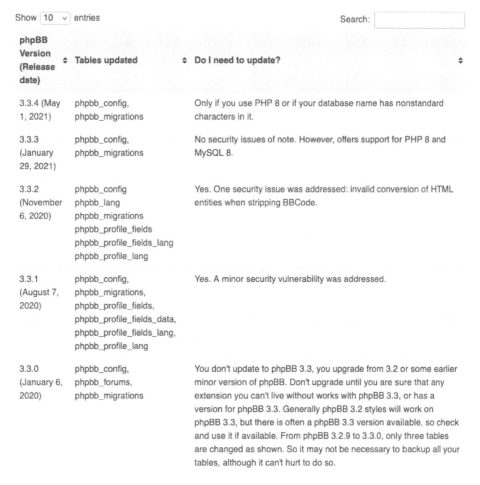

phpBB 3.3 (Proteus)

Show 10 ∨ entries   Search: [   ]

phpBB Version (Release date) ⬍	Tables updated ⬍	Do I need to update? ⬍
3.3.4 (May 1, 2021)	phpbb_config, phpbb_migrations	Only if you use PHP 8 or if your database name has nonstandard characters in it.
3.3.3 (January 29, 2021)	phpbb_config, phpbb_migrations	No security issues of note. However, offers support for PHP 8 and MySQL 8.
3.3.2 (November 6, 2020)	phpbb_config phpbb_lang phpbb_migrations phpbb_profile_fields phpbb_profile_fields_lang phpbb_profile_lang	Yes. One security issue was addressed: invalid conversion of HTML entities when stripping BBCode.
3.3.1 (August 7, 2020)	phpbb_config, phpbb_migrations, phpbb_profile_fields, phpbb_profile_fields_data, phpbb_profile_fields_lang, phpbb_profile_lang	Yes. A minor security vulnerability was addressed.
3.3.0 (January 6, 2020)	phpbb_config, phpbb_forums, phpbb_migrations	You don't update to phpBB 3.3, you upgrade from 3.2 or some earlier minor version of phpBB. Don't upgrade until you are sure that any extension you can't live without works with phpBB 3.3, or has a version for phpBB 3.3. Generally phpBB 3.2 styles will work on phpBB 3.3, but there is often a phpBB 3.3 version available, so check and use it if available. From phpBB 3.2.9 to 3.3.0, only three tables are changed as shown. So it may not be necessary to backup all your tables, although it can't hurt to do so.

Figure 9.2: Tables changed during an update are documented on my website

In the last chapter, I demonstrated various ways to back up the database.

The phpBB Group does not mention that updates generally update the database minimally, leaving most tables unchanged. So, you can save a lot of hassle by backing up only the tables that will be changed by the update, instead of all your tables. To help you out, I keep a page on my website that indicates the tables you need to backup:

https://www.phpbbservices.com/do-i-need-to-update/

Figure 9.2 is just a snapshot because the page is updated with every release.

For most updates, you only have to back up the phpbb_config and the phpbb_migrations tables. These tables are guaranteed to change with an update.

To use this page, look at the version you currently have installed. You can see it when entering the Administration Control Panel. For example, if you have version 3.3.1 and the latest version is 3.3.4, then examine the rows for version 3.3.2, 3.3.3 and 3.3.4. You only need to back up the tables for these versions.

You can make a backup inside phpBB:

ACP > Maintenance > Database > Backup

I recommend you download the backup created and check its integrity and completeness, using techniques discussed in the last chapter.

Back up the files

You can save some time by backing up only the files in phpBB that contain data.

If you use this approach, make sure that you have a reference copy of your current version of phpBB in case you need to recover the board's software to your earlier version of phpBB. If you need a reference copy of an older version of phpBB, use this URL:

https://download.phpbb.com/pub/release/3.*mm*/3.3.*mmm*/phpBB-3.*mm.mmm*.zip

where *mm* is the minor version of phpBB (like 3 in 3.3) and *mmm* is the micro version of phpBB (like 7 in 3.3.7.)

Here is an example for downloading a full archive of phpBB 3.3.7:

https://download.phpbb.com/pub/release/3.3/3.3.7/phpBB-3.3.7.zip

Back up the following files and folders:

- **config.php**. The instructions warn you not to overwrite this file, but it's a critical file. It's easy to accidentally delete it and can be a pain to restore, so you might as well back it up. It contains the key information that connects your board to your database.

- **/ext**. Your extensions are here. If the folder gets deleted during an update, then there will be errors when going into the Manage extensions page. That's because the extensions' software is missing, while the database will still show them as installed.

- **/files**. All your post and private message attachments are in here.

- **/images**. Any uploaded avatars, smilies, icons and ranks are uploaded here.

- **/store**. Your database backups and other persistent data files are written here.

- **/styles**. If you don't use the prosilver style, back it up. If you use only the prosilver style, back this up if you made any changes to the prosilver style that will need to be reapplied.

An arguably faster approach is to use your web host control panel's file manager to create an archive of your entire board. If you do this, be careful to select all files and folders for your board. Also, make sure the archive is stored somewhere outside of your board's folder, or download it. Expand the archive on your computer to make sure it is complete.

Warning: on large boards with many attachments, making an archive could exceed your allowed file space. If this happens, use the web host control panel's file manager to delete the partial archive, skipping the step to move it into the trash. Then use FTP to download the files.

Note: If you make a database backup in phpBB, the resulting archive is placed in the /store folder. By saving the store folder when backing up files, you are also saving the database.

Update method (previously Full package method)

This is the typical method used to update phpBB and the only method recommended by the phpBB Group. After much trial and error with the other methods, it's the only way I use when doing updates for clients. The instructions are on the **Check for Updates** page in the ACP, but only if there is an update available.

ACP > System > Automation > Check for updates

These are a set of expanded steps that I use for my clients. phpBB's instructions assume a generic installation of phpBB, which I don't assume. So I recommend these procedures instead.

1. **Disable your board: ACP > General > Board configuration > Board settings > Disable board > Yes**

2. **Back up the necessary database tables**. Use the process discussed above and in Chapter 8. You don't need to backup all your tables in most cases.

3. **Back up the files**. Use the process discussed in the last section and in Chapter 8. It can't hurt to back up everything, but you may choose to backup only the data files.

4. **Download the latest version of phpBB**. The latest version of phpBB is available on phpbb.com on its **Downloads** page:

   https://www.phpbb.com/downloads/

   Typically, the zip file archive is downloaded. A bz2 archive is also available.

5. **Expand the archive on your computer.**

6. **Delete items from the archive**. The main approach here is to delete certain files and folders from the new version that you download from phpbb.com before you upload it. These files and folders must be removed:

   - config.php
   - /files folder
   - /images folder
   - /store folder

   Double-check that you did this correctly because otherwise you may lose information.

7. **On your website, delete all files from your board EXCEPT for:**

- The config.php file

- The /ext folder

- The /images folder

- The /files folder

- The /store folder

- The /styles folder

8. **Upload all the files**. Make sure you upload to your phpBB root folder. Thousands of files are uploaded, so the process will take some time.

   An install folder is uploaded as part of this process. As soon as it is uploaded, your board is effectively disabled. phpBB will notice its presence and show the user a message saying the board is unavailable.

9. **Check the file permissions**. The cache folder must have 777 permissions (for Linux systems), or be publicly writeable. The /files, /images/avatars/upload and /store folders should also retain 777 permission settings too. Other folders should have 755 permissions. Ordinary files normally have 644 permissions. Ideally, the config.php file will have 640 permissions.

10. **Run the update program**. There is a link you can use in Step 8 of the instructions at **ACP > System > Automation > Check for updates**.

Figure 9.3: Update database screen

11. You can also use:

http://forums.myspecialdomain.com/install/app.php/update

phpBB will detect that you've already uploaded the files, so you only need to update the database. See Figure 9.3.

Press **Submit**. This will start a script that makes the necessary changes to your database. At least two things will happen:

- The phpbb_config table will be updated to indicate the updated version of phpBB.

- The phpbb_migrations table will record each migration program that was successfully completed.

The update program may make other changes to the database too depending on the features of the new release. All of these update programs are in the /phpbb/db/migration/data folder.

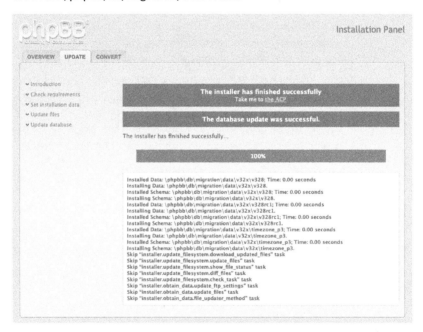

Figure 9.4: Running the database upgrade program

If you are curious, you can see what these programs actually do and what tables they affect. For example, the v330x folder contains migration programs for version 3.3.x, but not 3.3.0. There are typically one or more release candidate programs such as v336rc1.php that are run before the main script is run, v336.php in this case. These programs may call other programs which you can read.

When complete, you should see a screen telling you the installer has completed, and a list of the actions taken will appear in a window (Figure 9.4).

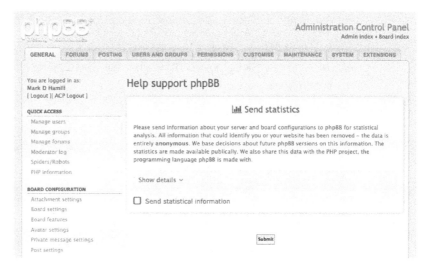

Figure 9.5: Administration Control Panel initial screen after an update

Clicking on the link to the ACP will give you the Help support phpBB screen (Figure 9.5). You may also see a checkbox to optionally enable the Viglink extension.

You can share your board's statistics anonymously with the phpBB group by clicking the **Send statistical information** checkbox.

Press **Submit**.

12. **Remove the install folder**. If you don't, you will get a warning when you go to the main Administration Control Panel screen because your board is disabled. You can use FTP or your web host control panel's file manager.

13. **Update any styles and language packs**. Skip this if you are using the prosilver style with no changes and the British English language pack only. See sections of Chapters 5 and 6 for procedures for installing styles and language packs.

You can upload the newer version of the styles and language packs, overwriting the old files. Language pack files and folders are uploaded to your phpBB root folder. Style files and folders are uploaded to the styles folder.

If you made changes to the style, they will need to be reapplied. To get around this problem, see Appendix C: Creating a custom style.

You should not need to disable the old style and language pack first.

14. **Optionally, update out-of-date extensions**. The update program might update some extensions for you. Otherwise, see Chapter 6 for more details on updating extensions.

    The old version must be disabled, its files removed, the new files uploaded correctly, and each extension re-enabled. This process is detailed on the Manage extensions page: **ACP > Customise > Extension management > Manage extensions**

15. **Re-enable the board**: **ACP > General > Board configuration > Board settings > Disable board > No**

16. **Test**. Navigate around your board to make sure it is behaving correctly. You might want to make and delete a test post.

In the event of a major error, both your files and database prior to the update are stored and can be reloaded. See Chapter 8 for the methods you can use.

Advanced Update (previously Changed Files) method

This method should only be used if you added code changes to phpBB's base code that need to be retained. You are prompted individually if you want to retain your code changes if they are in any of the changed files.

Using this method, except for the /vendor folder, you upload only files that have changed between your current version of phpBB and the latest. These are stashed temporarily inside the /install folder.

On the phpbb.com **Downloads** page, you select the **Advanced Update** tab.

You must first select your current version of phpBB from the dropdown control. See Figure 9.6.

Figure 9.6 - Advanced Update (choose current phpBB version)

After picking your current version from the dropdown, press **Select**. On the next screen click on the link for the archive type you want, either a zip or a bz2 archive (Figure 9.7). The archive will be downloaded.

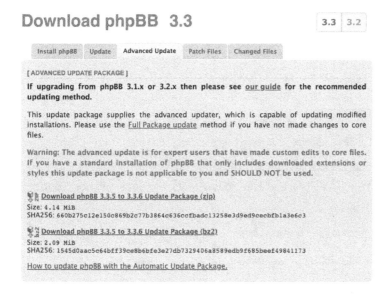

Figure 9.7 - Advanced Update (select archive type)

Expand the archive you downloaded. Note that the archive contains three folders: docs, install and vendor. (Figure 9.8)

Name	Date Modified	Size	Kind
> docs	Mar 14, 2022 at 4:17 PM	--	Folder
∨ install	Today at 7:14 PM	--	Folder
app.php	Mar 14, 2022 at 4:17 PM	2 KB	text document
> convert	Mar 14, 2022 at 4:17 PM	--	Folder
index.html	Mar 14, 2022 at 4:17 PM	226 bytes	HTML text
phpbbcli.php	Mar 14, 2022 at 4:17 PM	2 KB	text document
phpinfo.php	Mar 14, 2022 at 4:17 PM	300 bytes	text document
startup.php	Mar 14, 2022 at 4:17 PM	10 KB	text document
∨ update	Today at 7:14 PM	--	Folder
index.php	Mar 14, 2022 at 4:29 PM	2 KB	text document
> new	Mar 14, 2022 at 4:29 PM	--	Folder
> old	Mar 14, 2022 at 4:29 PM	--	Folder
> vendor	Mar 14, 2022 at 4:26 PM	--	Folder

Figure 9.8 - Advanced Update archive

If you open the install folder, you will see an update folder. Inside the update folder you will see new and old folders. The file names and folder names inside these new and old folders will match. These contain the old and new version of each program that was changed.

The vendor folder contains third party libraries phpBB uses. These are wholly replaced with every release, so there will be thousands of files inside this folder.

You must follow most of the steps for the full package method. Refer to the full package method for details. The actual steps are:

1. Disable your board

2. Back up your database

3. Back up your files

4. Delete the vendor folder. If using FTP, this may take many minutes as there are thousands of files to delete. It's faster to delete it using your web host control panel's file manager.

5. Upload the install folder in the archive

6. Upload the vendor folder in the archive

7. Optionally, delete the docs folder on your server then upload the new docs folder

8. Make sure the cache folder has public write (777) permissions

9. Run the install script following the same procedures as with the full update approach. However, you need to pick the **Update filesystem and database** radio button before submitting the form.

   http://forums.myspecialdomain.com/install/app.php/update

10. Depending on your file permissions, you can choose whether to:

    - Download an archive with the modified files. With this approach you later upload these, overwriting phpBB's files.

    - Update files with FTP. You must provide a set of valid FTP credentials for your server for this to work.

    - Update files with direct access. This will only work if you can write to these files.

11. Click the **Update files** button

12. If you chose the download an archive option, you now expand that archive and upload it to your phpBB root folder with FTP, choosing to overwrite files with the same name.

13. Upon successful completion, remove the install folder

14. Update any styles and language packs

15. Optionally update any extensions

16. Re-enable your board

17. Test the board

Patch files update method

There is not much to say about this method except that if you are familiar with Unix patch files, you can use it. It's designed for those who have made changes to phpBB's code that need to be kept with an update.

If you use this method, you should still backup your database and files first. You should also disable the board before starting and re-enable it afterwards.

On phpbb.com's **Downloads** page, you select the **Patch Files** tab then download either the zip or the bz2 archive. This is then expanded.

Inside, you will see a list of .patch files, one for every version since phpBB 3.1.0, with a naming convention similar to that used for the advanced update method. These .patch files are essentially instructions that indicate snippets of code to find, change, add or delete based on changes to be made to them. The Linux `patch` command can read them and take necessary actions to delete, add or modify the changed lines of code. You will be prompted to make a decision on how to apply a particular patch.

While this patches the necessary files, if you use this method, you still need to upload the install and vendor folders in the archive.

There is also a complicated command you have to execute from the command line on your server using SSH:

```
patch -cl -d PHPBB_DIRECTORY -p1 < PATCH_NAME
```

PHPBB_DIRECTORY is the directory path that your phpBB installation resides in, for example /var/www/mydomain/phpbb, or a relative path from your current directory. PATCH_NAME is the relevant filename of the selected patch file. An example of how this might look if you were in your board's main directory and the .patch file was uploaded to it would be (all on one line):

```
patch -cl -d ./ -p1 < ./phpBB-3.3.0_to_3.3.7_patch
```

You will be asked to make decisions on whether to retain customizations in your code. It's possible that you will have to revise or remove the code to make it work correctly. So this process assumes a high level of understanding on the PHP programming language.

Afterward, you can delete the .patch file.

You still need to update the database, which the phpBB group recommends doing from the command line:

```
php ./bin/phpbbcli.php db:migrate --safe-mode
```

The phpBB group discourages the patch method of updating. You shouldn't entertain this approach unless you are a skilled Linux administrator and have the requisite PHP programming skills. If you have these skills, you can figure out this method.

Even so, it is somewhat problematic. You may encounter HUNK FAILED errors. This is why if you made code changes to phpBB, the phpBB Group recommends using the Advanced update method instead, which offers a more failsafe approach.

Changed files method

With this method, rather than uploading 4000+ files in the full archive of a new release of phpBB, you upload only the files that have changed. However, the vendor folder must be uploaded in its entirety, even though typically the libraries in the vendor folder don't change much or at all between releases. The vendor folder is huge with about 2500 files. So while this reduces the number of files uploaded somewhat, it won't speed up the time for doing an update that much.

Given that you might have changed some files since your last update or upgrade, the phpBB Group does not recommend this approach, as this could leave old software on your machine.

The steps for using this method are:

1. **Download and expand the latest archive.** On phpbb.com's **Downloads** page, you select the **Changed Files** tab then download either the zip or the bz2 archive. This is then expanded.

2. **Extract the archive containing the changed files you need.** As with the patch files update method, inside the archive you will see a number of files. In this case, each is an archives containing the changed files needed since the release. For example, assuming you downloaded a zip archive, if you downloaded the phpBB 3.3.7 changed files archive, all the file changes between phpBB 3.3.0 and 3.3.7 would be in an archive phpBB-3.3.0_to_3.3.7.zip. Expand this archive. In this case the folder would be named phpBB-3.3.0_to_3.3.7. Inside you should see a number of folders.

3. **Upload three folders.** The **docs**, **install** and **vendor** folders need to be uploaded to your phpBB root directory. The docs and vendor folders are wholly replaced. To be safe I would first remove the docs and vendor folders with FTP or a file manager before uploading the new folders. (The install folder should not be there.)

4. **Upload the changes files.** In the example in Step 2, the folder uploaded would be phpBB-3.3.0_to_3.3.7. These files would then be uploaded to your phpBB root directory, overwriting the old files.

5. **Run the database script.** Ex:

   http://forums.myspecialdomain.com/install/app.php/update

   Press the **Submit** button and allow the script to finish.

6. **Remove the install folder.** If you don't, you will get a warning when you go to the main Administration Control Panel screen because your board is disabled. You can use FTP or your web host control panel's file manager.

7. **Update any styles and language packs.** Skip this if you are using the prosilver style with no changes and the British English language pack only. See sections of Chapters 5 and 6 for procedures for installing styles and language packs.

   You can upload the newer versions, overwriting the old files. If you made changes to the style, they will need to be reapplied. To get around this problem, see Appendix C: Creating a custom style. You should not need to disable the old style and language pack first.

8. **Optionally, update out-of-date extensions**. The update program might update some extensions for you. Otherwise, see Chapter 6 for more details on updating extensions. The old version must be disabled, its files removed, the new files uploaded correctly, and each extension re-enabled. This process is detailed on the Manage extensions page: **ACP > Customise > Extension management > Manage extensions**

9. **Re-enable the board**: **ACP > General > Board configuration > Board settings > Disable board > No**

10. **Test**. Navigate around your board to make sure it is behaving correctly. You might want to make and delete a test post.

Upgrading phpBB

Introduction

As mentioned, upgrading is when you move from one minor version of phpBB to another, such as from 3.1 to 3.3, or 3.0 to 3.3.

The instructions will vary based on your current minor version of phpBB. For example, moving from 3.0 to 3.3 is more complicated and time consuming than moving from 3.1 to 3.3.

A summary of the upgrade process to phpBB 3.3 is on the phpbb.com website:

https://www.phpbb.com/support/docs/en/3.3/ug/upgradeguide/

We'll go through it in detail in this section.

Risks of upgrading

A lot more will happen in an upgrade compared with an update, so it's inherently a lot riskier.

An upgrade from phpBB 3.2 to 3.3 is relatively simple and largely risk free. The discussion below is more focused on upgrades from phpBB 3.0 or 3.1 to the latest version of phpBB 3.x.

An upgrade from 3.1 to 3.x is more challenging, and upgrades from 3.0 can be even more challenging. In these cases, it's a good idea to warn users that the board may be down for a day or so. It's also a good idea to schedule the work for non-peak times, particularly if your board tends to be busy.

During upgrades, particularly from 3.0 or 3.1, hosting resource limits are much more likely to occur, especially on shared servers. This is because upgrades typically do a lot more work, and the board's database may change a lot.

In about twenty percent of the cases I encounter, these problems are so severe that I end up downloading the database to my machine, converting it there, then uploading it back to the server.

With upgrades from 3.0 or 3.1, the more posts you have, the more likely you are to encounter resource limitations. I often see them when a board has 200,000 to 500,000 posts.

You can reduce the likelihood of these limitations by upgrading from the command line. This requires SSH privileges. Using SSH is challenging if you are not technically inclined, but is covered in this section.

Planning for an upgrade

Successful upgrades are a result of careful planning.

When phpBB 3.2.0 was released, many boards were upgraded immediately, and administrators found their styles and many of their extensions didn't work.

Don't upgrade until you:

- Verify there is a version of your style for the new version of phpBB, unless you are comfortable using the default prosilver style. Check the free styles in phpbb.com's **Customisation Database**. Make sure you open the **All branches** dropdown and select the current minor version of phpBB:

  https://www.phpbb.com/customise/db/styles-2

- Verify if there are versions of your extensions that will work for the new version of phpBB, unless you can tolerate waiting for a compatible extension to become available, which might be forever. In phpbb.com's **Customisation Database**, make sure you click the **All branches** dropdown and select the current minor version of phpBB:

  https://www.phpbb.com/customise/db/extensions-36

When upgrading my clients, the client will frequently take the risk of using a version of an extension or a style that is not yet approved, if discussion on the extension's support page indicates an earlier version works on the new version, or if there is a stable version available that is not yet approved. Since it can take months for the phpBB Group to review a style or extension, this often becomes a pragmatic approach and an acceptable risk. The phpBB Group though would discourage this approach.

You also need to check the newest version of phpBB's system requirements and make sure your hosting can accommodate them. The system requirements for phpBB 3.3 are at:

https://www.phpbb.com/support/docs/en/3.3/ug/quickstart/requirements/

Note your version of PHP. You can see it in the ACP. If it's not on the main screen, look for it under:

ACP > General > Board configuration > PHP Information

For phpBB 3.3, you must have at least PHP 7.1.3 enabled for your board.

You also should decide whether to upgrade using a browser or from the command line. It's generally safe to upgrade using a browser if:

- Your board is relatively small

- You are upgrading from phpBB 3.2 to 3.3

Seriously consider upgrading from the command line if your board is large (200,000 plus posts) *and* you are upgrading from phpBB 3.0 or 3.1 to phpBB 3.x. If all this is true and your board has more than 500,000 posts, you should use the command line.

To use the command line, you will need to:

- **Get SSH credentials to your server**. If you don't have any, you can create these in your web host control panel. The host should provide detailed instructions for properly connecting with SSH, including the IP or domain name to use, ports, usernames, passwords and private/public key requirements, if any.

- **Configure SSH**. Windows users can download and use Putty. Newer versions of Windows 10 can support SSH if the feature is enabled. It is accessed from the command prompt. Mac or Linux users have a terminal application built in to their operating system. They will use it to run the ssh command.

- **Find the path to your board on the web server**. You may be able to infer it from the file manager in your web host control panel. Or, it may take a support ticket with your web host.

- **Learn some basic Unix commands**. You will need to learn cd (change directory), ls (list files), pwd (print working directory) and chmod.

- **Read up on how to upgrade from the command line and what to expect.** From your board's root folder, you will need to execute the following command:

```
php ./bin/phpbbcli.php db:migrate –safe-mode
```

The full command line interface is documented at:

http://area51.phpbb.com/docs/dev/3.3.x/cli/index.html

Special preparations for upgrading from phpBB 3.0

When you upgrade phpBB from version 3.0, you have some additional things to think through and prepare for:

- **Your style will probably need to be replaced.** If you used the prosilver style, no worries. Otherwise, there is a good chance that your current style is not available for the current version of phpBB. You can view a list of styles here:

https://www.phpbb.com/customise/db/styles/board_styles-12

Open the dropdown to see what styles are available for your new version of phpBB.

When you find a style you want to use, download it and then expand the archive.

A lot of my clients had the old subsilver2 style carried over from phpBB 2's subsilver default style. It's no longer available because it is not responsive. The closest style to it is the Allan Style-SUBSILVER style.

- **Your mods (modifications) will not work.** Instead, you will use extensions. So, you need to analyze the modifications you have installed and see if there is an equivalent extension for the version of phpBB to which you will upgrade.

A number of functions handled by mods are now built in. For example, there are more effective built-in spambot countermeasures, so if you were using an antispam mod, you probably won't need an antispam extension.

Make sure you install only approved extensions that will work on the new version of phpBB. Look through phpbb.com's **Customisations Database** for the phpBB version you will upgrade to, search for relevant topics and ask questions.

Sometimes an extension author will stop working on an extension. Sometimes a version for the latest version of phpBB is in development.

- **Your database should be cleaned up before you upgrade.** Be prepared for this extra work. We'll cover the program to use to clean up your database properly.

- **Any custom code changes you made will be lost.** Trying to reapply these changes in the latest version of phpBB probably won't work. This is because phpBB's programs have changed so massively. If you're lucky, someone will have developed an extension that handles the functionality you added by hand to your old version.

Running an upgrade

1. **Disable your board: ACP > General > Board configuration > Board settings > Disable board > Yes**

2. **Back up your database's tables**. If this is an upgrade from phpBB 3.0 or 3.1, you must back up *all your tables*. It's the only way to fully recover! For upgrades from 3.2 to 3.3, you might want to check my Do I need to update? web page because the number of tables changed is relatively small.

3. **Back up all your board's files**. See the process in the Full update section. But since this is an upgrade, you *must* back up everything if you need the ability to fully revert to the old version.

4. **Deactivate all styles except the prosilver style and make prosilver the active style**

   - For phpBB 3.1+:

     o If the prosilver style is not enabled, it can be enabled: **ACP > Customise > Style management > Install Styles > prosilver.** Then select prosilver as the default style: **ACP > General > Board settings > Default style > prosilver**

     o All other styles should be deactivated too. **ACP > Customise > Style management > Manage styles**

   - For phpBB 3.0:

- o If the prosilver style is not enabled, enable it: **ACP > Styles > Style management > Styles > prosilver.** Then select prosilver as the default style: **ACP > General > Board settings > Default style > prosilver**

- o All other styles should be deactivated too. **ACP > Styles > Style management > Manage styles**

5. **Make a note of any license keys for your modifications.** Certain phpBB 3.0 mods, most typically Cleantalk and Tapatalk, require that you to enter license keys to use them. You will have to reenter the keys when you install the extensions, so write these down as they are likely to get erased. Usually these will be found in modules on the .MOD tab in the ACP.

6. **If you are upgrading from phpBB 3.0, remove mod-related changes from the database.** If you've never installed any mods, you may be able to skip this step, but you might encounter errors during the upgrade, so I recommend doing it anyway.

Figure 9.9: Support Toolkit for phpBB 3.0, database cleaner screen

a. Download the Support Toolkit (STK) for phpBB 3.0 from https://www.phpbb.com/support/stk/. Note that the STK won't work if you upgraded PHP to version 7 already. Presumably you can enable a version of PHP 5 temporarily.

b. Expand the archive on your computer.

c. Inside the archive, upload the stk folder to your board's root folder, so a stk folder is inside it.

d. Start the Support Toolkit with a URL similar to the following:
    http://forums.myspecialdomain.com/stk

e. Click on the **Support Tools** tab.
    Select the **Database Cleaner** link (Figure 9.9).
    Note: If you get a "Parse error: syntax error, unexpected 'new' (T_NEW)" error, you are running PHP 7. You should downgrade your PHP temporarily to any version of PHP 5 available, typically 5.6. You should be able to do this in your web host control panel.

    Press **Continue**, which will disable the board. What you see next depends on what the Support Toolkit detects. It will show you the tables that may need adjusting, which usually includes the phpbb_mods table. Any checked tables will be dropped. See Figure 9.10.

Figure 9.10: Support toolkit, database cleaner screen

f. Press **Continue** again to start the database cleaning process. You may get multiple screens where you are asked to make some decisions on whether to keep or add various tables or table columns, depending on what the program finds. The database cleaner compares your tables, table columns and configuration variables with a reference phpBB 3.0.14 installation, and will ask you to make decisions about any variances. You may also be asked to reset permissions and roles to the defaults and remove any report reasons you added.

If a mod you were using is available as an extension, you plan to enable the extension, *and* you want to retain any settings from the mod, the database cleaner will point out the additional tables and columns. You should retain these but tell the program to remove others. Many extensions ported from modifications have scripts that can carry these settings into the extension. You should check the extension's FAQ to see if this is in fact the case. If it is not, you can use the STK to remove tables, columns and configuration variables created by the mod.

When complete, you should get a message summarizing the work done.

g. The STK previously disabled your board, but reenables it on exit. You should disable the board again to ensure consistency: **ACP > General > Board settings > Disable board > Yes**

5. **Disable applicable extensions**. For phpBB 3.1 or higher, disable extensions incompatible with the version of phpBB you are upgrading to.

You can click on the **Details** link for an extension to see what version of phpBB the extension author asserts the extension should work with:

ACP > Customise > Extension management > Manage extensions

See Figure 9.11 as an example. This extension asserts that it will work with any version of phpBB equal to or greater than 3.2.0, including 3.3 when released.

Requirements

phpBB Version: >=3.2.0

PHP Version: >=5.4.7

Figure 9.11: Example of an extension's version requirements

Click on the **Disable** link for the extension to disable it.

7. **Set British English as the only enabled language pack**. If you aren't using any other language packs, you can skip this step. *Note: You aren't actually deleting these from the file system; you are just disabling them.*

    - phpBB 3.1+: **ACP > Customise > Language management > Language packs.** Disable any non-British English language packs. Enable the British English language pack if it is disabled.

    - phpBB 3.0: **ACP > System > General tasks > Language packs.** Disable any non-British English language packs. Enable the British English language pack if it is disabled.

8. You should set the default and guest style to prosilver, if you haven't done this already: **ACP > General > Board configuration > Board settings > Default style > prosilver**

9. **Download the phpBB 3.3 Full Package archive**. You can do this from phpbb.com's Downloads page.

10. **Extract the contents of the archive to your computer and open the phpBB3 directory**.

11. **Delete the following files from the package:**

    - The config.php file

    - The images/ directory

    - The files/ directory

    - The store/ directory

12. **On your website, delete all files from your board except:**

    - The config.php file

- The /ext directory, if it exists. (It won't exist for an upgrade from phpBB 3.0.)

- The /images directory

- The /files directory

- The /store directory

- Any other files you added outside of phpBB. For example, it you have a favicon, you might want to retain this file, a robots.txt file if it exists, or a PHP error log file.

13. **Upload the contents to your board's directory**. Move the files from your computer to your board's directory. You may be prompted to overwrite the remaining files. If prompted to merge or overwrite directories, choose to overwrite them. Use FTP to upload them.

14. **Check folder permissions**. The /cache, /files, /images/avatars/upload and /store folders should be publicly writeable, i.e. 777 permissions on Linux-based systems. Change if needed.

15. **Change your config.php file, if necessary**. phpBB 3.3 won't work with PHP 5. So if upgrading from phpBB 3.0 or 3.1, look at your config.php file. If the you see the line:

```
$dbms = 'mysql';
```

then change it to:

```
$dbms = 'mysqli';
```

16. **Change your version of PHP if needed.** phpBB 3.3 works on PHP 7.1.3 or higher, and that includes PHP 8.0 and 8.1. phpBB 3.2 works on PHP 5.4.7 through 7.2. You can usually change the version of PHP you are using in your web host control panel, sometimes only for the directory containing phpBB.

If you are using other software on your site, this other software may stop working or show errors if you change the PHP version. If you are using WordPress and keeping it regularly updated, it should not be an issue. If you have older software, like Joomla, you may have issues; so if it's an option, limit the PHP version you choose to affect just to your board folder.

17. **Upgrade the database.** This is where the bulk of the work is done. Your phpBB database has to be upgraded to add new tables and columns expected for the new version. Rows may be added to some tables too, or deleted from some tables, particularly the phpbb_config table. Some data munging occurs too. This is a process that could take only a few seconds when updating from 3.2 to 3.3. But when upgrading from other versions on very large boards, it can take hours. You can do this either from a web browser or from the command line.

Using a browser, go to the install folder, ex:

http://forums.myspecialdomain.com/install/app.php/update

- The **Update database only** button should be the only choice. So press **Submit.**

- Wait for the progress bar to reach 100% and for a message indicating that the update has completed. *Note: If you don't see a progress bar, don't panic. It's nice to see a progress bar, but eventually the screen will show the percent completed.*

From the command line:

- Connect to your web host with Putty or the Command Prompt (Windows) or Terminal using SSH.

- Navigate to your board's root folder using the cd command

- Execute the command:

```
./bin/phpbbcli.php db:migrate --safe-mode
```

or if that doesn't work try:

```
php ./bin/phpbbcli.php db:migrate --safe-mode
```

Note: in some cases, the php command will execute an older version of PHP than the one you need. You will see an error if this occurs. You may need to point it to the path where your version of PHP exists. Your web host can provide this information. You must run a version of PHP compatible with the version of phpBB that you are updating to.

- Since you are at the command line, no windowing will appear. The status of actions will appear as text when completed. Red text will appear if an error occurs and the update will stop. You should fix any underlying problem, then issue the command again. It should resume at the point of failure.

- When done, type `exit` and press **Enter** or **Return** to close the SSH connection.

You may get error messages that stops the upgrade. If they appear, it is most likely because you have run out of allowed resources, such as the maximum time a script can run or the maximum amount of database resources you can use. Often waiting fifteen minutes or an hour will reset the clock, allowing you to resume.

Occasionally, there will be error messages that point to an inconsistent database that the upgrade program can't resolve. With the right preparation, this is unlikely to happen. But if it occurs, you may need to work with a phpBB consultant such as myself. You can also seek support on the support forums on phpbb.com. Generally, it involves going into the database using a tool like phpMyAdmin and fixing the error, which can be inferred from the error message, and then restarting the database upgrade.

Sometimes just restarting the upgrade program will work, particularly if it's a matter of running out of resources, which is a temporary condition. The upgrade program keeps track of steps that were completed successfully and won't repeat them. If this seems to be working, keep trying. You may eventually complete the upgrade.

Tip: If it stops repeatedly with a timeout error message, you may want to use the CLI (command line interface). First delete any io.lock file in your board's /store folder and restart. You can do this with FTP or using your web host control panel's file manager.

When completed, you will either get a green dialog box reporting successful completion, similar to Figure 9.5, or on the command line you will see a green successful completion message. When using a browser, the green dialog box should include a link to the ACP. Go into the ACP regardless.

18. **Check the search index and remake it if necessary.** If you were using the MySQL fulltext index as your search index, the update script may drop it. This means you may need to remake your search index.

If you need to re-create the search index, you should see a message to this effect going into the ACP.

First, check to see what search indexes were retained, if any: **ACP > Maintenance > Database > Search index**

Look in the value column. If all show zero posts indexed, you will have to make a new search index. Even if the value is not zero, you may not have all posts in the search index.

You can create an index on this page by pressing the **Create index** button for the kind of index you want. The more posts you have, the longer it takes. In the case of boards with hundreds of thousands of posts, it can take hours.

I've seen timeouts occur when creating the search index. You should get a pop-up dialog box to show that work is underway. The pop-up dialog box will disappear when the index is complete. But if there is a timeout, it will remain, and you will have to close it manually. Often, if you refresh the page, you can restart the search index, but it can feel frustrating.

If pressed for time, choose the MySQL fulltext index, as it is considerably faster than creating a phpBB Native index.

You can change the search index that phpBB uses: **ACP > General > Server configuration > Search settings > Search backend > Search backend**

19. **Remove the install folder.** If you don't, your board will remain disabled, and you will get a warning when you go to the main Administration Control Panel screen. You can do this with FTP or through SSH with an appropriate command.

20. **Remove AutoMOD modules, if necessary.** Upgrading from phpBB 3.0? See if an ACP_CAT_MODS tab appears in the ACP on the far right.

    If this happens, it's probably because AutoMOD was installed when the board was running phpBB 3.0. AutoMOD was a tool that made installing mods on phpBB 3.0 easier. The AutoMOD software is gone, but the modules it used are still in the database. These need to be manually deleted, working your way from the bottom up to the ACP_CAT_MODS category. Start at: **ACP > System > Module management > Administration Control Panel > ACP_EXT**

21. **Remove any other errant modules that may still exist.** Check each page in the ACP to see if there are any modules that don't have a language string

associated with them, like ACP_CAT_MODS. They are hard to miss these since they will look so off. If so, delete these modules using procedures in the last step. Check through the MCP and UCP modules as well using the module management software.

22. **Install any styles and language packs.** You can skip this if you are using the prosilver style with no changes and the British English language pack. See sections of Chapters 5 and 6 for procedures for installing styles and language packs. You may also want to apply a logo or additional styling. You can analyze any style changes by comparing your backup of your style with a reference version of that style.

23. **Recommended best practices.** These steps are optional, but based on my experience they should be done immediately after an upgrade. Refer to Chapter 5 for details, which are covered as part of installing phpBB.

    - Disable the Contact page to prevent Contact page spam: **ACP > General > Board configuration > Contact page settings > Enable contact page > Disabled**

    - If upgrading from phpBB 3.0, add a home page link, if you want that feature because your board is part of a larger website: **ACP > General > Board configuration > Board settings > Main website URL**

    - Set up an effective spambot countermeasure. The default spambot countermeasure is GD image, which is not very effective. Consider changing it to either the Q&A or a reCAPTCHA countermeasure. **ACP > General > Board configuration > Spambot countermeasures**. Since most of these countermeasures require that your server be able to communicate with the Internet, check your PHP settings: **ACP > PHP Information**. Search for "allow_url_fopen". If it's not set to On, change your PHP (not phpBB) configuration to allow it. Most web hosts have a control Panel interface where this and other PHP settings can be changed.

24. **Fix the reCAPTCHA spambot countermeasure, if applicable.** If you were using reCAPTCHA as your spambot countermeasure, note the following:

    - For an upgrade to phpBB 3.3, if you are using reCAPTCHA V2 Checkbox CAPTCHA, you will need to change it to reCAPTCHA V2 Invisible or reCAPTCHA V3. You will need to go to Google's reCAPTCHA site and generate a new set of keys for the new CAPTCHA.

- For an upgrade to phpBB 3.2, you will need to set the reCAPTCHA V2 Checkbox type CAPTCHA. phpBB 3.1 used the old reCAPTCHA V1 CAPTCHA, which was quickly compromised.

- In either case, you then need to enter these new keys: **ACP > General > Board configuration > Spambot countermeasures > Installed plugins > reCaptcha**

25. **Add or upgrade extensions.** See Chapter 6 for more details. If you want, you can add these later. For extensions you disabled, if there is a newer version, you might want to install the newer versions now to regain that functionality. Some extensions won't work if you don't upgrade them to one that works with your newer version of phpBB.

26. **Reenable the board**: ACP > General > Board configuration > Board settings > Disable board > No

27. **Test**. Navigate around your board to make sure it is behaving correctly. You might want to make and delete a test post.

28. **Store an archive**. Place a copy of your old files and extracted database in a safe place offsite. You never know what may happen! It's not a bad idea to store a backup of your files and database immediately after the upgrade as well.

Chapter 9 – Handling versioning

Chapter 10 | Troubleshooting

The nice thing about phpBB is that it tends to work reliably and predictably, so much so, it can make you complacent. Then suddenly something happens—your board comes crashing down, weird errors appear on the screen, things just slow down, or a cryptic HTTP error pops up.

As the administrator, you get to fix these issues, or at least instigate getting issues fixed. In this chapter, I'll share many of the general techniques I use when trouble strikes.

Troubleshooting strategies

When your board's behavior changes, there are five approaches to fixing the issue:

- **Search for an answer**. Go to phpbb.com and place a search query in its search field. Most likely, someone has had the same issue and has shared how it was fixed. In many cases though, the solution you found may be years or a decade old and may not work for your version of phpBB.

- **Use phpbb.com's support forums**. Go to phpBB's support forum, explain your issue in detail and hope for the best. Generally, you will get useful and timely help there. However, support is provided only for the current version of phpBB, or for any previous minor version of phpBB not more than a year old. Use the template they provide when asking for support.

- **Hire a consultant**. You hire someone like me to puzzle through the issue and affect a solution. You can hire me if I'm available, but phpBB also has a Wanted! forum where you can post for paid help.

- **File a support ticket with your web host**. Unfortunately, few web hosts have phpBB troubleshooting skills. But if the root issue is related to their infrastructure, they may be able to fix the underlying issue.

- **Try to fix it yourself**. This depends on your web and IT skills. I'll talk about ways to find the underlying cause and give some examples of how I solved certain issues that came up for clients. From these, you may be able to decide if your issue is something you can handle.

Why does good software break?

It can be frustrating when errors happen. Since phpBB is carefully tested, when something breaks, it's most likely not a bug in phpBB. What are the typical overarching issues that cause these problems? Here are the ones I most often have seen over the years with my many clients.

Technology upgrades

Some change in your web-hosting environment has broken phpBB or is no longer optimal.

Procrastination could also cause problems. If you continue to insist on running phpBB 3.0, at some point, things will blow up. It could be because your web host made PHP 7 the new default, and phpBB 3.0 is not certified to work with PHP 7. Or it could be that they are using a version of PHP that sometimes won't work well with 3.0, such as PHP 5.6, or some PHP default setting was changed and affected phpBB. This is why I stress how important it is to update your phpBB version in a timely manner. It is the best way to reduce issues from happening.

Web technologies regularly change, so your board should keep up with the times too. You can't stop people from using a smartphone to access your board. You can't stop them from using a different browser or a newer version of their new browser. And you can't expect web hosts to forever maintain old versions of common software like PHP on their infrastructure. Keeping old PHP versions accessible ultimately makes problems for web hosts.

Success

Boards can break if they become too successful too quickly. If you go from a small backwater board to one that gets hundreds of posts a day, your hosting plan may no longer be adequate. Success can cause users to suddenly see HTTP error pages, or messages that tell you too many resources were used, generally due to shared hosting limitations. Sometimes these are due to spammers, who have sensed a vulnerability, or malicious bots inflicting a denial-of-service attack.

Earlier in the book, I discussed ways to manage higher traffic, but those will take you only so far. At some point, you may need to upgrade your hosting to a package that can handle the increased traffic that your board is getting.

Shared hosting

Shared hosting is generally cheap, but it *is* shared. You are likely one of dozens of clients that your web host has on one machine. Web hosts will do their best to maximize their profits while hopefully not driving away customers. Some do this better than others.

If you are seeing too many resources used error messages, things just suddenly run slowly, you are getting regular timeouts while working on your board that never happened before, or you regularly see various HTTP error pages, it's usually due to shared hosting limitations.

Aging hosting infrastructure

The root cause may also be old machines in your web host's server room.

From where you sit, you have no way of knowing how old your host's hardware is. It may be using highly fragmented and slow disk drives or may not have enough memory, causing it to use virtual memory by writing memory to disk, which is relatively slow. Obviously, replacing hardware costs money. The good hosts will do this regularly; the bad hosts will see if they can get away with it and hope they don't lose too many customers.

Older hardware is not necessarily bad, but it is more likely to have issues, just like an old car.

Security issues

It's possible for malware (malicious software) to get on a server. I've had many clients with malware issues. For example, I've discovered that sometimes key phpBB programs have had malware injected into them; obviously after phpBB was installed from a security-tested release. The presence of a PHP eval() statement at the top of a file is a sure sign you've got malware. Comparing your phpBB software with a reference version can uncover malware issues.

The better web hosts proactively keep malware off their machines by regularly scanning files on their servers. But as mentioned earlier in the book, sometimes security solutions cause problems. Integrated security solutions can be managed too tightly or configured incorrectly, affecting open-source software like phpBB. Probably ten percent of the problems I troubleshoot are issues like this.

Space issues

As your board grows, it consumes more space. Topics, posts, private messages, attachments and videos are all recorded in the database or the file system and take up space. So, the more content on your board, the more phpBB and your server have to manage. At some point, it becomes like a juggler with one too many balls in the air, and it can cause it to all come down.

Obviously, phpBB will try to do use space as efficiently as possible, but over time, the volume of the content it manages can stress databases and hardware. Sometimes you hit a quota limit for overall database or file space, and because most web hosts won't send you quota limit warnings, you are surprised when it happens.

Software bugs

This is actually rarely the cause of an issue, at least if you keep your board regularly updated. phpBB is very complex software, so despite its rigorous pre-testing, it's not unusual to discover new bugs or security issues in the latest release, most of which are very obscure. Still, you might experience some of these. If you do, a search query on phpbb.com will probably uncover discussions by plenty of others with the same problem, and hopefully will offer a workaround or solution.

It's also possible that your web host is using older versions of software like MySQL or the web server, which may have bugs that haven't been patched.

Non-LAMP technologies

phpBB works with many different databases and web servers. But it works best on servers with a normal LAMP (Linux, Apache/nginx, MySQL/MariaDB and PHP) software stack. So, if you have a choice in hosting:

- Prefer a server operating system that runs on a Linux kernel and is widely used, like CentOS, Ubuntu, RedHat or Debian

- Prefer Apache or nginx as the web server

- Prefer MySQL or MariaDB for the database management system

If you can, avoid Microsoft IIS web server, and avoid Microsoft, Postgres, Oracle and SQLite as the database management system. This is not because Microsoft technologies and these other database management systems are inherently inferior. However, they are rarely used with phpBB so they are more likely to experience obscure issues.

If you are using Microsoft server technologies, often your web host can move you to a standard LAMP stack. Moving the tables in your database management system from one type to another can be tricky and require specialized tools and expertise.

Try purging the cache first

Just purging your phpBB cache may solve the problem:

ACP > General > Purge the cache

This doesn't work all the time, but should be tried to see if it works. It may only work temporarily.

Why would this work? The files in the /cache folder are actually programs created dynamically. They might reference old versions of SQL statements, old passwords and the like. By purging the cache, it forces phpBB to re-create these files, which may include more correct configuration information.

While not recommended by the phpBB Group, you can purge the cache outside of phpBB. You do this by removing all files in your board's /cache/production folder. This tends to take a while. A faster way is to use your web host control panel's file manager.

Warning: if you delete the file queue.php in the /cache/production folder, all emails queued to go out (such as new topic notifications) will be permanently lost. So you might want to except the queue.php and queue.php.lock files unless queue.php's file size is zero bytes.

If you delete the entire cache folder, make sure to re-create it and give it publicly writeable (777) permissions. The owner and group for the folder should match the owner and group for other folders and files on the board. The Linux `chown` command allows the ownership of files and folders to be changed.

Where to look for clues

The error message itself

If phpBB throws an error message, this is a great clue. Unfortunately, error messages are meant for geeks and are generally confusing to everyone else.

A generic HTTP 500 application error or similar HTTP error is not of much help. But if it gives a reasonably useful message, doing a web search may point to solutions. If it points to a program and a line of code, then a web search referencing this information could help undercover the root problem.

Try searching the error message you get on phpbb.com. Optionally, you can also constrain a search engine to return results only on phpbb.com as follows:

```
search terms site:phpbb.com
```

phpBB's error log

If phpBB can trap an error, it will, and it will record the error in its error log, with most recent errors showing first. Unfortunately, while it may show errors that occur, phpBB won't tell you that there are new errors it has trapped. You have to check the error log periodically instead.

ACP > Maintenance > Forum logs > Error log

Also, unfortunately, there are plenty of errors that phpBB can't trap because they occur somewhere else. But its error log is definitely a place to check if problems are happening.

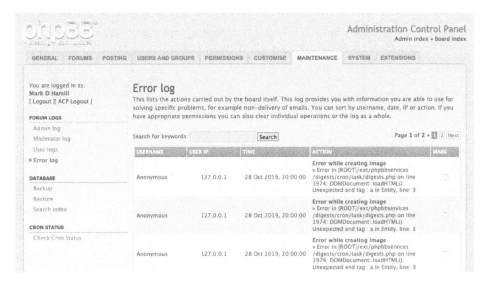

Figure 10.1: phpBB's error log

The log will indicate the date and time of the problem, an error message and who experienced it. If it says "Anonymous" for the username, this means a guest's actions triggered it, i.e. someone not logged in. See Figure 10.1, which shows an error log for a phpBB 3.2 board.

PHP error log

Since phpBB is written in PHP, there is usually an accessible PHP error log that can be read that could contain important clues. Its location depends on how your web host has configured PHP, so you might have to ask your host where it is or hunt for it.

Sometimes in your board's root directory, you will find a file called error_log. This is not part of phpBB, but is where PHP may decide to write PHP errors encountered by scripts in this folder. Sometimes it has a different name, like php_errorlog. Sometimes it's in a special folder, such as /var/logs that is not easily seen. Sometimes a web host control panel will contain a link to a PHP error log, which makes it easy to read.

You may be able to download it and read it offline, look at it using SSH, or read it in your web host control panel's file manager. Recent errors are of the most interest. See Figure 10.2.

```
[03-Apr-2019 17:59:21 UTC] PHP Parse error:  syntax error, unexpected end of fil
e, expecting variable (T_VARIABLE) or ${ (T_DOLLAR_OPEN_CURLY_BRACES) or {$ (T_C
URLY_OPEN) in phar:///chroot/wp-cli/vendor/wp-cli/wp-cli/bin/wp-cli.phar/vendor/
wp-cli/eval-command/src/Eval_Command.php(37) : eval()'d code on line 1
[04-Apr-2019 12:08:04 UTC] PHP Parse error:  syntax error, unexpected end of fil
e, expecting variable (T_VARIABLE) or ${ (T_DOLLAR_OPEN_CURLY_BRACES) or {$ (T_C
URLY_OPEN) in phar:///chroot/wp-cli/vendor/wp-cli/wp-cli/bin/wp-cli.phar/vendor/
wp-cli/eval-command/src/Eval_Command.php(37) : eval()'d code on line 1
[13-Jun-2019 13:16:42 UTC] PHP Parse error:  syntax error, unexpected end of fil
e, expecting variable (T_VARIABLE) or ${ (T_DOLLAR_OPEN_CURLY_BRACES) or {$ (T_C
URLY_OPEN) in phar:///chroot/wp-cli/vendor/wp-cli/wp-cli/bin/wp-cli.phar/vendor/
wp-cli/eval-command/src/Eval_Command.php(37) : eval()'d code on line 1
[19-Jun-2019 06:52:08 UTC] PHP Parse error:  syntax error, unexpected end of fil
e, expecting variable (T_VARIABLE) or ${ (T_DOLLAR_OPEN_CURLY_BRACES) or {$ (T_C
URLY_OPEN) in phar:///chroot/wp-cli/vendor/wp-cli/wp-cli/bin/wp-cli.phar/vendor/
wp-cli/eval-command/src/Eval_Command.php(37) : eval()'d code on line 1
[08-Aug-2019 10:58:41 UTC] PHP Parse error:  syntax error, unexpected end of fil
e, expecting variable (T_VARIABLE) or ${ (T_DOLLAR_OPEN_CURLY_BRACES) or {$ (T_C
URLY_OPEN) in phar:///chroot/wp-cli/vendor/wp-cli/wp-cli/bin/wp-cli.phar/vendor/
wp-cli/eval-command/src/Eval_Command.php(37) : eval()'d code on line 1
[08-Oct-2019 11:40:31 UTC] PHP Parse error:  syntax error, unexpected end of fil
e, expecting variable (T_VARIABLE) or ${ (T_DOLLAR_OPEN_CURLY_BRACES) or {$ (T_C
URLY_OPEN) in phar:///chroot/wp-cli/vendor/wp-cli/wp-cli/bin/wp-cli.phar/vendor/
wp-cli/eval-command/src/Eval_Command.php(37) : eval()'d code on line 1
```

Figure 10.2: PHP error log

From SSH, you can read the bottom of the error log with the `tail` command, i.e.:

```
tail error_log
```

or to get the last 50 lines of the file:

```
tail -n 50 error_log
```

Tip: if there is a file like error_log in your phpBB root directory, a similar log for the ACP is usually in the /adm folder. So, look for ACP errors there.

Since most errors are a result of PHP code executing incorrectly, this is generally the most useful log for troubleshooting these sorts of problems.

Web server error log

The web server also keeps a log of errors. It shouldn't catch PHP errors, but it should capture web server errors.

Figure 10.3: cPanel error log interface

Most web host control panels come with a tool that allows you to see the bottom of the web server's error log, with most recent errors showing first.

In this example using cPanel, it is found in a Visitor Stats group (Figure 10.3).

Opening the error log will show the most recent errors. You may have to scroll horizontally to see the details of each error message. See Figure 10.4.

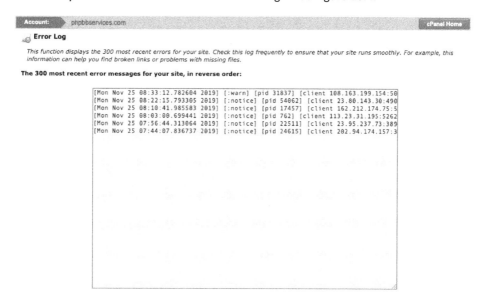

Figure 10.4: cPanel error log

Bear in mind that the web server log captures errors of interest only to the web server, not PHP or general program errors. If you get HTTP errors, it can contain clues to help solve the issue.

Here are some common HTTP errors and what they could mean in diagnosing your problem.

- **400 – Bad request.** The URL may have some garbage in it, such as using htt://
  instead of http:// or a bad/misspelled parameter in the URL, such as
  using ?viewtopicc.php instead of ?viewtopic.php.

- **401 – Unauthorized.** If you use HTTP authentication and you fail
  authentication, this will show up. It might also happen if a user makes too many
  invalid username/password entries.

- **404 – Not found.** The page requested could not be served, perhaps because the
  page name does not exist. Usually, some part of the path in the URL was
  incorrectly typed.

- **500 – Internal server error.** This is usually due to lines in a PHP program that
  could not be interpreted correctly. So, there may be a syntax error in a phpBB
  program or in a phpBB extension's program, or your board is being run with a
  version of PHP that it is not tested to run on. When this occurs, it's the web
  server's way of saying, "this problem is due to some program I'm trying to run,
  and it failed."

- **503 – Service unavailable.** This is usually a temporary condition, and could
  indicate that a denial-of-service attack is underway on the server or there is just
  a high usage of the site, and the web server can't keep up with demand.

Outside of a web server error log, you may also see an access log which includes
requests that were not errors. Here are some of these common non-error codes and
what they usually mean in the context of phpBB:

- **200 – OK.** This is not an error code, but is a web server's way of saying it served
  a web page with no errors or issues.

- **301 – Moved permanently.** This is often a result of the user requesting HTTP
  protocol but your webserver redirected the request to use HTTPS.

- **304 – Not modified.** The user hit the refresh button in the browser but no
  content has changed. The web server is telling your browser to serve content
  from its cache.

Solving issues

Solving issues involves fixing the underlying issue, which comes from an analysis of the behavior encountered and any clues provided by error messages that are recorded. Sometimes, a workaround suffices.

This book can't teach you how to fix every issue, or even to determine the cause of every issue. But I can use my experience to describe the issues that I most often see, discuss where the problem likely lies, and show how they can be fixed.

Avoiding issues

Again, the best way to solve issues is to avoid having them come up in the first place. This means investing time proactively to keep issues from occurring. Mostly, this means keeping your board up to date with fresh phpBB software. It also means updating extensions and styles when they have updates. You can also keep an eye on your web traffic and the resources you are using.

Figure 10.5: cPanel summary statistics

Your web host control panel may provide statistics on the resources you are using. For example, on my hosting, cPanel often provides a high-level overview in a sidebar. See Figure 10.5.

If you are close to maximizing your allocated disk space, or your *inode* usage is high, you may start experiencing problems. An inode is a file, folder or link to a file or folder that lives elsewhere and that the operating system has to manage. To do so efficiently, most hosting packages limit your number of inodes. If you are coming close to these limits, you might want to upgrade your hosting plan. Your web host probably won't tell you if you are getting close to using up your quota.

If you know the maximum size your databases are allowed to grow to, you can also see how much space they are using. If you have only your board's database size to worry about, you can see the space it's in a table on the main page. Scan for **Database size**.

For MySQL and MariaDB, the following SQL query will give you a bottom-line number for the size of all your databases:

```
SELECT ROUND(SUM(data_length + index_length) / 1024 /
1024, 1) "DB Size in MB" FROM
information_schema.tables
```

You can get this answer using a tool like phpMyAdmin. On the SQL tab, enter this search query. Compare the result with your database quota.

Some statistics you probably can't get. For example, if you are worried you will go over your outgoing email quota, with shared hosting there's probably no tool provided by your web host to let you know how many emails your domain sent. But there may be a tool that reports on how many emails were blocked from going out, or why. Look for an **Email deliverability** link in your web host control panel.

Some classes of hosting, particularly cloud hosting, may keep these sorts of statistics because you pay for the resources you use. On most shared hosting, the statistics will be partial at best.

Issue categories

Issues you encounter will fall into these general categories:

- phpBB bugs

- PHP integration issues

- Database issues

- Emailing issues. This is covered in Chapter 6. See *Reliably sending emails*.

- Hosting issues

If you can correctly categorize the issue, you may be able to solve the issue yourself.

phpBB bugs

Most phpBB bugs will appear in its error log:

ACP > Maintenance > Forum logs > Error log

Here's an example (Figure 10.6):

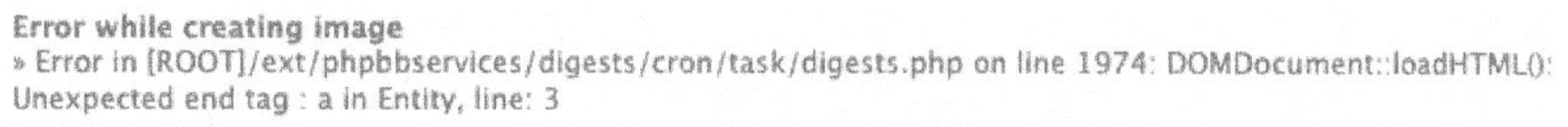

```
Error while creating image
» Error in [ROOT]/ext/phpbbservices/digests/cron/task/digests.php on line 1974: DOMDocument::loadHTML():
Unexpected end tag : a in Entity, line: 3
```

Figure 10.6: phpBB error log example

The program that failed was /ext/phpbbservices/digests/cron/task/digests.php, and a line number in the code indicates where the failure occurred. If you can read the program and know enough about PHP, you may be able to understand the issue and maybe fix it too.

The /ext folder means it's in the extensions folder, so the problem is due to an extension. The path also tells me the vendor of the extension is phpbbservices, and the extension name is digests. So, this is my digests extension, and the error points to a bug on line 1974 of the digests.php program in a /cron/task folder.

If you see a program name and a line number where it occurred, it's likely a bug in phpBB or a phpBB extension somewhere. In this case, searching for the term "Error while creating image" or "digests.php on line 1974" on phpbb.com might turn up a solution or workaround.

PHP integration issues

phpBB is written in the PHP programming language. A PHP interpreter parses every executed line of phpBB code and turns its English-like code into instructions that get executed by the central processing unit (CPU). Every line of code must make sense to this interpreter. If it doesn't, PHP should trigger an error, warning or information message. However, these are not always captured.

A PHP configuration file controls PHP's behavior. Exactly what features of PHP can be used vary from web host to web host, depending on how they configure and compile PHP.

In many cases, you can selectively override PHP settings in your web host control panel.

Figure 10.7: PHP interface in cPanel web host control panel

See Figure 10.7. In this cPanel instance, there are two interfaces for changing PHP and its behavior. Clicking on PHP Version Manager allows you to change the version of PHP to be used, either globally or for a particular folder. First, select the folder of interest.

Your interface may look different. See Figure 10.8.

The solution to some of these problems may be to change your version of PHP. For example, phpBB 3.2 is not certified to work with PHP 7.3 or 7.4. In this case, changing your version of PHP to 7.2 will likely solve the problem.

Sometimes analyzing the error will point to a solution that will work if you change certain behaviors in PHP. For example, PHP might need to be told, "It's okay to access URLs outside of my web hosting with HTTP POST requests." This is essentially what PHP's allow_url_fopen setting does. You probably won't have permission to edit PHP's master configuration file. But you can usually selectively override a setting or two.

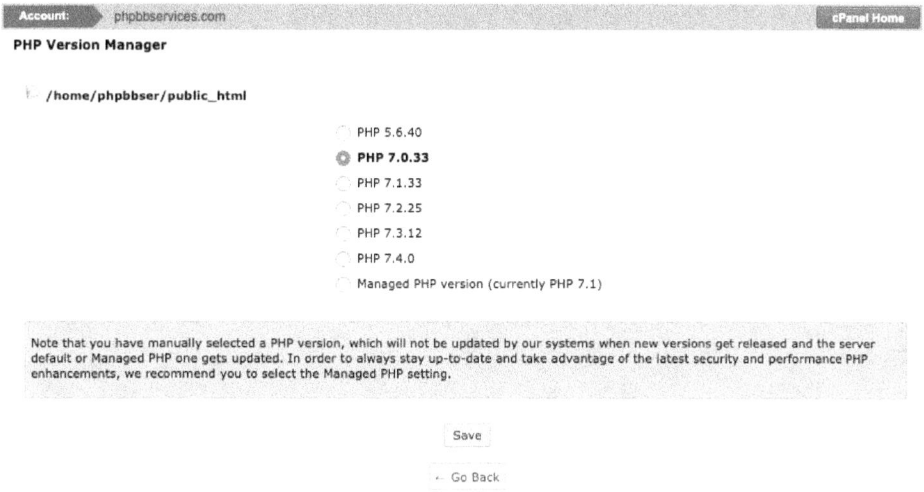

Figure 10.8: PHP version manager in cPanel

In this cPanel example, the **PHP Variables Manager** does just this. See Figure 10.9.

Figure 10.9: PHP variables manager in cPanel

In this case, I entered "allow_url_fopen" in the variable field, and then pressed the **Add** button. A set of radio buttons then appeared, allowing me to override the default setting. I chose **Yes** and pressed the **Save** button.

How does this override work? In this case, a php.ini file was created in the folder I chose. You may see something similar if you explore your web space with FTP or a file manager. If I look at the file in an editor, it shows the setting:

```
allow_url_fopen = On
```

In many cases, PHP is configured so that if a php.ini file exists in the folder where software will be run, it will read the file and override the default PHP setting using the instructions in the file.

I do tweaks like this regularly for my clients. In other cases, PHP will be configured to not allow settings to be overridden, so this won't always work. That may require a conversation with your web host's technical support people to see if there is another way to do this.

Reading phpBB's error log might show you an issue that amounts to a PHP integration issue. Here's an example. See Figure 10.10.

Email error
» **EMAIL/SMTP**
/forum/posting.php

Could not get mail server response codes.

Backtrace

Connecting to tls://email-smtp.us-east-1.amazonaws.com:465
LINE: 1139 <- 220 email-smtp.amazonaws.com ESMTP SimpleEmailService-d-B4C2B5NV0 MybeM8N297uZghbkjay7

EHLO ip-172-31-37-57.us-east-2.compute.internal
LINE: 1486 <- 250-email-smtp.amazonaws.com

LINE: 1486 <- 250-8BITMIME

LINE: 1486 <- 250-SIZE 10485760

LINE: 1486 <- 250-AUTH PLAIN LOGIN

LINE: 1486 <- 250 Ok

AUTH LOGIN
LINE: 1610 <- 334 VXNlcm5hbWU6

Figure 10.10: phpBB error log example

Can you figure out what the root problem is here? There are a number of clues:

- A reference to posting.php suggests it occurred when a user made a post.

- It has something to do with emailing because it talks about a mail server and gives the name of the email server.

- Looking further, from the name of the email server, it's located on amazonaws.com, which in this case is outside of the web-hosting environment. So, this board is configured to use a third-party service (Amazon Web Services) for sending email.

The likely culprit is that phpBB can't reach this server. It could be that a wrong set of SMTP credentials were used. But it could also be that the web host blocks outgoing calls to email servers.

Try sending a test email:

ACP > General > Client communications > Email settings

Does another error like this occur in the log? If so, it suggests that the SMTP settings are not defined correctly. You might want to check with your email service to see if you have the correct SMTP settings, and fix them. Or in this case, you might want to check with your web host to see if it blocks requests to third party external email servers. If a test email works, it suggests this issue was transient.

Database issues overview

I've hinted at a general database issue that can occur: the space for your databases gets too big.

Most web hosts won't shut things down if this happens, but they might notify you that you've got a quota problem. You'll need to reduce its size (see the pruning discussion in Chapter 8), drop the search index or pay for a larger database quota. The latter may require a different hosting package.

Database issues may show up in phpBB's error log or in the PHP error log. The database tables affected are normally in the error message, often with the database query that failed.

Calls to the database are written in a language called *Structured Query Language*, or SQL for short. These SQL statements are embedded inside phpBB's PHP code. The phpbb_posts table is an example of a table phpBB will use frequently. It's a container for all the posts made on your board. Posts are added, updated, removed and read with SQL calls from phpBB.

On a stable board, it's unusual to suddenly develop database issues. This is because database management systems are all industrial strength, hence extremely reliable. And phpBB's code, with its embedded SQL statements, is well tested and reliable too.

Problems can occur through extensions, particularly unapproved extensions. They can also be introduced by upgrades and updates that were not done properly.

Database resource issues

On shared hosting and some virtual private servers, you can use too many database resources over a given time. Exactly what a "database resource" is can be murky, but it's usually units of work of some sort, like the number of database queries per unit of time, such as over one minute. If you use too many, you could get an error message.

Curiously, this often happens during upgrades to phpBB because a lot of changes are made to the database in a short time frame. Running the upgrade script again usually solves the issue.

But if your board is getting hammered by a lot of traffic, the error can occur regularly and be very disruptive. The result is usually a very ugly error message. Eventually the clock resets, and you are allowed to use more resources again. If it happens once, it is likely to recur periodically.

If this happens regularly, it may point to a larger issue. For example, if the traffic is due to a lot of malicious robots hitting your site, it might be possible to block them by blocking a range of IP addresses.

Your web host may be able to provide some insight into what's causing these issues, and perhaps solutions too.

Repairing and optimizing tables

The most typical issue I see where databases are to blame is due to running databases on older hardware. Tables that are frequently written to, particularly large ones can become corrupted.

No database can be more reliable than the machine it resides on. Moreover, on mechanical disk drives, large tables often scatter data all over disk platters, making gathering data a relatively slow process. With age, sectors on a disk drive can become problematic, affecting the whole table and generating SQL errors. It most typically happens on frequently read from and written to tables, like the phpbb_sessions table. In this case, the root problem is mechanical: the surface of the disk drive may be wearing off in certain highly trafficked tracks, or the disk head reading the disk can't quite read it reliably because of tiny changes to the gap between the disk head and the disk platter. This is becoming less of a problem now as hosts move away from mechanical disk drives to solid state drives.

MySQL and MariaDB tables using the MYISAM storage engine have a repair command that can help. But first, you need to know which tables have been affected. That can be inferred from the error message where the table is identified. It doesn't take much more time to run a repair on all your tables than it does with one table.

You can repair database tables using phpMyAdmin. In your database, select the table to be repaired by clicking on its checkbox. From the **With selected** dropdown at the bottom of the page, select **Repair table**.

From the command line, you can easily repair all the tables in a MySQL or MariaDB database. For example, if your database name is "forums" and your MySQL username is "forums," it can be done from SSH using the mysqlcheck program:

```
mysqlcheck -u forums -p --auto-repair forums
```

In this example, you will be prompted for your database password.

If you logged into the database and are at the mysql prompt, you can repair any table with the MYISAM storage engine with the REPAIR TABLE command. For example:

```
REPAIR TABLE phpbb_search_wordmatch;
```

Tables can also be optimized. Over time, lots of writing to a table can cause data to become scattered inefficiently. Optimizing the table will attempt to arrange the data and update the table's indexes so data can more quickly be retrieved and written. The syntax is very similar. For example:

```
OPTIMIZE TABLE phpbb_search_wordmatch;
```

This option is also available in phpMyAdmin in the **With selected** dropdown.

Some administrators will regularly optimize and repair their tables hoping to prevent problems and keep the database running with maximum efficiency. Creating a cron job, perhaps run weekly at 3 AM, could do this if it issues the correct command to the database.

Changing the storage engine used by your tables

Storage engines are used to store and retrieve data in tables. Each storage engine stores and retrieves data differently. MySQL and MariaDB have two principal types of storage engines: MYISAM and INNODB.

In newer installations of phpBB, you will most often see the INNODB storage engine used. On older installs of phpBB, the storage engine is usually MYISAM.

Figure 10.11 shows an example of the storage engines used in MySQL for some phpBB tables. These tables are using the MYISAM storage engine. I used phpMyAdmin (available in most web host control panels) to view the tables in a board's database.

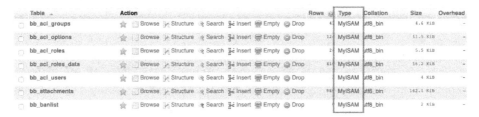

Figure 10.11: List of tables in phpMyAdmin showing storage engine used

The MYISAM engine is more likely to have problems than the newer INNODB storage engine. So, you might want to take the time to change the storage engine for these tables.

It's pretty easily done. However, since you are making major changes to the database you should:

1. Disable the board during the process, so users don't see any errors: **ACP > General > Board configuration > Board settings > Disable board > Yes**

2. Make a backup of the database.

3. After all tables are converted, re-enable the board: **ACP > General > Board configuration > Board settings > Disable board > No**

For example, to change the phpbb_acl_groups table from MyISAM to INNODB, execute this SQL. In phpMyAdmin, click on the SQL tab when in the database and enter it there:

```
ALTER TABLE phpbb_acl_options ENGINE=INNODB;
```

This works for a single table, but since there are more than seventy tables in phpBB, it can be tedious to do this for all of these tables.

If you have access to the information_schema database (which is typically granted), you can use this SQL query to create all the SQL needed. Substitute dbname with the name of your database in your board's config.php file:

```
SELECT CONCAT('ALTER TABLE ', TABLE_NAME, '
ENGINE=INNODB;')
FROM information_schema.TABLES
WHERE TABLE_SCHEMA = 'dbname' AND engine = 'MyISAM'
```

When run, you should get a list like this (only partial results are shown):

```
ALTER TABLE phpbb_acl_groups ENGINE=INNODB;
ALTER TABLE phpbb_acl_options ENGINE=INNODB;
ALTER TABLE phpbb_acl_roles ENGINE=INNODB;
ALTER TABLE phpbb_acl_roles_data ENGINE=INNODB;
ALTER TABLE phpbb_acl_users ENGINE=INNODB;
ALTER TABLE phpbb_attachments ENGINE=INNODB;
```

These SQL statements can then be copied and pasted. Use the SQL tab in phpMyAdmin for your database, or if you have command line access and are at the mysql prompt and are using your database, paste them there.

It's generally not a good idea to do all these in one batch. I recommend doing them in blocks of ten and seeing how it goes. Very large tables like the phpbb_posts and the phpbb_search_wordmatch tables should be done one at a time.

In most cases, it takes less than five minutes to change the storage engines for all your tables.

Hints at solutions to more complex database issues

A fair amount of the troubleshooting I do for clients is fixing other odd database issues. These fixes are too specialized and nuanced to describe here, so if they occur, you will probably have to seek out help.

Most of these occur or are introduced during incorrect upgrades or updates to phpBB. They usually amount to one of these things:

- **Data are missing in one or more tables**. The phpbb_config table maintains a lot of configuration information that phpBB uses to keep itself organized. For example, your board's title is stored as a row in this table. If a row it expects to be there is missing, or if a row it tries to insert is already there, an error will be triggered. Certain tables, like phpbb_acl_options, are used with phpBB's permission system, so rows missing in this table might trigger errors.

- **Columns are missing in one or more tables**. Extensions often add columns to tables. Missed migration steps in upgrades or updates may introduce these types of problems too.

- **Columns in tables may not have all the necessary attributes**. For example, phpBB may expect a column to have a default value for a newly inserted row when its value is not supplied, but the instruction for that is missing in the column's definition.

- **Indexes are missing**. Indexes are used to quickly find data in tables. A missing index can slow down the process of finding matching rows in the table because it may require the table to be read sequentially until the data are found. Missing indexes are at the root of a lot of board performance issues. To fix these issues, I check the indexes in a client's database tables with a reference database and add any that are missing.

Hosting issues

One other thing I tend to do for my clients, at least several times a year, is rehost them.

For these clients, their web host repeatedly lets them down. When it seems like you are spending more time dealing with the frustrations of hosting with your current web host, that's a sign you need to move to new hosting.

It's likely these hosts will either have lax security practices or too stringent security practices. Or, they are so busy keeping optimal hosting environments (particularly for WordPress) that they forget that one size doesn't fit all.

phpBB may be the most popular open-source forum solution out there, but it's minor for most web hosts. Most web hosts are far more concerned about the WordPress market, as it serves about forty percent of websites. So, they will pimp out their hosting packages to try to give the ideal WordPress experience, and in the process, give short shrift to other software solutions.

It could certainly be that you are using the wrong kind of hosting. In that case, you may have unrealistic expectations for your class of hosting. Shared hosting can work well if your board gets moderate use and the web host maintains its infrastructure properly. If you are expecting the capabilities of a virtual private server on shared hosting, this may be your fault. Appendix A discusses web hosting in general.

When your pain dealing with these issues gets too high, you will generally know it's time to rehost elsewhere. Fortunately, I tackle the process for rehosting in Appendix E.

Troubleshooting permission issues

I have noted before that phpBB's permission system is awesome. In one way though, it's a bit defective: it's hard to troubleshoot issues with permissions, particularly forum permissions.

The general problem is that a user can belong to more than one group, and different groups can have different permissions. In addition, users can be granted individual permissions. These permissions overlay each other, so it's hard to know which permission is causing the problem. Even if you know where the permission issue lies, it's hard to know how to fix it.

Seeing the problem

Figure 10.12: Test user permissions link

A little-known feature of phpBB is that administrators can experience a user's permission issues by temporarily assuming them:

ACP > Users and groups > Users > Manage users

Enter the username in the **Enter username** field and press the **Submit** button. In the **Overview** section, note the **Test out user's permissions** link. See Figure 10.12.

When you click on the link, you get a screen that confirms the user's permissions have been switched and provides instructions on how to undo these permissions to revert to your normal permissions. You also get a link to the Board's index.

You have to open the drop down on the navigation bar with your username on it to see a new link that allows you to restore your own permissions. See Figure 10.13.

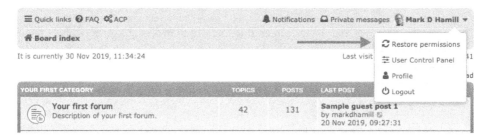

Figure 10.13: Restore permissions link

Now simply navigate around the board to see the issue from the user's perspective. When done, click on the **Restore permissions** link.

Understanding permission types

This was covered earlier in the book, but if you skipped it, here's a brief overview. A phpBB permission has one of three values that have the following meanings:

- o **YES** will allow a permission setting, unless it is overridden by a **NEVER**

- o **NO** will disallow a permission setting, unless subsequently is or previously was overridden by a **YES** permission

- o **NEVER** will completely disallow a permission setting for a user. It cannot be overridden by a **YES**

Essentially, when the NEVER permission is set, it becomes a blocker overriding any other permission, completely disallowing the permission.

As we learned earlier in the book, there are permission types for users in general, which also apply to groups. There are separate classes of permissions for moderators and administrators. A final form of permission applies to forums only. Forum permissions allow more granular permissions, so users and groups may have different privileges in different forums.

Since it's the most complicated, we'll concentrate on examining and troubleshooting forum permissions, but they all work similarly.

Seeing all forum permissions for a user, forum and permission type

phpBB has a tool for seeing and troubleshooting forum permissions, but it can be difficult to find. In this example, I use my development board to see forum permissions for myself.

ACP > Permissions > Permission masks > View forum-based permissions

1. Pick the forum or forums you want. In this example, I used the forum "Your first forum". I then pressed **Submit**.

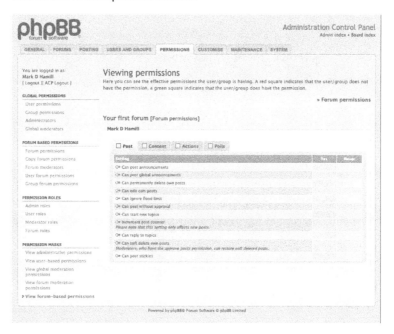

Figure 10.14: Viewing permissions screen

2. Next, I picked the user. There are various ways to do this with the interface for both users and groups. In this case, I put the administrator "Mark D Hamill" in the **Find a member** field and pressed the **View permissions** button below the field.

3. This brings up the Viewing permissions page (Figure 10.14). The colors you see on the permission tabs may vary from mine where the green squares in each of the tabs basically say, "This user or group has effective YES for ALL permissions under this tab." Recall that red means, "This user or group has NEVER or NO set for all permissions under this tab," and that blue means, "This user or group has a mixture of permissions on this tab and at least one YES permission." Green is an all-clear (all YES) signal.

4. I now want to check out a particular permission. You may have to hunt for the permission you want to check for the user and forum as it may be on a different tab. There is a tiny little icon to the left of each forum's permission. That's what you need to click on. In this case, I want to see how permissions are determined for the **Can start new topics** permission (Figure 10.15).

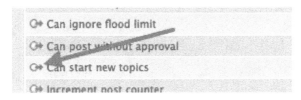

Figure 10.15: Selecting a permission to check

5. This brings up a popup window. If you don't see a popup window, you may have to tell your browser to allow popups for the domain.

6. This brings up a useful screen (Figure 10.16) where you can see how my permissions are being determined for this forum permission. phpBB applies permissions from top to bottom as shown.

Figure 10.16: Viewing a particular permission

Since I am both an administrator and a global moderator, I belong to both groups, each of which has their own group forum permissions.

- By default, the user's permission is set to **NO** access.

- But it is set to **YES** for the Administrators group, which overrides the **NO** permission, so the logic continues, and the next group I belong to is tested.

- It is set to **YES** for the Global moderators' group too, which I am in, so the net permission remains **YES**.

- It is set to **YES** for the Registered users' group in this forum too, so it's still **YES**. Remember that all users are in the Registered users' group.

- Finally, phpBB looks for any user-specific forum permissions (identified by my name, Mark D Hamill). None were found, so this permission is **NO**, but since it is **NO** and not a **NEVER,** the overall **YES** permission still applies. In most cases, user permissions are default permissions since user permissions must be explicitly set otherwise. phpBB will default to paranoid mode, so a default permission will be **NO**.

Fixing the underlying permission issue

With this tool, you should be able to determine where the root of the permission issue is and fix it. You'll see how the actual permission is derived, which helps determine how the permission issue can be fixed. Look in the **Who** column for the permission that is causing the root issue. Usually, it's a group permission that needs changing. The possible solutions are:

- A **NO** permission should be changed to **NEVER**, blocking everything.

- A **NEVER** permission blocks everything, so it should be changed to **NO. NEVER** can occur due to a role like No Access.

  Assigning the **No Access** role to a forum for the registered users group amounts to a full set of NEVER permissions for the group. This can block administrator permissions to administrator-only forums because administrators are also registered users and administrator forum permissions are applied *after* permissions for registered users. Clicking on the **ALL NO** links for these forums for the registered users' group would fix this sort of issue: **ACP > Permissions > Forum based permissions > Group permissions > Registered users**

- A **NO** or **NEVER** permission is incorrect and should be **YES.**

Adjust the group or user permissions for the forum privilege accordingly:

ACP > Users and groups > Groups > Group forum permissions or **ACP > Users and Groups > Users > User forum permissions**

Doing it with groups is preferred and makes it easier to keep your board consistent.

After making your changes, you can use the View forum-based permissions tool again to verify the result is correct, or use the feature in the Administration Control Panel to test out a user's forum permissions.

I am demonstrating troubleshooting forum permissions since it is the most complex type of permission, but this approach also works with user, moderator and administrator positions. There are links for each of these in the permissions mask group:

ACP > Permissions > Permission masks

The newly registered users group permission quirk

Figure 10.17: Newly registered users quirk

phpBB's built-in permission arrangement has some peculiarities. For example, newly registered users are also in the registered users' group. See Figure 10.17.

To me, this makes no sense. In the case of user "tester66," because they are in the newly registered users' group, the forum's permissions for newly registered users do not allow them to start new topics.

But because they are in the registered users' group too, they *can* start new topics, the exact opposite of what you would expect! While a newly registered user can start a topic, it will have to pass moderation before posting is allowed. This is because, by default, a newly registered user's first three posts require moderation.

How do you fix this, if you think it needs fixing? There are two approaches using:

ACP > Users and Groups > Groups > Group forum permissions > Newly registered users

- Select the **Advanced** link to fine tune the permission and set this permission to **NEVER** for each forum where you want it to apply.

- Change the role used by the newly registered users' group for the forums where this quirk exists, which is probably all of them. For this group and the particular forum, when in the **Role** dropdown, select **Newly Registered User Access**.

Figure 10.18: Newly registered users quirk, fixed

After changing the permission, you can see the result. Arguably, phpBB should be configured this way by default. See Figure 10.18.

You can also effectively turn off moderation of posts by newly registered users for all forums this way:

ACP > General > Board configuration > User registration settings > New member post limit > 0

Other tools

phpBB has a few other built-in tools to help solve issues and keep your board more orderly.

Reset or resynchronize board statistics

Right on the main page for the Administration Control Panel are a number of useful buttons focused on resetting and resynchronizing statistics, which can be helpful when trying to solve issues. **Purge the cache** is the one I most often use, but there are others that can be useful:

- **Reset most users ever online**. If this value looks suspiciously high, perhaps due to a spambot attack, this simply resets this value to 1. Over time as new traffic occurs, the number will increase.

- **Reset board's start date**. This sets the board's creation date to the current time, minus one second. This can be useful if you created a board that you extensively configured and tested, and want to give the board an official deployment date.

- **Resynchronize statistics**. This recounts the number of posts, topics, users and files. It's possible that the statistics have become incorrect. After pressing this button, the statistics shown will be correct.

- **Resynchronize post counts**. After pruning your forums, this will figure out the actual current post counts in various forums and topics.

- **Resynchronize dotted topics**. A *dotted topic* is a topic where the logged-in user has contributed at least one post. There is a little star in the topic's icon on the View topic page. On the index, it indicates the user contributed to at least one topic in the forum. If these look off, pressing this button will re-examine all posts so that dotted topic icons show properly.

- **Purge all sessions**. Sometimes sessions will stay around, leaving thousands of sessions in the phpbb_sessions table. This table is probably the most accessed table in phpBB and, in many ways, is its most crucial table. After this button is pressed, everyone should get a new session and may be required to login again.

You might want to change your session time after doing this: **ACP > General > Server configuration > Load settings > Session length**.

Resynchronize a forum's statistics

In addition, the Forums tab in the ACP has an easily overlooked **Resynchronise** button (in orange) for each forum. Clicking on it allows you to recalculate the statistics for a forum. On the board index, it will recalculate the number of posts and topics in the forum, and update the last post subject, last poster and last post time in the forum. **ACP > Forums**. See Figure 10.19.

Figure 10.19 Resynchronize forum button

Miscellaneous tools

Here are more tools that may be useful in the Administration Control Panel:

- **PHP Information**. This link is also on the Quick Access menu and provides a host of information on how PHP is configured on your server. This is very useful when you need to verify that a feature of PHP is enabled. It also provides some useful information, such as your type of operating system, the version of PHP you are using, your database management system and its version and the exact modules and extensions enabled for PHP on your server, including any that you explicitly enabled. This is also available at: **ACP > System > General tasks > PHP Information**.

- **Inactive users. ACP > Users and groups > Users > Inactive users**. This lists inactive users, i.e., those users that did not complete registration. Clicking the links for these users allows you to activate their accounts, send them a reminder email or just delete their accounts.

- **Customise tab**. This is your go-to place to add extensions, but also to enable or disable styles and language packs.

- **Maintenance tab**. You can manually backup your database here or restore a database backup you made previously, which could bring your board back to a stable place.

- **Mass email**. **ACP > System > General tasks > Mass email**. This provides an easy interface from which to send all your users an email, or all members of a group, or a list of users that you specify. *Only text emails can be sent.*

- **Extensions tab**. This ACP tab usually appears when your first extension is installed. Most extensions have administrator interfaces on this tab.

- **Forum logs. ACP > Maintenance > Forum logs**. There are four types of logs that record significant events in phpBB that you should review periodically. The error log is the most useful one because it documents many issues when phpBB goes awry, and, as discussed earlier in this chapter. This often provides clues on how to solve an underlying technical issue with phpBB.

Showing advanced diagnostic information

Before phpBB 3.3, it was possible to edit a line in your config.php file and phpBB would show various specialized diagnostic information in the footer of the web page. For example, you could remove the // at the start of this line:

```
// @define('DEBUG_CONTAINER', true);
```

Afterward, in the footer of the web page, you would see some diagnostic information (Figure 10-20):

```
Time: 0.544s | Peak Memory Usage: 17.3 MiB | GZIP: Off | Queries: 22 | SQL Explain
```

Figure 10-20 Advanced diagnostic information in the page footer

This information is quite technical in nature, so generally you wouldn't want this to show. However, if you have the technical skills, or are working with a systems administrator to troubleshoot issues, this information can be useful.

With phpBB 3.3, this setting in the config.php is ignored. However, its functionality is available elsewhere. Add these lines (shown in bold below) to the end of your /config/production/config.yml file:

```
imports:
    - { resource: ../default/config.yml }
parameters:
    debug.load_time: true
    debug.sql_explain: true
    debug.memory: true
```

Warning: you cannot use your tab key in this file. Lines containing spaces at the start require four spaces to be entered. These YAML (.yml) files cannot be parsed if tab characters are used.

After purging the cache (**ACP > General > Purge the cache**), you should see something similar to Figure 10-20 in the footer of board web pages, including in the ACP.

These features can be individually set to false in the config.yml file to disable their display. When all are enabled, the load time and server memory usage statistics are shown, as well as a link to information that shows the latest database queries and information on how they were executed, which can be valuable to database specialists as it can indicate if an index was used or not. See Figure 10-21.

QUERY #16								

SELECT u.username, u.username_clean, u.user_id, u.user_type, u.user_allow_viewonline, u.user_colour FROM (phpbb_users u) WHERE u.user_id IN (2, 48) ORDER BY u.username_clean ASC

ID	SELECT TYPE	TABLE	TYPE	POSSIBLE KEYS	KEY	KEY LEN	REF	ROWS	EXTRA
1	SIMPLE	u	range	PRIMARY	PRIMARY	4		2	Using where; Using filesort

Before: 0.06635s | After: 0.06660s | Elapsed: **0.00025s**

Figure 10-21 Database query diagnostic information

When enabled, this information will appear in the footer for all users, including guests. **Consequently, you should turn off the display of this information as soon as it is not needed.** After editing the config.yml file again, make sure to purge the cache.

The **SQL Explain** link contains the most potentially sensitive information, as it shows the database queries that were made recently including potentially sensitive information, such as the encrypted password for a user in the database.

Chapter 11 | The future of phpBB

We can't say exactly what the future of phpBB will be except that it will have a future. After all, phpBB 4.0 is in development.

phpBB has been the most popular forum solution for about twenty years now, as attested by the likelihood that you have used many phpBB boards over the years, even if you didn't know it was powered by phpBB. There are a lot of competing forum solutions out there, but phpBB hasn't gone away and has stayed popular, in spite of some of its limitations. Some of these other solutions have dropped by the wayside or aren't being updated, likely due to phpBB's dominance.

phpBB's technical issues

As you've learned, phpBB amounts to a very solid and comprehensive forum solution. However, the phpBB Group has a hard time introducing new features in a timely manner, mostly because it is so full of features already that must still work when new features are added. And since phpBB 3.1, it uses a new and more modern architecture, which includes a lot of professional third-party software, careful adherence to modern web standards, and sophisticated automated testing of builds in development. All this is good, but this also made phpBB more complex.

Yet, phpBB *is* based on PHP, a widely-used programming language but one that seems long in the tooth to many web developers. These days, PHP has lost a lot of its sexiness. Javascript frameworks seem to be taking over web development. phpBB includes some Javascript, but it is mostly a PHP application.

PHP gained favor about the time that the Perl programming language lost its luster, which means PHP's time may be limited if it reaches a point where, like Perl, it loses favor in a meaningful way.

Fortunately, PHP has matured in many other ways. For example, Symfony's PHP libraries are very popular. Many are used in phpBB. This went a long way to making PHP development very professional. As a developer, I can appreciate the many high-quality tools developed for PHP since its introduction, such as PhpStorm, an editor optimized for quickly and professionally creating PHP applications.

While PHP is not all the rage anymore, so much of the web runs on it. As programming languages go, it's relatively easy to learn, which bodes well for it, although writing good PHP programs takes more advanced knowledge. Like the COBOL language widely used in the 1970s, there may be no need to ever rewrite phpBB in a different language, just as many of those old COBOL programs are still around running banking applications.

WordPress, which runs about forty percent of websites, is also based on PHP. With WordPress using it, it's hard to see how PHP will ever go away. Speaking of PHP, Facebook is also reportedly mostly written in PHP.

As content management systems like WordPress dominate the market, administrators increasingly want bulletin boards that work inside these frameworks. That's why WordPress forum solution plugins, like bbPress, have gained a lot of traction while not having nearly the breadth of features that phpBB has.

All this to say that phpBB won't be going away for a very long time, if at all. It's been going for over twenty years. Since it is used on so many websites, it won't be easy for those on the platform to transition off it. Most administrators will keep upgrading phpBB rather than go through the hassle of moving their board to some other solution. Knowing there is a dedicated group of volunteers keeping phpBB going and providing top-notch, timely technical support helps too.

In short, phpBB should continue to be a top-notch and fully supported forum solution for the web, probably at least through 2030. However, as this book demonstrates, it is hardly intuitive to customize, administer and troubleshoot. In fact, most open source software solutions have similar issues, including the mighty WordPress platform.

I hope that if you have read this book through, you won't feel lost administering phpBB anymore. I also hope that I've succeeded in writing a friendly and useful book that empowers you to get the most out of the number one open-source forum solution out there.

We've indeed been down a lot of phpBB's rabbit holes. There are many more holes I could take you down, but I've taken you down the ones you most need to know about.

Check out my website

If you haven't been to my website, please pay it a visit. I keep a blog with regular posts, including many tips I have learned over the years. On my site, you can subscribe to receive emails whenever I make a post. It's an easy way for me to share what I am learning with you.

https://www.phpbbservices.com

You can also write me at mark@phpbbservices.com. Fair warning: I won't troubleshoot your problems for free, but you may be able to hire me.

I hope to update this book regularly, at least once a year, and to offer discount prices for new versions of this book to purchasers of previous editions. If there are topics that you'd like me to discuss in future editions of this book, please let me know.

Thank you for reading!

Appendix A | phpBB and Web Hosting

What is a web host?

A *web host* is an organization or company that provides the machines and network connections that serve content to the web. Typically, this is the World Wide Web, but it doesn't have to be. Sometimes the hosting is internal to a company or organization.

A web host does the heavy lifting and provides the infrastructure for your website, generally in exchange for your money.

In this appendix we look at what's involved in hosting phpBB, in case you are new to hosting.

Getting a domain

A *domain* is the URL of your website without the prefix, such as myspecialboard.com.

It's generally a good idea to get a domain before you get web hosting. To get a domain, you need a *domain registrar*, which acts as a broker between you and ICANN (Internet Corporation for Assigned Names and Numbers.) ICANN is an organization that oversees the whole domain registration process for the Internet. These days, everyone and their grandmother seem to be selling domains, usually as a reseller for a bigger authorized registrar.

Most web hosts also provide domain registry services. You can buy your domain from them (or, more accurately, *through* them), and they will host it for you on their machines.

Why have a registrar different than your web host? If your web host exasperates you, you can do a quickie divorce. Move your files and database to a new host, change the nameservers for your domain and you are done. Changing registrars, though, tends to be a hassle, and the more domains you have, the larger the hassle it is. By selling domain services, web hosts are not just offering one-stop shopping, but are trying to make it hard, or at least awkward, to take your business elsewhere.

315

phpBB's system requirements

Since you plan to put phpBB on a domain, make sure your host can meet its system requirements. This is almost never a problem, but check to make sure. As of this writing, phpBB 3.3.7 is the current version of phpBB.

phpBB 3.3 requires:

- A web server or web hosting account running on any major Operating System with support for PHP

- A SQL database system, one of:

    o MySQL 4.1.3 or above (MySQLi supported)

    o MariaDB 5.1 or above

    o MS SQL Server 2000 or above (via ODBC or SQLSRV PHP extensions)

    o Oracle

    o PostgreSQL 8.3+

    o SQLite 3.6.15+

- PHP 7.1.3+ with support for the database you intend to use

- getimagesize() function enabled

- The following PHP modules:

    o json

    o XML support

    o Corresponding PHP module for the database system you intend to use

- The following PHP modules are optional, but will provide access to additional features.

    o zlib Compression support

    o Remote FTP support

    o GD support

What kind of hosting do you need?

Before buying hosting, think about what sort of hosting you need. If you are just starting out, cheap shared hosting is probably fine. You can migrate to more expensive solutions in time. But if you anticipate putting up a site that will quickly get huge amounts of traffic, you need to carefully think through your hosting choice. Hosting types fall into four general categories. Which type do you need? See Table 1.

Hosting type	Advantages	Disadvantages
Shared	• Inexpensive	• Others using your shared server may impact your site's performance • Strict resource limitations on the number of files, CPU seconds, email quotas and size of databases may affect your site. Find out what they are before signing up.

Hosting type	Advantages	Disadvantages
Virtual private server (VPS)	• You have complete control over the resources you are buying • You can install any software on it that works for your server's operating system • Generally, resource limitations aren't encountered • Less expensive than a dedicated server. Prices usually start around $50/month • You are guaranteed your share of the machine's resources. They can't be taken away or used by someone else. So, you can expect a consistent level of performance.	• Although control panels like WebMin or Plesk may be provided to help manage your virtual server, it really helps to have technical skills, particularly Linux or Windows server administration skills. In fact, it's often required. • If you don't have these skills, you might have to pay someone to maintain your virtual server.

Hosting type	Advantages	Disadvantages
Dedicated server	• The entire machine is yours exclusively • It's very unusual to run out of computing resources • Response time is typically very fast	• Expensive. Machine rentals generally start in the hundreds of dollars a month. • Although control panels like WebMin or Plesk may be provided to help manage your server, you will have to maintain the server yourself, or hire someone to do it for you

Hosting type	Advantages	Disadvantages
Cloud (Amazon Web Services, IBM Cloud, Google Cloud, Microsoft Azure, etc.)	• Offers scalable computing on demand • You pay only for the resources you actually use • You can pay for redundancy across multiple data centers. This would require real-time database replication, an advanced topic not discussed in this book. • Security patches and operating system upgrades are generally done for everyone with the same package. But check to make sure. • You may be able to use containers to host phpBB	• Can be complex to set up. phpBB is not easily installed and configured in the cloud. There is a free Bitnami package that can ease the installation of phpBB. • phpMyAdmin or similar database tools may not be provided. You will likely have to install these yourself. • Setting up SSL certificates and email accounts tend to be complicated. It helps to be tech savvy. • You get little or no hand holding, so you either need excellent technical skills or need to have these on standby, generally for extra cost

Table A-1: Hosting types

Prefer Linux hosting

As a practical matter, I strongly recommend Linux-class hosting for phpBB. Linux is a name for the operating system's kernel (core system), so the actual operating system using the kernel will be something like Ubuntu, CentOS, RedHat or Debian.

From my observations, phpBB just works better and appears faster on Linux. Unless you need to support Microsoft technologies like ASP, there is no advantage to choosing Microsoft software for your hosting. Unlike Microsoft's operating system, which costs money to license, the Linux distribution is almost always free, so Linux hosting tends to be less expensive. Also, it's much less hassle to set file permissions using Linux conventions.

Prefer MySQL or MariaDB

phpBB is almost always installed on MySQL or MariaDB, so there is generally no compelling reason to use some other database management system. Either one is fine. Postgres is also often available and is a fine alternative choice. MySQL and MariaDB community editions are essentially identical in terms of functionality; plus, community editions are free. If you are using Windows hosting, avoid using Microsoft SQL Server database if you can. Both MySQL and MariaDB can be installed on Windows servers.

Prefer nginx or Apache web servers

The web server software your host provides will likely be either nginx or Apache, and either is fine. nginx tends to have the edge these days over Apache. If you get Microsoft hosting, you'll probably have to use their web server: IIS.

Deciding on a new host

The good news is that web hosts are commodities now. The competition is fierce, so prices can be quite low. But finding a good and cheap web host may be impossible.

How do you find a good web host? Ask around! I put my current recommendations on my phpbbservices.com rehosting page. You are welcome to investigate them and see if they meet your needs. If so, please use my affiliate links.

When I last rehosted, I did what most people do: I asked around. You will get a lot of opinions. Most people aren't that technically inclined though. Your friend's cheap shared hosting might be fine for their modest needs, but insufficient for running a phpBB bulletin board.

Fortunately, I was already a member of a local technical mailing list. Periodically, we trade our experiences with hosts, good and bad. Based on these discussions, my experience working on hosts for many clients, and the extent of my need, I chose Dreamhost's shared hosting.

I chose Dreamhost's shared hosting for a number of reasons, but mostly because I needed something reasonably inexpensive but reliable. I didn't need a lot of fancy features or a lot of horsepower. I also chose it because of its end-to-end solid-state infrastructure and because it was privately owned. One of my previous hosts was a company that buys and consolidates web hosts purchased. That event turned my good shared hosting into a bad experience. I wanted to avoid having it happen again.

But things change pretty quickly in the hosting business. Many hosts are moving to virtual hosting, which means they are getting rid of their server rooms and are hosting in a public cloud, such as Amazon or Google. For example, GoDaddy has been moving to Amazon Web Services. This has some advantages for them as far as cost and profit, and maybe for clients in terms of higher reliability. But it also means their hosting features must fit the constraints of the cloud vendor they use.

The sad truth is that generally web hosting is a low profit, high volume business. A great host today could become a bad host tomorrow. While virtual hosting may increase reliability, arguably these web hosts add little value by outsourcing the hosting. If you have the skills, you might want to skip the middle man and directly contract with a cloud provider instead.

If you know people who have hosting with requirements like yours, ask them if they are satisfied with their hosting.

Do not rely on websites with reviews, as many of these have fake reviews and will push you toward hosts that they have marketing agreements with. Appendix E talks about rehosting but gets into criteria that are important in choosing a host too. You might want to read that appendix.

Competition is good, so when you have a list of candidate hosts narrowed down, do some basic research on their pricing and limitations. In particular look at quotas on outgoing emails, number of email accounts allowed, limitations on database size, file storage size and bandwidth quotas.

Once you have signed up for hosting, you should get an email from the web host that will get you started. In general, you will get a control panel you can use on the web to help you set up your web space.

One action you will have to do at some point is point your domain to their hosting. If your web host is also your registrar, there should be nothing to do.

You should get a pair of *nameservers* to use from your web host. You'll have to go to your domain registrar and fill in the nameserver fields for your domain. It may take a few hours for the domain to connect to the hosting across the Internet.

Appendix B | Setting up and using File Transfer Protocol

FTP (File Transfer Protocol) is a standard protocol for transferring files over the Internet. As an administrator, you will need to use FTP periodically to upload new versions of phpBB, to back up files to your local computer, etc. You may need it to download file from your server too, such as database backups.

Creating FTP credentials in a control panel

When you sign up for web hosting, you are usually given a set of FTP credentials. If not, your web host control panel should have an interface for creating these and additional FTP credentials.

For the cPanel control panel, look for FTP Accounts, usually inside a Files group (Figure B.1).

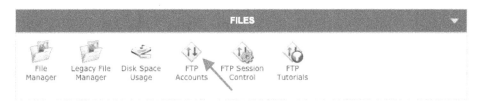

Figure B.1: Files group in cPanel with FTP accounts link

You will be led to a screen where you can create FTP accounts by filling out the following fields:

- **Directory name**. You should change the directory name because it will usually default to a folder that places the user in "jail." Files can't be uploaded or downloaded anywhere else. The directory should be at least the folder where your bulletin board's files are stored and possibly at a higher level, such as the web root folder or your home folder.

- **Quota**. Because you will be uploading lots of files for phpBB, you should specify an unlimited quota for the account. Otherwise, if you exceed your quota, additional files cannot be uploaded.

After creating the account, if you are confused about the exact credentials to use with FTP, look for the **Configure FTP Client** or similar link on the page and click on it (Figure B.2).

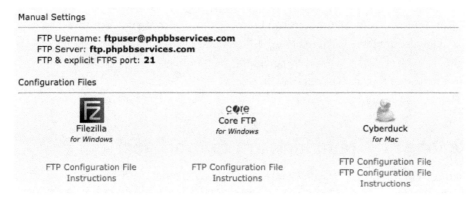

Figure B.2: FTP configuration instructions page in cPanel

Connecting with FTP using FileZilla

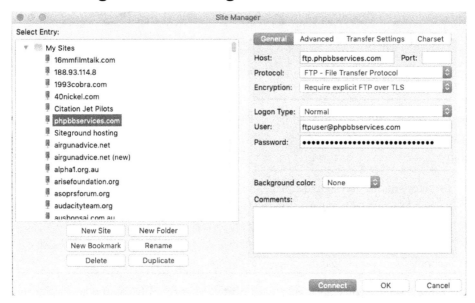

Figure B.3: FileZilla Site Manager

Typically, you install a program on your computer to help you transfer files with FTP. Technically though, it's not necessary if you have command line access. The `ftp` command (and other commands like `scp` and `rsync`) can transfer files too, but it's easier to use programs because they have a graphical user interface.

There are a number of FTP client programs out there. FileZilla is probably the most often used program because it is supported on virtually every operating system, it's free and it's maintained. FileZilla can be downloaded from https://filezilla-project.org.

I will show the process using FileZilla.

Using FileZilla's Site Manager

In FileZilla, you can use the **Site Manager** (far left button on the toolbar) to record your FTP credentials. This way, if you need to access the site again, it will be quick because all the credentials are stored.

When you click on the **New Site** button, you get to name the site in the Site Manager. (Figure B.3) I tend to use the domain name for the site's name.

Fill in the fields as follows:

- **Host**. Use the host name provided by your web host. Sometimes it's the domain name, often prefaced with "ftp." or sometimes it's an Internet Protocol (IP) address, like 123.45.67.89.

- **Port**. Generally, this is left blank. FTP uses Port 21 and is assumed. Secure FTP (SFTP) normally uses Port 22 and is assumed when you select SFTP. On occasion, you are instructed to use another port. Change the port if directed to do so by the web host.

- **Protocol**. Use **FTP** normally, but **SFTP** (Secure FTP) is better, if that's an option, since all communication is encrypted. Secure FTP uses SSH (Secure Shell) to create a secure connection. The FTP protocol is always used, just through a secure tunnel: SSH.

- **Encryption**. This field will only appear if you are using standard FTP. Select "Require explicit FTP over TLS" first, then try the others. If none of them work, try "Use only plain FTP (insecure)." If you use plain FTP, your credentials and files are sent unencrypted, which is a security vulnerability. With the other options, https (SSL) is used to identify you and transmit files. Note that this type of encryption is largely functionally identical to SFTP, as an encrypted connection is used.

- **Logon type**. Select **Normal** or **Ask for password** depending on your preference. If you use **Normal**, FileZilla will store the password on your machine, which could be a security concern.

- **User**. Enter the username you were given or created. Often it must be appended with an @ sign followed by the IP of the server or the domain name.

- **Password**. If you want FileZilla to remember the password, enter the password you were given or you created. If you selected **Ask for password** this field will not appear, but you will be prompted for the password when you try to connect.

Now press the **Connect** button. You may have to try some variations of your settings before it connects reliably.

Occasionally, some tweaks are needed to get FTP to work reliably. The most common tweak is to use enable **passive FTP mode**. In FileZilla, this setting can be found when you press on the **Transfer Settings** button.

Using key encryption with FTP

If your host requires a cryptographic public key to connect, then you must provide the public key to your web host and keep the private key on your computer.

Sometimes your web host will provide a program that lets you create public and private keys. If you don't have any keys already, you can generate them on the web host, then copy these into a text editor and save them an appropriate file name.

Sometimes you need to create these keys on your computer. From the command prompt (the Terminal program) the `ssh-keygen` command is used to create these keys. Sometimes you must create a passphrase when creating keys. If so, store the passphrase somewhere secure.

Any keys stored on your computer have some special requirements:

- On a Mac, keys are usually stored in a hidden folder: /Users/*username*/.ssh.

- On Linux, keys are usually placed in your home folder in a hidden .ssh folder too, for example /home/*username*/.ssh.

- On either Linux or a Mac, the file must have its file permissions set to 600, which is typically done from the terminal with the `chmod` command. You may need superuser privileges to set the file permissions, so you might have to preface `chmod` with `sudo`.

- On Windows 10 with PowerShell enabled, keys should be stored in C:\Users*username*\.ssh

- FileZilla can keep a set of your SSH keys: **Settings > Connection > SFTP > Add key file**

- In FileZilla's Site Manager, if you select the SFTP option one of the **Logon Types** is **Key file**. If you use this approach, use the **Browse** button to locate the private key that corresponds to the public key that your web host has. The key file identifies you uniquely, so you don't need to enter a username or password.

- If you create the key with a passphrase, you will have to enter the passphrase when connecting.

Using FTP

Transferring files with a program is generally very intuitive, but it depends on the program. See Figure B.4 for Filezilla's file transfer screen.

Uploading is the process of moving a file on your local machine to somewhere on the Internet. *Downloading* is the opposite: getting a file from the Internet and storing it on your local machine.

The files on your local machine are in a window in the left pane, and files on your server are in a window in the right pane. There are navigation controls to let you move between folders locally or remotely with ease.

If you see a file with two periods (..), this is a navigation link that will take you to the parent folder of the current folder. Consequently, you can't upload or download these files. Double-clicking on the link will take you to the parent folder.

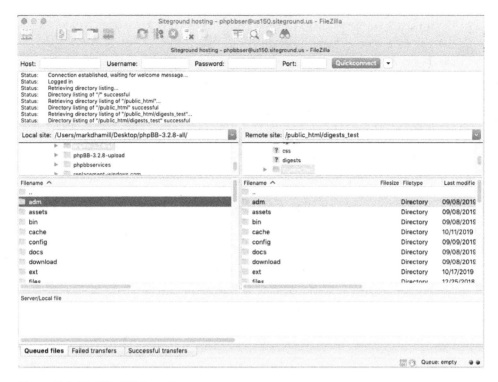

Figure B.4: FileZilla FTP transfer screen

In FileZilla, folders (also known as directories) are shown with a folder icon. Double-clicking on the folder will take you into that folder.

To upload and download a folder and all the files in it, you can:

- Double click on a file or folder. If done in the local window, it is uploaded. If done in the remote window, it is downloaded.

- Drag the list of files and folders from the local window to the remote window to upload, or from the remote window to the local window to download.

- Click on an item. Then right-mouse click on it and select the upload or download option.

You can also move blocks of files by holding down the SHIFT or CTRL keys for the range of files or select the files wanted. Holding down the SHIFT key then clicking on the first and last items selects a range; holding down the CTRL key then picking files or folders by clicking on them allows you to pick individual items. On a Mac, use Command instead of the CTRL key.

You often need to change the permissions on a file or a folder. In FileZilla, right-click on the file or folder, then select the **File Permissions** option.

FTP cautions

You do need to take care when moving files, as you can overwrite something or delete files permanently that are not backed up. FileZilla will warn you if you are about to do this, unless you tell it not to. *Always double-check your assumptions.* You need to make sure that you are uploading to and downloading from the correct folder.

Look out for files that failed to transfer. In FileZilla, they will show on the **Failed transfers** tab in the transfer queue window, if this is enabled. When this happens, it's usually a result of an FTP timeout on the server. These files should be noted and their transfer tried again until success. In FileZilla's transfer queue window, you can right-click on files and put them back in the queue again, then restart the queue on the **Queued files** tab by right-clicking on the tab.

Appendix C | Creating a custom style

When you update phpBB to the latest version, you will often discover that your custom logo or various style changes that you tediously made to phpBB are gone, or partially gone because they were overwritten. It's a common problem and one reason that many board owners defer updating phpBB.

You can end this hassle by creating and installing your own *custom style*. Using this approach, your custom style inherits most of its styling from a primary phpBB style. Then you selectively override the primary style's CSS, HTML or Javascript with your own changes. This way, when the primary style you use is changed, you don't lose your custom changes. This also ensures that your styles and templates use the most current and approved code, which often includes security patches.

In this appendix, I will show how you can do this.

Overview of steps required

The basic approach is:

1. Make a note of all the changes you made to your style.

2. Reload your preferred style.

3. Create a custom style that inherits from your preferred style.

4. Selectively override the preferred style's stylesheet directives. This is best done by creating a stylesheet.css file for your custom style and placing your style customizations there.

5. If you changed some templates, place the custom version of these templates in your custom style's template folder. Frequently, board owners will make changes to overall_header.html and overall_footer.html.

6. Install the custom style.

7. Make the custom style the primary style.

8. Test and refine.

Let's delve into each step to see how this is done.

Make a note of all the changes you made to your style

You probably know what these changes are, but if you have any questions, you can use a file comparison tool like WinMerge (for Windows) or kdiff3 (for pretty much any operating system) to compare your files with a reference version.

1. Download the current style folder where you made all your custom changes, such as /styles/prosilver.

2. Download the reference version of your style that you are currently using.

   - **prosilver or free styles on phpbb.com.** Note your style's version number: **ACP > Customise > Style management > Styles**

     Next, on phpbb.com select Customise, then Styles from the site's menu. Search for the style name. If you don't see your style version on the style's home page, click on the Revision tab near the bottom of the page.

   - **Paid styles.** If you own a paid style and you don't have it already, you may have to download it from the style author's website.

3. Compare your changes to the reference version of the style. Use a file comparison tool and note the changes you made, so they can be reapplied in the custom style.

Reload your preferred style

1. Make certain you have documented all the changes you made to your style. Once they are overwritten, you may not be able to recover them.

2. If you need to update phpBB, you might want to do this first. Bear in mind, if you do this, the default prosilver style will be updated. See Chapter 9.

3. You might also want to download the latest version of the style you are using, which will become the parent style. Otherwise, since you made changes to your preferred style, it's a good time to undo them. The simplest way is to upload the latest reference version of your style, replacing anything that's there.

4. Purge the cache: **ACP > General > Purge the cache**. If you don't see the plain style afterward, clear your browser's cache and reload the page.

Create a custom style that inherits from your preferred style

1. Create a folder in the styles folder for the name of your style, such as /styles/custom. Keep the folder name simple. Don't use any spaces in the folder name and keep the name all mixed case letters.

2. Create a style.cfg file in this folder. Copy the style.cfg file from your parent style's style.cfg file. Below is the code in /styles/prosilver/style.cfg for phpBB 3.3, which I used because my custom style inherits from prosilver.

```
#
# phpBB Style Configuration File
#
# This file is part of the phpBB Forum Software
package.
#
# @copyright (c) phpBB Limited
https://www.phpbb.com
# @license GNU General Public License, version 2
(GPL-2.0)
#
# For full copyright and license information,
please see# the docs/CREDITS.txt file.
#
# At the left is the name, please do not change
this
# At the right the value is entered
#
# Values get trimmed, if you want to add a space
in front or at the end of
# the value, then enclose the value with single
or double quotes.
# Single and double quotes do not need to be
escaped.
```

```
#
#

# General Information about this style
name = prosilver
copyright = © phpBB Limited, 2007
style_version = 3.3.0
phpbb_version = 3.3.0

# Defining a different template bitfield
# template_bitfield = //g=

# Parent style
# Set value to empty or to this style's name if
this style does not have a parent style
parent = prosilver
```

3. In my example, I changed "name = prosilver" to "name = custom." Since I want to inherit from prosilver, I left the "parent = prosilver" line unchanged.

    If you are changing a style other than prosilver as the primary style, you need to change the parent style to the correct style name. It must match the parent folder's name in the styles folder. You might also want to edit the copyright, style_version and phpbb_version lines. If it's only for your own use, this is not necessary. Here are my changes (highlighted):

```
# General Information about this style
name = custom
copyright = © Mark D. Hamill
style_version = 1.0.0
phpbb_version = 3.3.0

# Defining a different template bitfield
# template_bitfield = //g=

# Parent style
# Set value to empty or to this style's name if
this style does not have a parent style
parent = prosilver
```

4. Save the file, making sure it is in the root folder for the custom style, e.g.: /styles/custom/style.cfg.

Override the preferred style's stylesheet directives

1. Create a theme folder for your style. In my example, this would be /styles/custom/theme.

2. Create an images folder inside the theme folder. In my example, this would be /styles/custom/theme/images.

3. If changing the logo, upload the logo you will use to this images folder, in my example, this would be /styles/custom/theme/images. Make a note of the image's height and width, as you will need this later. Any special images that you will integrate into your style should go in this folder.

4. Create a file called stylesheet.css in the theme folder: ex: /styles/custom/theme/stylesheet.css

5. I also recommend creating a template folder. You may or may not need it, but it doesn't hurt to have one, ex: /styles/custom/template

6. To inherit styles from your parent style, you need an @import statement at the top of this file.

    Generally, you just need to reference the stylesheet.css file in the parent style, which most styles have. You will have to amend the path so it finds the parent style's stylesheet files. In the case of my @import line, I added "../../prosilver/theme/." The ?v=3.3 indicates the version of the phpBB style expected, so it may have to be changed. The first line of your stylesheet.css file would look something like this (all on one line):

    ```
    @import
    url("../../prosilver/theme/stylesheet.css?v=3.3");
    ```

    Note: The "../../" in the syntax means "ascend to the parent folder, then ascend to its parent folder. The instruction then descends into the prosilver folder, then descends into its theme folder and reads the file stylesheet.css; all its styles are read first.

Note: If the stylesheet you inherit from does not inherit from prosilver, you may have to first add the @import statement above for prosilver so your custom style can find all the styling it needs.

7. Any style changes you want to override should now be appended to the end of your custom style's stylesheet.css file. In the example of replacing the logo, in the prosilver style, you would normally edit the .site_logo CSS class in colours.css and common.css. In my case, I added these lines at the end of my /styles/custom/theme/stylesheet.css file, which provides the correct image to use for the logo and its proper dimensions:

```
.site_logo {
    background-image: url("./images/mark.jpg");
    width: 181px;
    height: 229px;
}
```

8. I then saved the file stylesheet.css with my changes.

Obviously, there are lots of other style changes you could make besides changing the logo: background colors, changing the default widths of content containers, using different font styles, etc. You should know what these are based on the file changes you researched, and should try to consolidate all style changes in the stylesheet.css file for your custom style. Simply tacking on each, in turn, to the bottom of the file, usually works.

If you are unfamiliar with the CSS syntax, here is a great reference with easy to try out examples:

https://www.w3schools.com/css/default.asp

It's also a good idea to run your CSS through a CSS validator. The CSS validator will check to see if it is syntactically correct. Fixing these errors will ensure your stylesheet will work correctly across all browsers. The Worldwide Web Consortium provides just such a validator: https://jigsaw.w3.org/css-validator/.

Changing templates

Template files serve your board's content. They contain HTML but can also contain CSS and Javascript.

The HTML describes the contents of the page, not how it should look. CSS (Cascading Stylesheet commands) styles handle the look and are normally placed in a .css file in the style's theme folder. But sometimes CSS statements are embedded inside HTML files between <style> and </style> tags. Javascript can also be embedded in a HTML file inside <script> and </script> tags, or in certain HTML tag attributes.

phpBB templates usually contain *template directives*. These are expressed as HTML comments and can insert dynamic content into a web page, such as post text pulled from the database. HTML comments begin with $<!--$ and end with $-->$.

Template inheritance

Unless you create your own template for your custom style, the templates in the parent style's template folder will be used if they are present. So, if you need to modify a template, you need to create your own version in your custom style's template folder, such as /styles/custom/template.

For example, you could create an overall_header.html template for your custom style, but if you don't, the overall_header.html template for the parent's style will be used instead. If the template does not exist in the parent style's template folder, it will be retrieved from the grandparent style's template folder, which usually is /styles/prosilver/template. All styles should ultimately inherit from the prosilver style. A few styles exist only in the /styles/all folder. This folder will be checked if the template file is not found anywhere else.

First, copy the template from the parent style's template folder to your own custom style's template folder. For example, you might copy

/styles/prosilver/template/overall_header.html to /styles/custom/template/overall_header.html.

Next, add, delete or change the HTML or Javascript in your version of the template to get the behavior you want.

To test template changes, you must first purge the cache: **ACP > General > Purge the cache**. You might also need to purge your browser's cache.

You don't want to make changes to the template in your parent's style. The whole point of creating a custom style is to insulate your custom changes from base styles.

Template events

Creating custom template pages should be avoided if possible. This is because most templates have template events inside of them. For example, the template overall_header.html in the prosilver template folder has this template event:

```
<!-- EVENT overall_header_head_append -->
```

What is a template event? Remember, in HTML anything between a <!-- and a --> is a comment. phpBB's template engine looks for patterns in these comments. If it sees the word EVENT in the comment, it examines the rest of the line, which shows the event's name, overall_header_head_append in this example.

This event is an opportunity for a phpBB extension to add HTML, CSS or Javascript markup dynamically at this location. When you view the source of your web page, you should see the dynamically inserted HTML, CSS or Javascript placed at the event's location. Of course, not all events will be used. In fact, most are unused.

New events could be inserted into future versions of a style's templates. These new events are principally for new extensions, which request them.

If you don't add these new events to your templates, it's possible that a newer version of phpBB or an extension won't be able to hook into your custom template, because the new event doesn't exist.

So, if you create a custom template, you should periodically look at newer versions of the parent's template and see if new events were added to it. If so, you should replicate these new events in your version of the template too.

Editing template files

If you have a custom template, you add, modify or remove the code to affect the markup you want. Fortunately, the names of the templates indicate their purpose. overall_footer.html, for example, appears on all pages and places the HTML seen at the bottom of all pages outside of the ACP.

Read Chapter 7 for the example of inserting some StatCounter code to understand how to edit a template file.

Modify your custom template pages as needed, but do so minimally. You need to be careful to insert only valid HTML, CSS or Javascript as appropriate. If the code is invalid, it may not display or take the actions you expect. In particular, check your template changes on mobile devices to ensure the look correct.

Major template changes require an understanding of HTML syntax, and how CSS interacts with HTML tags.

It's a good idea to validate the HTML source for the resulting page to make sure its syntax is correct. This also ensures that it will render correctly across all browsers. The Worldwide Web Consortium provides a tool to do this:

https://validator.w3.org/

Fix any errors found.

If you introduced any Javascript, you need to test these manually. The debugger built into your browser's Inspector tool can help you see these errors, which provide clues for fixing invalid Javascript.

Install the custom style

ACP > Customise > Style management > Install Styles

To install the new style you created, select it ("custom," in my example) by pressing the corresponding **Install style** link.

Make the custom style the primary style

ACP > General > Board configuration > Board settings

You generally want your new custom style to become the default style and the guest style. You may optionally want to set the override user style option to **Yes**, and then submit the form.

Test and refine

If you made only stylesheet changes, you should not need to purge the cache. However, if you make subsequent changes to any templates, first purge the cache, and then test:

ACP > General > Purge the cache

If you don't see the style changes, try deleting your browser's cache, then reload the page.

As noted elsewhere in this book, services like CloudFlare or your web host may have a caching solution enabled for your domain. So, if these suggestions don't work, look to see if you are using these services and purge its caches. With that, the new style should be seen.

Approach when upgrading phpBB

This custom style approach may not work correctly when upgrading. An upgrade is when you go from one minor release of phpBB to another, such as from 3.2 to 3.3. This is because styles typically undergo major changes between minor versions.

You can see if it will work by changing the style.cfg file to reference the new version of phpBB you will be using.

You can, of course, go through the process of creating a new custom style again if this approach doesn't work. Most of your changes to an older minor version should work on the new version.

For your custom templates, it helps to check the templates for the previous version of phpBB of the style you inherited from with its reference. For example, if you have a custom version of navbar_header.html and your style inherits from prosilver, compare the prosilver version of navbar_header.html for the new version of phpBB with the one from your last version of phpBB 3.2.x that you upgraded from.

This is a good example because this particular template changed quite a lot between phpBB 3.2 and 3.3, so if your version of navbar_header.html doesn't have these changes to MICRODATA the breadcrumb menu will not lay out properly.

Appendix D | Converting to phpBB from other forum solutions

The benefits and hazards of conversions

Not all bulletin board solutions are phpBB. Given phpBB's features and its dominance in this market, some board administrators may want to move their boards to phpBB.

Can this be done? The answer is a firm maybe. If it can be done, it's likely to be painful. It could be expensive too if it is done professionally.

To find out, you have to do some research on phpbb.com. Enter an appropriate search term for your current bulletin board software, like "vBulletin convertor," and start reading.

You can't merge a converted board with an existing board. It's virtually impossible to merge two boards together. Hopefully, someone will write a database merge program to do this. It's such a daunting endeavor that it's no surprise no such program exists, as far as I know.

A *convertor* is a program written to ease the conversion from a non-phpBB forum solution to phpBB. If a convertor is available, it likely exists for older versions of phpBB only. In addition, it may require a version of the non-phpBB forum solution that you aren't using. This is because the programmer who wrote the convertor hasn't updated it. And if it works for an older version of phpBB, you need to create a phpBB board to work on that older version. After a successful conversion to phpBB, you then will want to upgrade phpBB to the current version.

Consequently, conversions are problematic and technically challenging, with all sorts of potential issues that could arise. Unless there is a recent convertor written, you are better off finding a phpBB consultant such as me to do the work for you.

Even with a skilled consultant, conversions are always problematic and risky. This is because no forum solution is identical to another as features differ. Someone has to puzzle through these differences to see what is possible and write a conversion script. Then you hope it's correctly implemented.

You are likely to find issues with even the best-written convertor program. For example, phpBB stores post text in the database in an odd format with a lot of markup inside of it, which gets translated on the fly to HTML. A program that converts a post's text on a non-phpBB board to this kind of markup is challenging and complex to write.

Then there are numerous referential integrity issues that come with relational databases. Keys in one table must match keys in another table for the table joins to work properly. Moreover, phpBB's permission system is feature rich but cryptic. Most permissions are stored as bit flags in a database column.

In short, conversions are not for the faint of heart. But generally, if you are determined, have perseverance and possibly a large checkbook then it can be done. And having your board in a robust, open-source forum solution like phpBB has some long-term advantages.

How the conversion process works

Someone has to write a convertor program. This convertor is written to a certain version of phpBB, usually a version of phpBB 3.0. So, you first have to set up a version of phpBB that works with the convertor. Check the convertor's instructions to see what version of your forum software it was written for.

This is becoming harder to do because phpBB 3.0 runs on earlier editions of PHP 5, and it's hard to find web hosts that support these versions. It's easier to install a local web-hosting environment with these older versions of PHP and do your conversion there.

For example, XAMPP is a local web server environment with an Apache web server, a MariaDB database management system and PHP. You can install it on Windows, Linux or MacOS. On the XAMPP downloads page, if you dig for it, you can find older versions of XAMPP that contain the PHP version you need.

To know what you need, you must look at the system requirements for the version of phpBB required by the convertor. Use of higher versions of PHP is problematic at best. System requirements are in the /docs folder of the phpBB version, in the INSTALL.html file.

A default installation of phpBB for the version needed by the convertor should be done first, before copying in the convertor file. You can find older versions of phpBB in this SourceForge repository:

https://sourceforge.net/projects/phpbb/files/

After installing the needed version of phpBB, the conversion script is copied to phpBB's /install/convertors folder.

Once the convertor is in the right place, when you run the installer, it will appear on the **Convert** tab. The installer is run by appending /install to your board root path in the URL.

Assuming the convertor program runs without errors, you should carefully check the result by running the converted board. Try making topics and replying to posts to see what happens. If you had a permission system working, make sure it is working correctly. The convertor may have some manual steps you must do before or after the conversion, so read its instructions carefully.

If a thorough test verifies that all is in order, then you can try upgrading the board to the latest version of phpBB using instructions in Chapter 9. It is likely that errors will be encountered because few convertors are perfect. If they occur, errors will require analysis to fix. A fix may be technically possible but too time consuming or costly to attempt.

So, unfortunately, conversions are very iffy.

Converting phpBB 2 boards

One convertor exists out of the box: a convertor for old phpBB 2 boards, which became obsolete in 2007 with the release of phpBB 3.0.

Technically, this should be considered an upgrade. But phpBB 2 and phpBB 3 are so completely different that a convertor was created to handle this work. Fortunately, with the right preparations it works very well and will leave you on the current version of phpBB.

Except for the attachments mod, phpBB 2 modifications (mods) are not supported. So, if the attachment mod is installed and you have attachments, they will be copied over. This is why the whole /images folder needs to be publicly writeable for conversions.

But there might be an extension for phpBB 3 that has equivalent functionality to your phpBB 2 mod that you can install after the conversion completes.

It's possible that a phpBB 2 mod's changes to the database will cause errors during the conversion. If it happens, these will require troubleshooting. Normally, these issues don't occur, but if they do, the error message will hopefully provide a clue to the solution.

Pick a new style

The old subsilver style is not available for phpBB 3.x. It has been replaced by prosilver. See Chapter 6 for the details on picking styles. If the style is not prosilver, download it and expand it.

If you are enamored with subsilver style's layout, the closest equivalent is the AllanStyle-SUBSILVER style. The CleanSilver and SE Square styles also have subsilver's boxy look.

PHP implications

phpBB 3.3 requires a minimum of PHP 7.1.3. phpBB 2 was designed on versions of PHP up to 5.2, though it often worked on PHP 5.6. Consequently, when converting a phpBB 2 board, the old board can no longer be used. That's a shame because when you convert a phpBB 2 board, it is copied. If an old version of PHP is available on your hosting, you could leave it around in a different folder in read-only mode.

Disable your phpBB 2 board

The good news is that you don't need to make a backup copy of your phpBB 2 database. Your converted board will use a new space and hopefully be placed in a separate database, so data is copied and munged by the convertor.

But the board should be disabled first so you don't lose any posts.

1. Login to your phpBB 2 board as an administrator.

2. Select the **Go to Administration Panel** link at the bottom of the index and authenticate if needed.

3. See Figure D.1. In the left sidebar, select **General Admin > Configuration.**

4. On the General Configuration screen, select **Disable board > Yes.**

Figure D.1: Disabling a phpBB2 board

5.   Press the **Submit** button at the bottom of the form.

Upgrade PHP

I assume you will be converting directly to phpBB 3.3. You will need a version of PHP 7.1.3 or higher. You can switch the version of PHP in your web host control panel. If not, you may need to file a technical support ticket with your web host.

Once you have upgraded PHP, your old board should no longer work. Attempts should bring up many errors.

Create a new database

Creating a new database is technically not required, but highly desirable.

If you don't create a new database, use a different table prefix from the old board for the database tables. For example, if the old table prefix was phpbb_ (the default), you could make the new table prefix phpbb3_, so it's pretty obvious which tables contain the new board's data.

Creating a database for phpBB is discussed in Chapter 4. The procedures are the same even though this is a conversion.

Upload phpBB into a temporary folder

I suggest creating a board_new folder and uploading it there. Remember to make sure the folder permissions for the converted board are correct. The /cache, /files, /images and /store folders must be publicly writeable. The config.php file may need to be so as well.

Install phpBB with the defaults

Follow the procedures in Chapter 4 for installing phpBB. Do not create any forums or do any other customization upon completion. Use all the defaults. The convertor will overwrite these, so it's wasted effort. **Stop at the step where you would delete the install folder.** You will need this folder to run the conversion.

Run the conversion

Append the install folder to the URL to bring up the install program again, ex:

https://www.myspecialdomain.com/board_new/install

Figure D.2: Convert link

A **Convert** tab should appear. Click on it. Then click on the **Convert** link. See Figure D.2.

After checking for correct file permissions, the convertor brings up a screen where you must enter connection information to the phpBB 2 database. This may be a bit confusing to figure out. You need to know:

- The name of the phpBB 2 database, and the database username, its password and the table prefix, which can be found in the old board's config.php file.

- The relative path to the phpBB 2 board from the location of the new, temporary board.

Figure D.3: Specifying the phpBB2 database settings for a conversion

See Figure D.3. In this case, the old board is in a /phpbb2 folder off my web root folder. Since the new board is in a /board_new folder off my web root, the relative path requires going to the parent folder then descending into the board folder.

This is a Linux-based server, so the correct path is ./../phpbb2.

- ./ means "start at the current folder."

- ../ means "ascend to the parent folder."

- phpbb2 means "now descend into the phpbb2 folder to find the old board's files."

I chose to say **Yes** to the question **Refresh page to continue conversion**. This way, I don't have to press the **Continue** button at the bottom of a page when a page's work is completed. The page will refresh automatically after three seconds.

Pressing **Submit** will trigger a multi-page conversion process with nine primary steps and a number of additional steps where the converted data is resynchronized.

How long the process takes depends on the size of the board being converted and the speed of the hardware being used. A recent conversion I did on a board with 120,000 posts took about forty minutes. Of course, the preparation time took considerable time too. In another example, a board with 3.9 million posts took 30 hours! I kept my machine on for two nights while it crunched away at the task.

Generally, the conversion happens without errors. But if an error occurs, hopefully the error message will give a clue on how to fix it. When fixed, unfortunately you have to start all over again. So, this kind of conversion *can* be very tedious, but usually isn't.

Remove the install folder

When complete, you should remove the install folder for the new board using FTP or your web host's file manager.

Test and refine the new board

Test the new board by logging in with your old credentials. You may have created a new set of credentials to create the board, but the convertor will overwrite these, so log in using your old administrator credentials.

You should re-create the search index. The search index that exists contains only the one post from the sample post. **ACP > Maintenance > Search index**. Delete the phpBB Native Fulltext index. If you want to use a different kind of search index, change it at **ACP >**

General > Server configuration > Search settings. Then go back to the search index page and create the search index selected.

As with any other phpBB installation, I think you should also disable the contact form and set up an effective spambot countermeasure.

You can also add a new style and any extensions you want to. Follow the same procedures, as you would for a new board, as discussed in Chapter 6. If you are in a hurry, you can save these steps for later after you move the board.

Archive the old board

The old board should now be archived.

It's best to create an archive of both the converted board's files and database. See Chapter 8 for procedures for doing backups. There is no need to back up your old phpBB 2 board because it was never altered.

You might also want to drop the old board's database, since it is taking up space. Just make sure you don't drop a different database!

When you are done, remove or rename the folder containing the old phpBB 2 board. In my case, it was a /phpbb2 folder. This can be done with FTP or using your web host control panel's file manager. The latter is easier.

Move the new board to its new resting place

In my example, the converted board is in a board_new folder. Typically, you want to move all the new files to the old location, so the board's URL is unaffected.

Before moving though, change the following settings:

- **ACP > General > Server configuration > Cookie settings > Cookie path**. Change this setting to reflect the board's final location, if the cookie should not apply to the whole domain.

- **ACP > General > Server configuration > Server settings > Script path**. Change this setting to the new location on your file system.

- **Purge the cache**. Moving the /cache files takes extra effort, so why not purge them first? The cached files will also reference the old location of the board, which might lead to errors when you bring up the converted board in its new space. **ACP > General > Purge the cache**

Next, move the files.

While this can be done using FTP, it's very time consuming and tedious because there are so many files. If your board is in a folder, it's much simpler to rename the folder using FTP or your web host control panel's file manager. In my example, you would rename board_new to phpbb2, because the old board was in a phpbb2 folder.

Bring up the newly converted board

To start the converted board, simply type in the URL of your old board to bring it up again. It should come up without error. If things look off, you may need to clear your browser's cache.

If you can't login, delete your cookies for the domain and purge your browser's cache.

If you want to add a different style or any extensions, you can do it now, or add these as time allows. The board should be usable.

When everything is looking and behaving the way you want it to, re-enable the board:

ACP > General > Board configuration > Board settings > Disable board > No

Appendix E | Rehosting

If you are dissatisfied with your web host, you can move your hosting elsewhere, and your phpBB board with it.

Appendix A discusses hosting in general, with a summary on the four major kinds of hosting out there: shared, virtual private, dedicated and cloud. It also discusses domains and some of the general attributes of hosts. It doesn't discuss how you move your board from one set of machines to another across the Internet, or how to tell if a new host is sized properly for your needs.

The good news is that many web hosts will move your domain and its databases for free. I'll get into the steps on how you can do this yourself.

But some web hosts are sloppy when moving content. For example, they'll move files but not the database. Or they will move both but not connect software like phpBB properly. Many steps, like creating new email accounts and pointing your domain to the new hosting, are for you to do.

I'll assume you haven't picked a new host yet and offer an approach for intelligently finding the right host for your sites and your board.

Gathering your hosting statistics

A board is usually just part of a website. And you may host more than one domain on a host.

So, when searching for a new web host, you usually need to start with a set of statistics that describes the totality of your hosting needs. Your new host has to meet your current and future requirements.

A set of statistics will inform you just how much you use in hosting resources. They will serve as a basis for conversations with candidate hosts.

Key statistics needed

There are some key statistics that help determine the sort of hosting you need:

- **Hits**. These are anything on your web pages that is served by your hosting: the web page itself, images, CSS files, Javascript files and other miscellaneous files embedded or linked by the web page. Note that some things may be served from others places, such as Javascript libraries. They don't count as hits.

- **Page requests**. This is the number of HTML pages and text files served.

- **Emails sent or received**. phpBB can send a lot of email notifications. The more users and posts over a period of time, the larger the number will be. It may be impossible to get an exact number of emails sent and received, but you'll likely have an idea of the range of emails sent.

- **Your webspace size**. This is the overall size of all the files used by your domains on your current hosting. The size of the files that make up the operating system are normally not included but may need to be if you don't use shared hosting. Getting the size of your public_html or similar folder with your web content generally suffices, plus the size of your databases. Sometimes subdomains are placed outside of the public_html folder, so if you have subdomains like this you will have to include their space in your statistics too.

- **Number of inodes**. Inodes mean the number of files, folders, and files that link to the location of other files. In many ways, an inode count is more important than knowing your overall webspace size. These days, webspace is pretty cheap. But there's a real cost to managing the files and folders the operating system must track. Web hosts typically set a limit on the number of inodes you are allowed, based on your hosting package.

- **The aggregate size of all your databases**. In Chapter 10, I discussed a way to get an accurate size of your databases, as this is not usually provided. It might show up in your web host control panel. If you can't find it, you might want to file a support ticket with your web host to get the current size of all your databases.

Determining your webspace and inode statistics

Figure 10.5 in Chapter 10 showed summary statistics that may be provided for you in your web host control panel. If you are lucky enough to have this, there are some key statistics provided:

- **Disk space usage**. This is your webspace size, but if it looks huge it may include the operating system's files too.

- **Inode usage**

If you don't have access to this information in your web host control panel, file a ticket with your current web host and ask them.

If you have access to SSH, you may be able to run commands to get these values. Give these numbers a reality check if they look wildly off. If you are using virtual private, dedicated or cloud hosting, the count will include your operating system and its large number of files. Look at the df and du commands. The -i flag should return the number of inodes.

Determining your hits and page requests statistics

Surprisingly, external web statistics sites like Google Analytics are not very useful for rehosting purposes. There are many page requests made that may not be recorded by these packages. For example, page requests by search bots are often not counted. These numbers matter because it's work that a web server has to do.

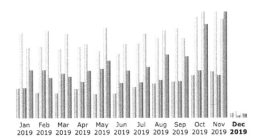

Month	Unique visitors	Number of visits	Pages	Hits	Bandwidth
Jan 2019	3,502	9,987	21,701	50,175	871.22 MB
Feb 2019	2,982	8,409	34,313	62,332	729.79 MB
Mar 2019	2,955	8,074	31,625	60,277	754.03 MB
Apr 2019	3,413	8,359	25,826	52,777	855.89 MB
May 2019	2,818	7,922	34,928	64,480	1.02 GB
Jun 2019	2,847	7,514	25,131	52,830	861.03 MB
Jul 2019	3,611	8,739	25,339	60,411	926.51 MB
Aug 2019	4,045	9,361	27,078	62,673	1.12 GB
Sep 2019	4,262	10,529	26,283	56,860	1.09 GB
Oct 2019	5,037	11,905	34,017	75,736	1.66 GB
Nov 2019	5,414	12,421	30,372	70,983	1.88 GB
Dec 2019	532	704	1,425	3,181	71.54 MB
Total	41,418	103,924	318,038	672,715	11.73 GB

Figure E.1: Awstats report for a domain

AWStats is usually available in your web host control panel and can give you a good set of metrics for a given domain. See Figure E.1. An annual report is useful with monthly averages. There may be other statistics packages too, like Webalizer that should give similar information.

AWStats will only give you statistics for a single domain, so if you have multiple domains on your web host, you need reports from each and then you total them.

Except on cloud hosting, bandwidth is not usually charged, but your new host may ask, so it's good to have this statistic.

Note your email accounts and email forwarders

After you rehost, you will want to re-create any email accounts and email forwarders for your domains. These should be re-created on the new hosting. Make a note of all your existing email accounts and email forwarders. If you keep email on your web host, unless you export your email, these emails will likely be lost with rehosting.

Decide the type of hosting you need

You should read Appendix A if you haven't already to look at the features of each of the four major classes of hosting.

Often you will feel the need to move to a higher class of hosting because of problems on the current host. However, if your statistics suggest your current type of hosting is fine, then you might want to shop for better hosting of the same type.

Picking a new host for rehosting

The hardest parts of hosting are probably figuring out what kind of hosting you really need, and then figuring out which company deserves your business.

The hosting business doesn't help matters. Most specialize in obfuscation, so it's hard to know if the hosting you select represents a good value. Most of us don't want to pay premium prices if we don't have to, and especially don't want to pay premium prices for hosts that don't deserve the label.

Look at your statistics and compare them to the published quotas of web hosts' hosting plans to get a general idea if the host will work for you.

Before making a decision, call each host's sales department on your final-candidates list to ask questions. In particular, it's important to find out about their policy and quotas for outgoing emails, number of inodes, CPU seconds and maximum database space size.

Also, think about anticipated growth. If with a move you are already using eighty percent of inodes allowed on the new host, the new host may not be a good fit because you might easily add 20% more files and folders over the course of a year or two.

Moving to a new host

Purchasing hosting

Once you have chosen a new host, you obviously need to purchase a hosting contract. Most give thirty days to back out with a full refund if they aren't working out for you. You should check what their refund policy is.

You can save money with a long-term hosting contract. Since it's a new host, you probably don't want to commit too much money. I go initially with a one-year contract. If after a year of good service, I may choose a multi-year contract for additional savings.

Previewing your new domain

There's a neat little trick that tricks your browser into using the new hosting even if the domain isn't yet pointing public traffic there. It involves temporarily configuring your computer so that it checks its local *hosts file* for your new hosting.

On Windows, you need to edit this file as an administrator:

```
c:\windows\system32\drivers\etc\hosts
```

On Linux or a Mac, you edit the /etc/hosts file as the root user. Since it must be done as a superuser, you usually precede the command with "sudo." This example assumes you are using the nano text editor, but you can change it to vi if you prefer that editor:

```
sudo nano /etc/hosts
```

Basically, you need to add a line in the file that associates the IP of the new host with the domain name, and then you save the file. Your new web host will provide you with an IP to use. Place a tab character between the IP field and the domain field:

```
108.163.199.172 mydomain.com
```

If you want to temporarily comment out the change, precede it with a # and save the file:

```
# 108.163.199.172    mydomain.com
```

In nano, you press CTRL-O (the letter) to save your changes and CTRL-X to exit the editor. (Note to Mac users: *Do not use the Command key instead!*)

Then open any browser on your machine. The new hosting should come up when you use your domain name. If you see errors, you have a clue on how to troubleshoot them. You will probably get a boilerplate new hosting page.

Moving your domains' content

Many hosts will move your files and databases for you for free. Doing this yourself is generally an unnecessary hassle, so take them up on it if they offer. Hosts are also less likely to make mistakes.

This is usually not an option for non-shared hosting plans. These classes of hosting come with the expectation that you know what you are doing and can move the files and databases yourself, but it doesn't hurt to ask.

Before moving anything, you should disable your board(s) plus any other software your domain uses, such as WordPress. This is to make sure you don't lose any content during the rehosting.

You move your files and your databases separately. Moving files requires either a lot of downloading and uploading, or if you have SSH privileges, the Linux scp (secure copy) or rsync programs can do a lot of the hard work for you succinctly.

Databases need to be exported to text files, generally compressed, moved, uncompressed and loaded into a new database. This process is discussed in Chapter 8.

If you do this yourself, you will have to create a number of databases: one for each board you are moving and possibly for other systems you use, like WordPress.

Each software application will require some tuning. Most likely, you will need to edit the config.php file for your board to give it the new correct database name, database user, machine name and database user password that you set up in your new web host control panel. Yes, it can be quite a hassle, which is why you want to let the new host do the moving for you, if possible. It might even be worth paying them.

Even then, you will end up doing some of the work. You may need to change a configuration file and reset folder permissions as well. You may also have to change some file and folder permissions.

Also consider whether you want to retain your web server's log files. These contain historical information about all your web hits. If so, move them too. If the web server is the same between hosts, it may be possible to include these old statistics in the new statistics package your new web host uses.

Always test emailing after rehosting. Change the SMTP settings to those provided by your new host:

ACP > General > Client communications > Email settings

Chapter 6 discusses in detail how to set up and troubleshoot emailing issues with phpBB.

If you have email accounts for your domains, you will need to create new email accounts and email forwarders on the new hosting. If you access these accounts through mail clients, you will need to change your email clients' SMTP information to retrieve emails from the new hosting.

Re-enable phpBB and your other software

Since you disabled your board before rehosting, you should re-enable it. Any other software you moved over, such as WordPress, should be re-enabled when it is behaving normally on the new hosting. Of course, test each software package to make sure it is working correctly.

Changing the DNS settings

Undo any changes you used for testing your domains from the hosts file.

When all your domains are running smoothly, you need to go to your domain registrar. Point the domains to the nameservers for the new hosting. Then wait.

These changes generally take an hour or less these days; your DNS changes need to spread across the Internet, and that just takes time. You can tell if the DNS switch worked by using the ping command for your domain from your terminal. Observe if the IP matches one assigned by your new host.

Cancel your old hosting

If you can get a refund for any unused part of your old hosting contract, try to get it. You can formally cancel your old hosting or let it lapse at the end of your hosting contract. The latter can be useful if you missed moving over any files. If you set your hosting up for automatic renewal, make sure to change this setting.

Congratulations! The long hassle of rehosting should finally be over.

About the author

Mark D. Hamill bears no known relationship with the actor Mark Hamill, the skater Dorothy Hamill, the late journalist and novelist Pete Hamill, or any other Hamills of any renown. Except, Mark *is* a distant ancestor of Rep. Patrick Hamill, who served in Congress 1869-1871, representing Maryland's 4th congressional district.

Prior to *Star Wars*, his life was much easier in that his name brought no questions but was frequently mispronounced. Mark notes (and he is not making this up) that he used to work next to a man named Abraham Lincoln.

Mark's interest in phpBB comes from the days of electronic bulletin board systems. Back in the 1980s and 1990s, before the Internet became popular, people explored cyberspace by dialing up "bulletin boards" using modems attached to their computers. These boards were generally a spare PC in someone's basement connected to a separate phone line. He hung out on a number of these boards in the Washington D.C. area and became good friends with many of the people on these boards.

As the Internet took hold, the old dial-up bulletin boards died, but new ones were created on the web. For a while, Mark maintained a board for his online friends using EZBoard, a hosted website that ran boards. But eventually, he saw no reason not to run his own bulletin board. He looked around, found phpBB around 2001, bought some hosting, and moved as many of his online friends there. Initially it was set up on old phpBB 2 software. He transitioned to phpBB 3.0 when it was released in 2007. He kept the board up until it died a natural death in 2009. As a result of all of this, Mark grew to become something of an expert in phpBB.

In the 2000s, Mark learned to write modifications to phpBB, that extended the built-in functionality. His first modification, Digests, was approved for phpBB 2 in 2003. He's kept it and evolved it into an extension all these years. In 2007 he created a feed modification, Smartfeed, that was subsequently turned into an extension too. Mark currently has a number of extensions both approved an in development including Spam Remover, Filter by Country, Selective Mass Emails and SCSS Compiler.

In 2006, Mark got hit up to do some work for a charity who had a phpBB board. Once he realized people were happy to pay him money for his services, a side hustle was born. Along the way, he kept improving his skills in phpBB.

About the author

Mark has a long career as an IT professional, mostly with the federal government where he earned his programmer stripes. Computer stuff pretty much consumed him, which let him advance quickly within the ranks, leading to technical leader positions and eventually an enterprise-scale web application manager.

In 1999, he received a Master's Degree in Software Systems Engineering from George Mason University. From 2004 to 2014, he managed the U.S. Department of the Interior's most active website, USGS Water Data for the Nation, which is very much still around. During his tenure, he introduced USGS water web services to complement the Water Data site.

He retired from the federal government in 2014 on a cushy pension, and in 2015, moved to Florence, Massachusetts where he happily resides with his wife and two cats. He still helps clients with phpBB-related work. You can see his website at https://www.phpbbservices.com and can hire him as well.

Mark has done a lot of adjunct teaching at local community colleges, teaching IT courses for Northern Virginia Community College and Greenfield Community College. When not doing phpBB consulting, he runs a local WordPress meetup. He is working to get the City of Northampton, Massachusetts to create a municipal network. Mark is not a Comcast fan.

Mark is grateful to the many fine people who run the phpBB project, who have educated him and put up with some of his exasperating tendencies. He's also grateful to the hundreds of customers who have trusted him with their phpBB boards and for their money that supplemented his income, and mostly went toward fancy vacations.

Index

www.ingramcontent.com/pod-product-compliance
Lightning Source LLC
LaVergne TN
LVHW081514050326
832903LV00025B/1482